4 Plymouth People

EMPLOYMENT

Tackling long-term unemployment in Plymouth is the job of the city's Employment Zone.

The Zone, which began as one of the Government's five pilot zones in February last year, aims to target its help toward the 1,900 or so over 25s in the city who have been jobless for more than a year.

The zone also aims to help people with disabilities, people in need of literacy and numeracy support, ex-offenders and lone parents.

Jobseekers are helped into work in four main ways:
- by advice and support
- training
- intermediate employment (short term jobs to help them back into the job market)
- business rehearsal (preparation, advice and support for setting up a business).

So far the the prototype zone has been one of the most successful and has already helped more than 450 unemployed people with its individually focused approach.

Applicants have either started some form of employment or job-seeking activity such as training or preparation for setting up a business.

The Zone aims to support 995 people before March 2000, either by helping them find work or providing a qualification which will improve their job prospects.

Jobseekers can find more information about Employment Zone schemes at Job Centres or by calling Plymouth 674070.

FACT ZONE

Who:	The Employment Zone Joint Venture Partnership: Prosper, the City Council,CFE, Chamber of Commerce, CFE and the Employment Service
What:	tackling long-term unemployment
When:	Feb 1998 until 2000 with the possibility of extension
Where:	all Plymouth
Why:	unemployment amongst over 25s is high in the city
How much?	£1 million a year

The Action Zone will bring real benefits to everyone who uses the city centre.

As part of a Zone project a team has been hired to act as "City Centre representatives".

They will provide a point of contact on the street for locals, tourists and firms, as well as report problems such as litter.

They will receive on-the-job training, including an NVQ, with the aim of finding a full-time job afterwards.

Project manager Victoria Little is pictured with Mike Betts, chair of the Plymouth Retailers Group.

A photographer is teaching in Bangladesh thanks to the Employment Zone.

Kirsten Claire, 53, who lives on the Hoe, was able to gain a teaching qualification to enable her to teach students English as well as photography at the South Asian Institute of Photography in Bangladesh.

With the help of her Employment Zone personal advisor, Diane Ball, and the City of Plymouth Training and Employment, Kirsten was able to take a four week intensive course and gain a certificate.

The 16-hour rule for benefits claimants does not apply for Zone clients.

Kirsten said: "The Employment Zone scheme helped me as I did not fall under the remit of other funding support opportunities because I was aged over 30. Being able to gain a qualification will really help support my work in Bangladesh."

Spring 1999

G FOR A FUTURE

GOING UP: Education chair Jack Jones and children at Leigham School watch progress on the new building which will replace the one destroyed by fire in 1997.

ovision for adult learning.
The way the Council provides oney for schools is also changing th school governors having even eater responsibility for running hools.
Meanwhile schools have roduced literacy and numeracy urs as part of a bid to improve e attainment of all children.
Councillor Jack Jones, chair of e Education, said: "We make no es about the fact we are making ucation a priority. This will mean ending on Plymouth schools will increasing substantially for the ond year running.
"We have seen a lot of progress our first year as an education thority and schools are seeing e benefits of new teachers and provements to buildings. This is mething we will be building on

INVESTING IN PUPILS

More is being invested in the education of Plymouth children, young people and adults than ever before as these figures show:

✔ This year the City Council will be spending around £25 per pupil more than last year
✔ An extra £5.5 million will be invested in the Plymouth education service this year.
✔ Plymouth has secured an extra £870,000 this year for extra teachers to reduce class sizes in infants schools.
✔ next year Plymouth will be spending nearly £500,000 of Standards Fund money on improving literacy, £235,000 on improving numeracy and £175,000 on Summer Literacy and Numeracy Schools. More than £1.3 million will be spent on computing in schools.
✔ Last year the city secured nearly £1.3 million of the Government's New Deal for Schools programme for refurbishment work on schools. Work at schools included new science labs, new toilet facilities, art rooms and classrooms.
✔ The City Council has bid for £3.1 million of New Deal money for improvements to Plymouth schools for the coming year.

NEWS in brief

Just pipped

The City Council supported PYPA 21 (Plymouth Young People's Agenda 21) this year clinched a second Green Apple Award for Environmental Best Practice at the Green Apple Awards.

In the category for Unitary Authorities they were only just pipped for the award of Britain's Greenest Council. Last year they were runners up in the category.

PYPA 21, which was launched four years ago, involves young people in decisions about the environment and quality of life.

The project is recognised as a leader in its field and has been quoted as an example of best practice by the UK Government, the United Nations and the Local Government Management Board.

Step training

A scheme providing teenagers with a stepping stone between education and employment has seen a big rise in the number of students achieving qualifications.

More than 740 students gained a vocational qualification through the Tamar Valley Consortium last year – a 20 per cent rise.

The Consortium of 18 schools and 19 training providers supplies vocational training for 1,000 post-16 students a year.

Contact the TVC on 769663.

Good planning

Plymouth is currently seeing one of the biggest ever public consultation exercises ever undertaken in the city.

Residents are being given a say about the city's future at a series of exhibitions at libraries and public events.

The Council is updating the Local Plan which sets out how land should be used in the city for the next 10 years. Public comments will be compiled into Planning Studies for each ward.

If your group would like to hold a Community Planning Studies event contact Peter Ford on Plymouth 304561.

Trailblazing

The *TEFL* Resource

Editor - David Leith
Production Editor - Ben Long
Production Assistant - Vikki Savage
Chief Contributor - Nick Brieger
Other Contributions - Martin Wragg, David Leith
Cover Design - Emma Whiting

Acknowledgements:

We would like to thank the following for their contributions and assistance: Peter 'Stan' Matanle *MA Cantab.*, Tim 'Briers' Brierly *Greene's, Oxon*, Sharon Spriggs (Trinity College, London), Helen Potter & Steve 'Meg' McKenna (UCLES), Jonathan 'BHA' Wescott, David 'Sporter' Porter, Mark 'Ranger' Bridger, Edward David, Brian 'Nobby' Horton, the staff of Anglesea Arms, Ian 'Rock' Stone, Mark 'Bruno' Brown, Jeremy Weeks, Michael 'MC' Prouten and everyone else however remotely involved for their support.

"Special thanks to Emiko and Vanessa for their patience and support" - **David & Ben**.

Although every effort and care has been made to ensure the accuracy of the information contained in this publication, the publisher and production editor cannot accept responsibility for errors or omissions.

Inclusion in this book is not intended as a recommendation or endorsement of individual organisations and we therefore disclaim any responsibility for the quality of training and recruitment practised by any training centres or other organisations included in the book.

© Zeitgeist Publications 1998. All rights reserved throughout the world. No part of this publication may be reproduced, stored in a retrieval system or transmitted in any form or by any means, electronic, mechanical, photocopying, recording or otherwise, without the prior permission in writing of the publisher.

ISBN 09527509-1-0

Published by Zeitgeist Publications, in association with Authentically English, 85 Gloucester Road, London SW7 4SS.

Read me first

Like most industries, the English Language Teaching has it's own language of acronyms and abbreviations which crop up with monotonous regularity. Following are just a few of the more well used to guide you, not only through this book, but also through the hallowed halls of English as a foreign language.

EFL - English as a Foreign Language - this refers to non-native speakers of English learning English. EFL is most widely used in conjunction with British English. In the US, this refers to teaching overseas only.

ESL - English as a Second language - in the US, this refers to people learning or teaching English as a second language. This includes EFL and immigrant English learners. In the UK, ESL is generally only used to refer to immigrant learners and not foreign students or overseas teaching.

ESOL - English for Speakers of Other Languages - another general term for EFL/ESL.

ELT - English Language Teaching/Training

TEFL - Teaching English as a Foreign Language

TESL - Teaching English as a Second Language

TESOL - Teaching English to Speakers of Other Languages.

It may seem, on initial inspection, that all these acronyms really mean the same things, however, they are usually used in specific contexts. To follow are some more abbreviations and acronyms that are in common usage including exam titles and associations.

ARELS - Association of Recognised English Language Schools - This is an marketing association of UK commercial EFL schools that have been recognised to attain a standard set by the British Council.

BASELT - British Association of State English Language Teaching - Association of UK state colleges and universities that have been recognised to attain a standard set by the British Council.

BATQI - British Association of TESOL Qualifying Institutions

CALL - Computer Aided/Assisted Language Learning

Cert. TESOL - Certificate Teaching English to Speakers of Other Languages - Trinity College Entry level qualification for TEFL

Cert. TEYL - Certificate Teaching English to Young Learners - Trinity College Qualification

CELTA - Certificate in English Language Teaching to Adults - Cambridge (UCLES) qualification. Entry level qualification for TEFL.

CTEFLA - Certificate in Teaching of English as a Foreign Language to Adults - Cambridge (UCLES) qualification which has been replaced with the CELTA.

Dip - Diploma

DTEFLA - Diploma in Teaching of English as a Foreign Language to Adults - Cambridge (UCLES) advanced qualification.

EAP - English for Academic Purposes - Learning/teaching English to enable further academic study in any discipline

ESP - English for Specific Purposes - English teaching for a particular field or industry etc. i.e. English for Engineers.

IATEFL - International Association of Teachers of English as a Foreign Language - UK based teachers association.

IELTS - International English Language Testing System - Exam to gauge level of English.

JALT - Japan Association of Language Teachers

JET - Japan Exchange and Teaching programme

LTCL (TESOL) - Licentiate of Trinity College London in Teaching English to Speakers of Other Languages - Licentiate Diploma in TESOL. This is the advanced qualification awarded by Trinity College London.

TESOL - Teachers of English to Speakers of Other Languages - this the acronym for the US Association for Teachers.

UCLES - University of Cambridge Local Examinations Syndicate - Exam Board which administers teacher and student EFL qualifications.

UODLE - University of Oxford Delegacy of Local Examinations

VSO - Voluntary Service Overseas

What do you want?

Welcome,

to the wonderful world of TEFL (Teaching English as a Foreign Language) and this, the long awaited Authentically English TEFL Resource.

For reasons political, economical, and historical, English is the most widely used medium for international communication. Businessmen, tourists and workers who do not share a common native language will invariably use English to communicate. The majority of Data storage, computer programming and radio communication systems rely on English. The results are simple, the ability to use and also teach English have become a valuable asset, as global demand continues to rise.

This book is designed to answer questions about TEFL, with forthright and frank advice from experienced EFL practitioners about starting, maintaining and furthering a career in English Language Teaching. It also provides an up to date and, as much as possible, comprehensive directory of relevant courses on offer in the UK.

The publication aims to become the benchmark in quality, value for money and comprehension of content.

I hope you find this book a useful and informative stepping stone into a world of endless possibilities.

So it starts here.....but it could lead on to anywhere.

David Leith
Editor

UNIVERSITY *of* **CAMBRIDGE**
Local Examinations Syndicate

Certificates and Diplomas in English Language Teaching to Adults & Young Learners

THE CERTIFICATES AND DIPLOMAS ARE:

- distinguished by the quality of the training provided by 250 established centres in over 40 countries worldwide

- more widely accepted by employers in the UK and overseas than any other international ELT qualification.

MAKE NO MISTAKE . . .

THERE ARE NO EQUIVALENTS

For further information please contact:

Helen Potter
The CILTS Unit
University of Cambridge
Local Examinations Syndicate
1 Hills Road
Cambridge
CB1 2EU
UK

Tel: +44(0)1223 553789
Fax: +44(0)1223 553086
e-mail: cilts@ucles.org.uk
http://www.edunet.com/ciltsrsa

Setting international standards
with the profession
for the profession

What's Inside?

1. What's EFL?
Explanation of EFL 8
Can I do it? 9
Advice for careers in EFL 10
Other methods of employment 12
Volunteering 14

2. Getting Started
Basic Qualifications 18
Summer school & UK work 20
Entry level qualifications 22

3. Further Qualifications
In service qualifications 26
University Courses 28
Short courses 33

4. Careers in TEFL
Advice for getting work 40
Outline of requirements 44
Further careers in EFL 48

5. Materials for Teaching and Learning
Introduction to EFL materials 54
Essential reading list 58

6. Associations in EFL
Explanation of associations in EFL 62

7. Directory of Centres
Certificate & diploma providers 68

8. Directory of Universities
Masters courses & University
Certificate & diplomas 90

9. Countries of the world
Top 69 TEFL consumer countries 100

10. Other Stuff
Contact details of Associations,
institutions, organisations etc. 126

Indexes
Index 140
Advertisers Index 144

a-e Authentically ENGLISH

The magazine for professional teachers of English...worldwide

"Could I have better directions to the resource centre"

Make sure you're prepared for teaching abroad!

Reviews, advice, topical articles, phtocopiable classroom resources, and much more.

For an annual subscripion to the magazine (4 issues), send a cheque or postal order for £17.50 payable to:
Authentically English, 85 Gloucester Road, London SW7 4SS
Tel: 0171 244 7301 Fax: 0171 835 0761

Section 1

What is *EFL?*

Explanation of EFL

"A look at the reasons behind EFL, what it is and where it's going"

page 8

Can I do it?

"The necessary qualities and potential career structure of an EFL teacher"

page 9

Advice for careers in EFL

"The job market and possible avenues of employment"

page 10

Other methods of employment

"Finding employment on your own and working with organisations & exchange programmes"

page 12

Volunteering

"Getting into a volunteer programme and where this can lead"

page 14

Explanation of EFL

A look at the reasons behind EFL, what it is and where it's going.

The English language originated in England and is now widely spoken on six continents. It is the first language of the United States, the United Kingdom, Canada, Australia, Ireland, New Zealand, and various small island nations in the Caribbean Sea and the Pacific Ocean. It is also an official language of India, the Philippines, and many countries in sub-Saharan Africa, where it has the status of second language. English is also the most widely studied foreign language throughout the world. As a result of its extensive use as a first, second or foreign language, it is also the most widely used language for international communication, i.e. one that two people communicate in when they cannot understand each other's native speech.

The press release for the launch of the British Council's English 2000 project summarises the position of English:

"World-wide, there are over 1,400 million people living in countries where English has official status. One out of five of the world's population speak English to some level of competence. Demand from the other four fifths is increasing. ...By the year 2000 it is estimated that over one billion people will be learning English. English is the main language of books, newspapers, airports and air-traffic control, international business and academic conferences, science technology, diplomacy, sport, international competitions, pop music and advertising."

Confusion sometimes arises over the terms used to describe English language teaching in different contexts. Acronyms most commonly used include: TEFL, TESOL and TESL.

1. TEFL (Teaching English as a Foreign Language) and TESOL (Teaching English to Speakers of Other Languages) effectively mean the same thing. Teaching is directed towards non-native speakers, often in commercial language schools both in the UK and overseas. Objectives of students will vary, but generally range from learning for leisure, e.g. improvement of general or conversational English to more focused study such as learning English for specific or academic purposes.

2. TESL (Teaching English as a Second Language) is also found in the UK and overseas, but the objectives differ from TEFL/TESOL. Usually classes in the UK take place in state schools and colleges with a high non-native speaking population in the local area. In the UK, TESL often involves teaching individuals from ethnic minority groups who require a level of English that will allow them to integrate into the country's educational, work and cultural environment. Overseas, TESL is the term most often used to describe a context in which English is the language of administration and communication between different language groups, for example Nigeria, Kenya and Singapore.

English Language Teaching, or ELT, is a term that is often used and covers TEFL, TESOL and TESL. This is an international term that is in common use.

In general, the ELT profession can be divided into state sector provision and private sector provision. As mentioned above, English is the most studied foreign language and English teaching can thus be found in state institutions at all levels - from elementary to higher education. In recognition of the importance of an early start to language learning, recent years have even seen the emergence of pre-school ELT. A global view, however, shows differing starting ages for ELT depending on the organisation of the education system and the importance accorded to English as a subject of study within the curriculum. The private sector acts either as a supplement or alternative to state provision. Private lessons and private language schools are ubiquitous; no other subject on the school curriculum receives as much additional provision. In Britain alone, the ELT industry is worth over £500 million a year, most of this generated by the private sector.

The precise scope of EFL teaching varies enormously between countries and between schools. Some focus on the formal teaching of grammar, vocabulary and pronunciation; others adopt a more communicative approach with the emphasis on developing fluency.

The sheer demand for ELT has led to a wide range of standards of provision particularly within the private sector. This, coupled with a lack of systematic regulation, has spawned a rather amorphous industry. At one extreme, language schools can set up and do business without any formal academic checks being carried out; at the other, institutes submit to regular, voluntary inspections to ensure quality standards. For the intending teacher of EFL, it is clearly preferable to practice in an environment where quality standards are upheld since these are likely to be linked to better working conditions and greater job security. To this end, there is a wide range of teaching qualifications for teachers of EFL. Each country sets out the requirements for local teachers working within its state institutions. For native speakers there is a wide range of qualifications:

- basic introductory (see page 18)
- internationally recognised (see page 22)
- qualified teaching (see Page 28)
- advanced (see Page 28)

In all, ELT is a liberal arts profession which has grown haphazardly into big business.

Footnote
Mailing lists (on the Internet) are topic-specific discussion groups. For those interested in ELT, a good starting point is to send the following e-mail message to **listserv@cunyvm.cuny.edu**:
info TESL-L
This will start the E-mail flowing

Discussion boards (on the Internet) allow those with a common interest to share ideas. EFL teachers should visit:
http://www.pacificnet/~sperling/wwwboard/wwwboard.html

To meet other teachers, go to:
http://www.eslcafe.com/phone4
http://www.classroom.net/contact/

Section 1 — What is EFL?

Can I do it?

The necessary qualities and potential career structure of an EFL teacher.

One assumption is that any native speaker can teach EFL. Generally speaking, this is true, but it is advisable to have some introductory training. In fact, many organisations which previously accepted untrained graduates are now demanding some form of EFL training as evidence of suitability. There is also an unofficial league table of native speech and your employment opportunities increase the higher your position. The European perspective is:

First Division	Second Division	Third Division
British English	Australian English	Indian English
American English	South African English	West African English
Canadian English		other varieties

Points can be lost or gained by deviating from the unwritten norms. For example, a British-English speaker with a strong local accent may lose points; an Indian with an American-English accent may enhance his/her position. In other parts of the world the table may look different depending on political alliances and business partnerships.

There are three distinct stages in the career of many TEFLers:

- the early years, characterised by short-term employment on foreign contracts
- the middle years, characterised by more permanent work either in the UK or abroad
- the later years, in a position of responsibility

Though many institutions will offer short-term contracts to unqualified teachers, for those interested in jobs offering better working conditions and greater security some form of qualification is a must.

One of the attractions of TEFL is the opportunities that it provides for foreign travel. Many people enter TEFL after completing their secondary or tertiary education, while making up their minds which career direction to follow. Some stay the course and make a career of it; others spend a few years in the profession before moving into other (more stable or more lucrative) fields. In either case TEFL can be a stimulating interlude or a lifelong commitment, providing opportunities for wide international contact.

While there is no single attribute which makes someone suited to TEFL, it is useful if you can demonstrate some of the following:

- an outgoing personality to motivate learners
- a sympathetic ear to deal with learning problems
- team spirit to get on with other teachers
- organisational skills to manage your teaching and your students' learning
- an interest in the English language
- a non-judgmental approach to cultural differences
- a curious mind.

On the academic front, those who have some experience of learning a foreign language often spend time as TEFLers. Many recruits to the profession come from graduates of modern languages. However, this is by no means a pre-requisite for the successful teacher. What is important is a sensitivity - to one's language and to one's students. The rest comes with training and classroom practice.

It is, of course, difficult to know whether TEFL is the profession for you. But as few institutions can provide you with a 'taster', it is more often than not a matter of signing up for an introductory course so that you can get you foot into the door. However, if you would like the opportunity of seeing TEFL (or TESL) in action you could ask:

- **a local private language school if you could observe some classes**
- **a local state school or college with a non-native speaking population if they have ESL classes you could observe**

Another avenue for gaining practical experience is as a helper or assistant social organiser on a summer course. Many established language schools employ additional helpers during the summer period to cater for the large influx of students that they (hope to) have. This type of work will bring you into contact with a large number of foreign students and their teachers. It will give you an idea of the students' backgrounds and their expectations, as well as giving you an opportunity to find out from their teachers about the rewards and frustrations of being a TEFL teacher.

For those who want to embark upon a TEFL training course, a number of options are open. A number of institutions offer short full time or longer part time introductory teacher-training courses. These courses, which cater for a variety of special needs, are exactly what they say, introductory. They do not lead to a generally recognised qualification to teach English as a foreign language (TEFL) but may be useful if you need to decide whether you are suited to TEFL as a career or as a lead up to a TEFL Certificate (see page 22). The duration of an introductory course is usually one week.

> *...TEFL can be a stimulating interlude or a lifelong commitment, providing opportunities for wide international contact.*

Section 1

What is EFL?

Advice for careers in EFL

The job market and possible avenues of employment

Prospective

TEFL teachers have various options open to them for employment in the UK and overseas. Different employers require different qualifications. Before embarking on a course of study leading to a specific qualification, it is advisable to check work requirements of employers in the countries you are particularly interested in. Some private school chains which have schools world-wide may offer employment following successful completion of their own TEFL training courses. However, these courses sometimes concentrate on the school's own teaching methods and materials and may limit your mobility between employers.

Voluntary agencies and religious organisations (see page 14) increasingly look for well-qualified candidates and often ask for a minimum of two years' post-qualification experience. Recruitment agencies will usually have a number of vacancies available at any given time. Generally, these agencies look for candidates with formal qualifications in TEFL and would normally expect the courses taken by applicants to have included a teaching practice element. A number of agencies recruit for their own chain of schools as well as for other employers.

Employment, especially during the early years, tends to be contract based. Contracts are usually for 9 months to one year, though longer and shorter ones are available. Before taking up a job offer, make sure you know the 6 'w's:

1. Who will you be teaching, i.e. the profiles of your students and the number in a class
2. Where will you be living and working, i.e. the location
3. What teaching materials and pedagogic facilities will be provided
4. When will you have to work, i.e. working days/hours and holidays
5. What will you be paid
6. What length will your contract be

Although the world is potentially your oyster, it is useful to know where the current demands for your services are likely to be. These are affected by various factors, including economic cycles and the need for internationalisation. Today's 'top spot' may be tomorrow's 'black spot' - politically and economically unstable with poor working and living conditions.

At present, employment prospects for EFL teachers in eastern and central Europe are expanding; however, work is generally poorly paid. Posts in developing countries have decreased considerably over the past few years because of a reduction in foreign aid budgets. A knock-on result of this has been that numbers of highly qualified teachers, many with up to thirty years' experience, have joined the market for TEFL jobs in other parts of the world. Other areas where employment prospects are good are Turkey, parts of East Asia (for example Taiwan, Vietnam and Korea), the Gulf, and most of Latin America. Demand for qualified and experienced EFL teachers is also set to expand in countries such as Australia and South Africa.

In general, salaries and employment prospects are not good in the profession and the demand that teachers be qualified, experienced and specialised continues to increase. The recognition of specific qualifications may vary between countries, though the RSA/Cambridge and Trinity College Certificate and Diploma (see

> *...prospective teachers would be well advised to research thoroughly the target country and the local institution...*

page 22 and 26) are the most widely accepted. Some countries also require teachers to have a degree or equivalent qualification. New entrants to the profession would be well advised to get reputable qualifications as early on in their careers as possible. Volunteer teaching programmes are a valuable source of experience for those new to the profession or seeking to expand their professional skills.

In the UK, all established language schools will require their permanent teachers to be qualified; however, there may be some opportunities for unqualified teachers during the summer rush as language schools scramble to find teachers to meet unexpected demand. Abroad, there is such an enormous range of requirements (set by the country, the education ministry and the schools themselves) that prospective teachers would be well advised to research thoroughly the target country and the local institution before committing themselves.

Though posts of responsibility (see page 48) and opportunities for promotion exist, there is relatively little in-built career structure within the profession. Many teachers move on to look for new opportunities (professional and geographical), rather than spending their professional lives working their way up within one organisation. The flatness of hierarchy provides few opportunities for professional advancement, and the absence of career progression means that one can spend one's life as a teacher at the chalk face

Schools often operate with relatively little infrastructure. They require few administrative staff or pedagogic facilities. Once they have rooms, furniture, teaching materials and some audio-visual equipment, they are ready to go. The main cost is the teachers required to provide English lessons. Therefore, organisations look to their teachers as income generators. The ubiquitous advertisements 'TEFL teacher required' indicate the availability of jobs rather than careers. Teachers of EFL can justly regard themselves as members of the second-oldest profession, able to provide their services in a truly international arena. In one sense, TEFL provides an international work permit enabling practitioners to travel the world and earn their keep; in another, it creates a sense of dislocation by belonging to a profession with few clearly defined standards and regulations.

As TEFL is a deregulated industry, there is an enormous variation in terms and conditions offered. In general, you command greater earning power as a qualified teacher, although there are many parts of the world where you will be accepted just on the basis of being a native speaker. For those wanting to work abroad, the most important factors are pay and the cost of living. These need to be balanced. As a novice teacher, you should not expect EFL to make you rich. However, you should ensure that your basic salary is at least enough to cover living expenses (food, accommodation plus some surplus for other expenses), though you may find that you need to give extra classes to pay all the bills. Before you leave on a foreign assignment, make sure that you have:

- **some written guarantee of work**
- **a description of your duties**
- **the number of hours you are expected to work**
- **the payment you are to receive**

> *....there are many parts of the world where you will be accepted just on the basis of being a native speaker....*

For many countries, some form of work permit or visa is necessary before you are allowed to enter or work. Find out the requirements from the local embassy/consulate and make sure that you have all the relevant documents. For more advice on finding work, see page 40.

REGENT

Regent Language Teacher Training

- Cambridge RSA CELTA Certificate in English Language Teaching to adults

- ARELS Certificate in Teaching 1:1

- Courses run throughout the year at Regent Oxford and Regent London.

For further information please contact:

**Regent Marketing, 14 Buckingham St, London WC2N 6DF.
Tel: 0171 872 6600 / Fax: 0171 872 6610
E-mail: 01562.744@compuserve.com**

The Other methods of employment

Finding employment on your own and working with organisations & exchange programmes

TEFL teachers are used to carrying out their own job searches, using the available formal and informal channels of information to gather details about vacancies or sending their CVs, unsolicited, to potential employers if they sense this will help them in their job search. In general, job seeking is a DIY (do-it-yourself) activity and both existing and intending TEFLers will need to demonstrate a degree of independence and determination to track down available and suitable jobs. While getting one's foot onto the first rung of the job ladder is a challenge, each subsequent change presents dilemmas, especially when moving from one country to another.

There are a number of sources you can use to find openings. English language newspapers and magazines in the country you intend to work, dedicated EFL magazines and papers such as the EL Gazette and the TESOL Newsletter are also useful. Recruitment agencies and national conferences such as JALT - Japan Association of English Language Teachers are other sources. Some countries have international centres which will post job opportunities on notice boards. Tourist information centres also collate details of schools. The English language version of a country's Yellow Pages is also worth a look.

Some organisations will do the job searching for you and provide you with a range of opportunities, or at least destinations. Some of these organisations are international chains which have schools or partnerships in different countries. An example is the International Language Centres (ILC) Group, a British-based private educational and training group with subsidiaries and associated companies in Britain, France, Czech Republic, Middle East and Japan, whose activities cover running language schools, company training programmes, teacher training centres and vacation courses in many countries.

The British Council, the United Kingdom's international network for education, culture and development services, offers English Language Teaching services worldwide through its schools, called Direct Teaching Operations. The British Council is widely regarded as a reliable employer.

The degree of welfare and support during the contract vary from organisation to organisation. Some of the services provided are:

- information on current vacancies through newsletters or bulletin boards
- job briefing by previous job holder
- country briefing before the assignment starts
- help with administrative matters, such as visas and work permits
- help with finding accommodation
- orientation course at the beginning of the assignment
- support of a professional organisation during the contract through in-house seminars, training courses, etc.
- help with finding a new job at the end of the contract.

In addition, some employers will help on the financial side with:

- travel at the beginning and end of contract
- trips to the UK during the contract
- insurance
- settling-in allowance

Another way into the profession is to follow the organisation's TEFL

> *...Some organisations will do the job searching for you and provide you with a range of opportunities...*

training course, which opens the door to working within the organisation. For example, successful applicants to Berlitz, one of the largest language organisations in the world, attend in-house training in the 'Berlitz method' and upon satisfactory completion of the training, teachers are employed within the organisation. Minimum entry requirement is a first degree or equivalent.

In addition to the private sector, another route is provided through state-sponsored schemes. The Japan Exchange and Teaching (JET) Programme invites young college and university graduates from overseas to participate in international exchange and foreign language education throughout Japan. The programme started in 1987 with the co-operation of the governments of the participating countries. In 1997, there was a total of 5,351 participants on the programme from the twenty-five countries. The JET programme seeks to help enhance internationalisation in Japan by promoting mutual understanding between Japan and foreign countries. The programme's goals are to intensify foreign language education in Japan, and to promote international exchange at the local level by fostering ties between Japanese citizens (mainly youth) and JET participants.

In the field of EFL, JET appoints Assistant Language Teachers (ALTs), who are placed mainly in publicly run schools or local boards of education. There are a very limited number of cases in which the participants are placed in private schools. ALTs engage

Section 1 — What is EFL?

in language instruction, the preparation of teaching materials and language-related extra-curricular activities under the guidance of teachers' consultants or Japanese teachers of the foreign language. Applicants must hold at least a bachelor's degree.

The Council on International Educational Exchange (CIEE) is a private, non-profit organisation dedicated to furthering international education and student travel. CIEE offers students a number of other international educational exchange opportunities, including International Study Programmes at universities in a number of overseas locations, with courses lasting from 3 weeks to one year.

As a result of the shortage of sufficiently trained English teachers in Eastern Europe, many state schools are recruiting foreign English teachers. Those interested should contact The Central Bureau for Exchange.

A final avenue is through educational consultancies which recruit EFL teachers as one of a range of services they provide. World-wide Education Service (WES) provides school inspections, advice and in-service teacher training to schools overseas and in the UK, as well as EFL recruitment.

The British Council English Language Information Unit
10 Spring Gardens,
London,
SW1A 2BN

The Central Bureau for Exchange
Seymour Mews House,
Seymour Mews,
London W1H 9TE

CIEE
52 Poland Street,
London W1V 4JQ

ELS *(American chain of language schools)*
ELS Language Centers,
5761 Buckingham Parkway,
Culver City,
CA 90230 USA

JALT Central Office
Urban Edge Building,
5th Floor, 1-37-9 Taito,
Taito-ku, Tokyo 110,
Japan

ILC
White Rock, Hastings,
East Sussex, TN34 1JY
Tel: 01424 720 109 / Fax: 01424 720 323

EL Gazette
Dilke House,
1 Malet Street,
London WC1E 7JA
Tel: 0171 255 1969 / Fax: 0171 255 1972

TESOL, Inc.
(Teachers of English to Speakers of Other Languages)
1600 Cameron Street, Suite 300
Alexandria, Virginia 22314-2751 USA
Tel: 703-836-0774 / Fax: 703-836-7864

For information on teaching without qualifications:
http://www.purdue.edu/oip/sa/work/teach1.htm

MASTER'S in TEACHING ENGLISH BY DISTANCE LEARNING
TESOL/TESP

Modular Programme

- Entry qualifications: First degree, normally, and 3 years' relevant professional experience.
- Start work whenever you wish, registering at any of 4 quarterly points during the year.
- Foundation module first, then modules can be done in any order, though we work out a Learning Pathway with you.
- You pay for modules as you request them: foundation/full £500, half £250, dissertation £1,250, total £5,000 (Supplement outside Eastern/Western Europe, total £6,000.) £600 discount for completion in 2 years.
- Weekend Seminar/Tutorial visits twice a year, fixed well in advance, to Aston Local Resource Centres in (currently): Spain, Greece, Turkey, France, Italy, Germany, Hungary and Japan; equivalent Study Days at Aston. Students from any location may attend any of these sessions. Support programme for students remote from these countries.
- You have your own Course Tutor at Aston, and Specialist Staff for each module.
- Personal support and feedback by e-mail/fax/phone/audiotape. Regular newsletter.
- No need ever to come to Aston, though you're very welcome if you do!

ASTON UNIVERSITY
Birmingham UK

Course Content

2-5 years for 100 credit accumulation
(Diploma: 50 credits)

Full modules 10 credits each
Foundation
Methodology
Course and Syllabus Design
Materials Analysis and Production
*Lexical Studies
*Text and Discourse Analysis
*Investigating Interaction in Context

Half modules 5 credits each
Language Testing
Distance Learning
Management of ELT
Teacher Development
Computational Linguistics
Grammar of Modern English

Dissertation = 25 credits

All assessment is by assignment (you can do the *modules by exam if you like).
You submit assignments at any of 4 quarterly points during the year, ie when you are ready.
Same certification/transcript as in-house degree at Aston.

The Benefits to You

Powerful professional development, publications maybe, promotion quite probably, and certainly new horizons. We have helped people to:

- add new dimensions to their teaching
- design new syllabuses and construct research projects
- publish papers in leading international journals
- move into management positions
- drive forward professional associations in their own country
- move on to a PhD
- set up their own company.

Wherever You Are:

You will belong to a worldwide network of Aston students and over 500 graduates which is held together by in-country events, through an international e-mail contact group, by a Newsletter for all Master's course participants, and by the half-yearly LSU Bulletin, in which you can publish research articles.

Contact:
MSc Secretary, Language Studies Unit,
Aston University, Birmingham, B4 7ET, UK
Tel: ++ 44 121 359 3611 x 4242
Fax: ++ 44 121 359 2725
E-mail lsu@aston.ac.uk

Volunteering
Getting into a volunteer programme and where this can lead

There are two ways into volunteering:
- by offering one's services on literacy programmes in communities where there are large numbers of immigrants (ESL).
- by working on a recognised volunteer programme abroad.

But remember that 'volunteer' does not necessarily mean 'untrained', and today many organisations require applicants to have qualifications and/or experience in TEFL.

If you are interested in the first option and live in an area with an immigrant population, you'll need to find out about the policies and provisions for ESL teaching. In the UK, your starting point will be the local education offices which are responsible for the provision of education in all state-maintained schools and colleges. From them you will be able to find out whether there is a need for volunteers.

If you wish to teach abroad as a volunteer, there are a number of organisations that you can approach. In the UK, the best-known is Voluntary Services Overseas (VSO). VSO is a charity that sends aid to developing countries - not in the form of money, food, clothing or equipment, but in the form of expert volunteers. VSO currently has 1950 qualified and experienced volunteers between the ages of 20 and 70 working in about half the world's poorest countries in Asia, Africa, the Caribbean and Pacific Islands. Volunteers work closely with local communities in order to pass on experience and skills that are not available locally. In ELT, recent job advertisements sought graduates both with and without TEFL qualifications for volunteer posts in China, Vietnam, Laos, The Maldives and Mongolia.

The Eastern European (EE) Partnership is an initiative by Voluntary Services Overseas and places selected graduate volunteers in Central and Eastern Europe and the former Soviet Union. Volunteers must be qualified teachers or have a TEFL qualification with two years' experience and are paid a local salary.

Christians Abroad has a World Service Enquiry desk for people of any faith, or none. It offers information and advice about opportunities to work overseas through a variety of different organisations, secular and Christian.

In the US, the Peace Corps remains a popular way for many people to go abroad, experience a new culture and teach English as a Foreign Language before returning to the US to work in state education. Posts are usually for two years and volunteers follow a training programme for between 6 months and one year before they leave. Volunteers must be US citizens with a college degree.

United Nations Volunteers (UNV) has about 2,000 volunteers worldwide. This organisation, which is an arm of the UN, recruits experienced professionals (normally 5 years' ELT experience) for a minimum of one year.

Another US organisation, Worldteach, sends volunteer teachers abroad for one-year terms of service. (The volunteers are expected to pay a certain fee). In addition, there are other programs which crop up from time to time. A good source of information on these programs is the magazine Transitions Abroad, address below.

Useful Contacts:

VSO Enquiries Unit
317 Putney Bridge Road
London, SW15 2PN
Tel: 0181 780 1331

EEP
Carlton House
27A Carlton Drive
London, SW15 2BS
Tel: 0171 780 2841

Christians Abroad
1 Stockwell Green
London, SW9 9HP
Tel: 0171 737 7811

Worldteach
Harvard Institute for International Development
1 Eliot Street
Cambridge, MA 02138
USA
Tel: 00 1 617 495 5527

Peace Corps
Room 8500
1990 K Street NW (PO Box 941)
Washington, DC 20526, USA
Tel: 00 1 800 424 8580
http://www.peacecorps.gov

UNV
Postfach 260 111
D-53153 Bonn
Germany

Transitions Abroad
18 Hulst Road
Amherst, MA 01004-1300, USA
http://www.transabroad.com/

Volunteers in Asia:
http://www.volasia.org

Volunteer work overseas:
http://www.purdue.edu/oip/sa/work/voluntr.htm

TEFL Teachers

"I was surprised by the size of the package."

How will the VSO experience translate for you?

On a Voluntary Service Overseas placement, you won't be expected to live on fresh air. We'll pay the full cost of your flight and VISA. There's a living allowance while you are overseas. You'll be entitled to pre-departure, mid-term and end-of-placement grants. We'll cover your pension and NI contributions. And there's a whole host of other valuable benefits.

You won't be poorer for the experience either. You will be bringing your skills to the heart of the developing world. Working at grass roots level. And sharing your knowledge with people whose livelihoods depend on you. With your placement lasting two years, you'll also have the time to build productive relationships with your students and see the results of your efforts. All in all, you'll return home a very marketable person - according to The British Council, "a two year TEFL placement with Voluntary Service Overseas makes an excellent career decision for the serious teaching professional."

We are interested in hearing from graduates with a TEFL qualification - a PGCE is not essential for all placements - and at least six months' experience. Vietnam, Mongolia, Ethiopia... these are just a few of the countries within which we have placements available.

VSO gives professionals the chance to share their skills with people in the developing world. But before you apply, ask yourself the following questions. Could you thrive for up to two years in unfamiliar environment on modest income? Are you flexible and someone who values human relationships? Are you entitled to unrestricted entry to the UK?

If you can honestly answer 'yes' to all these questions, please write to us, quoting reference AE/EE3S, and we will be happy to send you further information and answer any queries you may have. Contact: The Enquires Unit, VSO, 317 Putney Bridge Road, London SW5 2PN. Tel: 0181 780 7500 (24 hours). Website: http://www.oneworld.org/vso/

VSO

charity number 313757.

International House Teacher Training

International House has been running and certifying teacher training courses since 1962 and its original Introductory Certificate provided the model for what is now the RSA/Cambridge Certificate in English Language Teaching to Adults. International House trains over 3,000 teachers every year at fifteen centres around the world.

RSA/Cambridge Certificate (CELTA)

Probably the most widely recognised qualification for teaching English as a foreign language. This highly practical course is run at IH London every month throughout the year and very frequently at other IH centres in the UK and abroad. A choice of full-time and part-time courses is available.

RSA/Cambridge Diploma (DELTA)

Run full-time over 8 weeks at IH London, Hastings, Budapest and Barcelona and part-time over an academic year in IH Madrid, Barcelona, Lisbon and Rome.

IH London has run a distance training programme leading to the RSA/Cambridge Diploma since 1980. This programme, designed and developed by IH, is the only one on offer anywhere in the world preparing candidates for the Diploma.

There is also a written Examination Preparation course by correspondence to assist those candidates who did not pass the written Diploma examination and who will be re-sitting.

Teaching with International House

International House recruits around 350 teachers every year for its network of over 100 schools in 27 countries. Posts offer good salaries, airfares, paid leave and assistance with accommodation. Most are for initial periods of one or two years. All IH schools offer excellent educational support and back-up to their teachers and most have well-developed programmes of continuous in-service training.

IH offers an international career structure to its staff with many teachers transferring to another IH school elsewhere in the world at the end of their initial contract. A significant number of senior posts ranging from Senior Teacher to School Director are available every year.

For more information on our courses or for details on working for International House, contact us in London or at any of our schools worldwide.

International House

Argentina
Australia
Austria
Belarus
Brazil
Czech Republic
Egypt
England
Estonia
Finland
France
Georgia
Germany
Hungary
Italy
Lithuania
Former Yugoslav Republic of Macedonia
New Zealand
Poland
Portugal
Romania
Singapore
South Africa
Spain
Switzerland
Ukraine
USA

International House
106 Piccadilly London WIV 9FL Telephone 0171 491 2598 Fax 0171 409 0959
E-mail: 100733.511@compuserve.com

Getting *Started*

SECTION 2

Basic qualifications

"The benefits of packing a qualification along with your luggage"

page 18

Summer school and UK work

"The UKs thriving EFL market examined as an employment arena"

page 20

Entry level qualifications

"A look at pre-service and certificate teaching qualifications"

page 22

Basic qualifications

The benefits of packing a qualification along with your luggage

Whether you are new to the profession or have previous TEFL experience, you will find that schools are increasingly looking for teachers with qualifications. Qualifications break down into two categories:

- recognised
- unrecognised

Recognised qualifications (see section 3) cover a range of awards offered by:

- RSA/Cambridge
- Trinity College London
- university departments of education and other institutes of higher education. These postgraduate courses, leading to State Qualified Teacher Status (QTS), preferably with a TEFL component, are recognised for TEFL posts in the UK and abroad, and for TESL posts in the UK

Courses leading to unrecognised awards include a range of full time or part time introductory courses offered by both large and small institutions in the UK and abroad. Some of these courses are introductory, in that they are intended for pre-service teachers. They will provide a taster of TEFL and can be useful if you need to decide whether you are suited to TEFL as a career or as a lead up to a recognised TEFL Certificate. The duration of an introductory course can be from two days to one week. Other longer courses are also on offer, but these do not necessarily confer a recognised qualification at the end.

It is undoubtedly valuable to have a qualification. It can open doors to better jobs (better pay, greater recognition) with better conditions (security, holidays, etc) and better prospects (promotion). However, the worldwide ELT market does not attach equal importance to recognised qualifications. In some countries and among some employers, 'recognised' means qualifications from the authorised bodies listed above; in others, 'recognised' means having completed any relevant teacher training course.

So, what can one expect on an introductory course? These provide a taster to the profession. They are aimed at native speakers with a good educational background, but no previous teaching experience who need a quick introduction to TEFL methodology and language analysis before looking for or starting a job. The course will sketch out for you the world of TEFL, the requirements of learners and the expectations of employers. The TEFL methodology component will equip you with essential techniques for teaching a class, based around using a published course book. It should also provide you with some guidelines for coping with difficult learning situations. Finally, the language analysis component will cover the elements of language, ensuring that you can identify the basic building blocks, combine them into grammatical combinations and recognise inappropriate usage.

Having covered an introductory course and without any experience, prospective teachers face the challenge of finding their first job. At this hurdle their success in interviews will depend on their personality, the knowledge and skills derived from the course, and the current job demand. At times of high demand, for example during the peak summer months in the UK, it is much easier for the novice to get his or her foot in the door and get their first experience. In a supportive environment and among an experienced team, the enthusiastic novice can glean a lot from colleagues. On the other hand, being faced with one's first class can be a daunting experience, no matter how well prepared one is. That's why confidence (but not arrogance) and an outgoing (but not domineering) manner can help the inexperienced teacher cope with their first class.

Not all novice teachers can (or want to) work in the UK. In fact, for many, one of the attractions of the profession is the opportunity to travel. It is impossible to list the range of jobs available outside the UK, nor to categorise them in any meaningful way. Suffice to say

> "...It is undoubtedly valuable to have a qualification. It can open doors to better jobs, with better conditions and better prospects..."

that in most jobs you will be expected to teach in some sort of school setting. You may be working:

- **with young learners or adults**
- **with large classes or with individuals**
- **with beginners or with advanced**
- **motivated learners or unmotivated learners**
- **during the day and/or in the evening**
- **as part of a large team or on your own**
- **with prescribed materials or free to choose your own**

The list of permutations is extensive. That is why it is important to understand as much as possible about the job before you commit yourself.

A lot of information about working conditions abroad tends to be anecdotal. Valuable as they are as personal experiences,

anecdotes can distort the picture. Just as two people may have very different experiences of doing the same job or working for the same company in the UK, the same is even truer of working abroad where differences can easily become accentuated. There are a number of internet sites on which you can read, and post questions about working abroad. At the time of publication, the following sites provided opportunities for asking about and finding out about working conditions abroad:
http://www.eslcafe.com/jd/
http://tefl.com/bbs/index.sht

Following an introductory training course in an organisation which provides work after successful completion of their training course provides easier entry to the world of teaching. Organisations such as Berlitz, with a worldwide presence, offer their teachers employment 'upon satisfactory completion of the training'. Berlitz is one of a number of organisations which has its own method and materials. These customised materials provide the basis for teaching at different levels and on different programmes within the school, such as Business English. This approach creates a degree of uniformity within teaching since all courses at a certain level will be based around the same course book. The Berlitz training course, therefore, provides specific training in using Berlitz materials, as well as covering standard introductory issues for teachers joining the profession.
http://www.berlitz.com/berlitz_corporate/employment.html

While 'methods' were fashionable in the 60's and 70's, recent years have seen a move to a more eclectic approach. The focus has moved away from 'teaching' towards 'learning' and teachers are encouraged to develop a versatile set of tools for different learners and learning styles. Materials, too, have become more wide-ranging, offering teachers enormous choice (and sometimes confusion) by their sheer volume. For the novice teacher following an introductory course, it is important to cover some aspects of:

- **communicative methodology, and the way that this translates into classroom practice and is reflected in published materials**
- **the grammatical system and how to teach it in a participative way**

As English gains ground as an international language, there will undoubtedly be more and more opportunities for native-speaker teachers to find jobs abroad. Getting a toehold on the TEFL ladder is not difficult if one considers the total demand for teachers; however, for a good job one needs some basic training (on which to build), determination (to thoroughly investigate the job market) and luck.

> *...As English gains ground as an international language, there will undoubtedly be more and more opportunities...*

Websites of interest:

Centres for UCLES awards:
http://www.go-ed.com/ciltsrsa/centres.cfm

Distance learning programmes:
http://www.wfi.fr/volterre/distancelearning.html

TEACH ENGLISH OVERSEAS
CAMBRIDGE/RSA CELTA

St Giles Educational Trust

- **Four week CAMBRIDGE/RSA intensive courses all year round at our Brighton and Highgate centres**
- **Maximum of 12 participants per course**
- **Counselling service to help you find an overseas post**

St Giles College
51 Shepherds Hill
London N6 5QP
Tel: 0181 340 0828
Fax: 0181 348 9389
E-mail: lonhigh@stgiles.u-net.com

St Giles College
3 Marlborough Place
Brighton BN1 1UB
Tel: 01273 682747
Fax: 01273 689808
E-mail: stgiles@pavilion.co.uk

Courses also available at our San Francisco centre

We also arrange courses for overseas teachers

Over 40 years of the best in English Language Teaching

Summer school & UK work

The UKs thriving EFL market examined as an employment arena

In the UK, the TEFL summer season runs roughly from June to September. It is a period when language schools are traditionally very busy as they welcome students on their range of summer courses. The preparations for these courses start many months before, as schools gear themselves up for the summer onslaught. Most schools need to take on temporary staff to cope with the additional numbers.

Although general English courses take place throughout the year, in the summer period, schools may segment the market into different products.

Junior courses

Junior courses are short courses from 1 - 4 weeks for children and teenagers. The upper age limit on these courses is 16 - 17. The minimum acceptance age is steadily falling as parents try to give their offspring the competitive edge with a grounding in English and a visit to the UK. Where numbers permit, schools may subdivide their junior schools by age, for example, 13 - 17 year olds in one group and under 13's in another. Within each age range children will be grouped according to ability. Junior course programmes are usually based on combining language learning in the morning with activities in the activities. Activities include the range of sports facilities provided by the host institution, and excursions to places within driving distance of the school. In recent years junior course providers have begun to rent boarding schools for their courses. This has the advantage of providing a ready-made environment, with facilities for teaching, activities and residential accommodation. To staff these courses, schools need to employ a range of personnel, including teachers, carers and social organisers. Not all junior courses are residential and some schools offer host family accommodation either as standard or as an alternative to the residential package.

General courses

These courses are aimed at the adult market, covering the 17+ age range. They typically bring together learners of different ages, different backgrounds and different objectives. Students come for varying lengths of time - anything from 2 weeks upwards. Course providers have to balance these elements and try and keep all their students happy most of the time. Some offer a standard programme of general English Language lessons throughout the day. Others offer a varied diet, often combining the English Language component with other more specialised or more fun activities. These activities are frequently offered as options, especially during the afternoons, thus acting as a counter-balance to the morning programme. Options can cover anything from special varieties of English (English Literature, English for Business, Law, Medicine, Engineering, etc) to improvement activities, for example English plus Fashion and Design, English plus Computing to sports activities such as golf or tennis. Sometimes these combinations are formalised so that they are marketed as activity courses (see below).

Activity courses

These courses combine an English learning element (usually in the morning) with a more specialised focus in the afternoon. Examples are:

English plus Photography
English plus Literature
English plus Fashion and Design
English plus Computing
English plus Institute of Commercial Management Diplomas
General English plus Business English
General English plus Legal English
English plus Golf
English plus Tennis

The summer is a boom time for the EFL industry. The large operators often take on extra premises to cater for increased demand, particularly for junior courses. Smaller schools can expect to be busy catering for students from their established markets, as well as attracting learners from emerging markets, such as eastern Europe. In addition, summer schools spring up throughout the country - operating during the summer period and then closing their doors come the autumn. This part of the market is largely unregulated and, in the absence of any agreed code or imposed conditions for teaching staff in the EFL industry, their standards can be very variable.

Some universities and colleges of further education also offer summer vacation courses. With their main student population on holiday, they can provide both the environment and the facilities - classroom and sports. However, they usually need to recruit (additional) teachers who can manage and deliver the range of courses that they propose to offer. There are many providers, many locations, many courses and many durations on offer. A useful guide to the world of higher education can be found at:
http://www.studyuk.hobsons.co.uk/
http://www.feonline.hobsons.com/

Summer work overseas

The normal trend is for schools abroad, at least in Europe, to scale down their activities during the holiday period. Some operate on reduced staffing as their regulars take their summer breaks; others close completely when they reach the end of term (any time in June or July, depending on how the national holidays are organised). This means that there are fewer jobs on offer abroad, as students wishing to improve their language head towards the UK. However, there are some schools, particularly the larger ones, which offer special summer courses for the junior market. In addition, there are international camps, attracting students from all over the world, where some instruction in English may be on offer.

The run-up to the summer involves a lot of preparation. In terms of recruiting staff, some schools have their 'regular' summer teachers, trained EFL teachers who perhaps work as state school teachers at other times of the year or British teachers who return to the UK during the summer to visit family and friends. However, schools do typically recruit additional staff. Depending on the size of school and the number of positions to be filled, schools may advertise either in the local or national press. This recruitment can start any time after Christmas and continue right up to the summer, as schools get a better idea of the number of students who have booked courses. Contracts can be anything from 2 - 10 weeks. Job duties can include one or more of the following:

- **teaching English**
- teaching other subjects (e.g. Literature) or running activities, such as sports
- **organising and/or participating in the social programme**
- looking after children on excursions
- **supervising (part of) the residential accommodation**

Summer courses need a lot of preparation, not only because of the numbers involved, but also because of the mixed expectations of learners. It is important for teachers to remember that students come for a mix of study and pleasure. Getting the balance right can be a problem in the classroom, as the teacher tries to provide a varied and stimulating mix for the diverse group.

Other problems that teachers may have to contend with on junior courses are:

- **naughty children**
- spoilt children
- **homesick children**
- criminal children
- **conflict with the local population**

These are all areas which may need to be dealt with sensitively yet firmly. They can test even the most experienced professional. For the new teacher they are part of the rich learning experience to be gained from TEFL.

For more information on junior courses, general and activity courses in the UK see:
http://arels.org.uk
http://www.englishinbritain.co.uk/
http://www.abls.co.uk/

For more information on schools worldwide see:
http://www.eslcafe.com/phone
http://www.petersons.com/summerop
http://www.studyabroad.com
http://www.u-net.com/eflweb/tefl121.htm

Teacher's Survival Kit

For more information and to receive our Oxford English Language Teaching Catalogue please contact:
Oxford University Press
English Language Teaching Department,
Great Clarendon Street, Oxford OX2 6DP
E.mail: elt.enquiry@oup.co.uk
http://www.oup.co.uk/elt

OXFORD UNIVERSITY PRESS

Entry level qualifications

A look at pre-service and certificate teaching qualifications

The Cambridge Certificates in English Language Teaching

The Cambridge Certificate in English Language Teaching to Adults (CELTA) is the standard initial recognised training qualification for those wishing to enter the profession. (Up to January 1997 it was called the RSA/Cambridge Certificate TEFLA (CTEFLA)). Considered to provide a well-balanced introduction to the theoretical and practical aspects of TEFL, this qualification is recognised by Ministries, employers, overseas public schools and colleges, ELT organisations and the British Council in Britain and in many other countries. A second award, the Certificate in ELT to Young Learners in Language Schools (CELTYL), is available both as a course in its own right and also as a two-week extension course (Certificate of Endorsement in ELT to Young Learners in Language Schools or CEELTYLLS) for CELTA graduates. (For further information on awards for young learners, see page 35).

Who are they for?

Native or bilingual speakers of English who wish to enter the profession. It is also suitable for practising EFL teachers who have no formal or practical teaching qualification.

Who offers them?

Approved centres throughout the world as part of a range of EFL teacher training schemes administered by UCLES under the joint title of RSA/Cambridge. In order to offer this course, centres must have their course and programme, staffing and facilities approved by UCLES. As from January 1998 you can study for:
CELTA at 176 centres in 35 countries worldwide
CELTYL at 6 centres, mostly overseas
CEELTYLLS at 9 centres, two in the UK

Private institutions (language schools) and state colleges, polytechnics and universities offer the CELTA. Quality is variable. Institutions with an established track record in ELT are likely to offer a better training programme, based on their own in-house approach to course development.

How long is the course?

For CELTA and CELTYL, about 100 hours' tuition offered either on a full time basis (typically over four weeks) or on a part time basis over a number of months. For CEELTYLLS about 50 hours.

What you need to enrol?

Candidates must be at least 20 years old by the start of the course and have a standard of education which would allow entry to Higher Education in their own country. Candidates must have competence in English, both written and spoken, that enables them to follow the course and complete all the assessed elements successfully. Previous teaching experience is an advantage, but is not required.

How much does it cost?

Course fees vary from centre to centre. Individual centres can provide details.

How do I pay for it?

State funding is not available for these courses. However, you may be able to get a Career Development Loan (CDL) from a participating bank to borrow up to £8,000 to study on a vocational course not longer than two years.

About the course

Syllabus areas
A significant amount of observation of classes and teaching practice, systematically integrated with the input sessions. The specific aims of the scheme are to enable candidates to:

1. develop an awareness of language and a knowledge of the description of English: meaning, form and function, grammar, vocabulary, pronunciation;
2. learn how the language and its elements fit into ELT practice;
3. develop an initial understanding of the contexts within which adults (CELTA) or children (CELTYL) learn English: educational backgrounds and traditions, motivations, learning styles.
4. develop familiarity with the principles and practice for effective English language teaching to adults (CELTA) or young learners (CELTYL/CEELTYLLS), including the roles of the teacher and the learner;
5. learn how to plan for effective teaching: course and lesson planning, selecting and adapting materials and activities, testing and reference;
6. develop basic techniques for managing the classroom: organising and directing classes for adult (CELTA) or young (CELTYL/CEELTYLLS) learners of English;
7. develop knowledge of and techniques in specific teaching procedures: introducing and practising language, checking learning, correcting errors, developing receptive and productive skills;
8. observe and practice teaching; give and get feedback on teaching
9. identify methods for self-assessment and opportunities for future development as professionals in ELT;

In addition, most course providers will advise trainees about jobs and the job market; some will also be able to offer job placements.

Assessment

There is no final exam. Assessment of each candidate's practical ability in ELT is carried out on a continuous basis and trainees are assessed in all the syllabus areas with particular emphasis being given to their ability to foster learning in their students. Candidates may also be required to produce several pieces of written work of a practical nature.

Results

Candidates are awarded the appropriate certificate (CELTA, CELTYL or CEELTYLLS), if they satisfactorily fulfil all the requirements of the scheme. They will have shown potential for further developments after the course, and an awareness of language learning problems and of classroom techniques.

Grades & Certificates

Grades awarded for CELTA and CELTYL: A Excellent, B Good, C Pass, D Fail. These grades are based on continuous assessment of teaching ability and potential, as shown in the teaching practice sessions and coursework. There are no grades for CEELTYLLS.

Other qualifications

The Certificate in the Teaching of English to Speakers of Other Languages is offered by Trinity College London. Aimed at pre-service native and non-native speakers (proficient users) with a good educational background, candidates must successfully complete a course approved and moderated by the College. Courses are offered at more than 50 centres in the UK and selected locations overseas. The course lasts a minimum of 130 tuition hours (on a full time or part time basis) exclusive of any distance learning or assignments. In addition, the course contains a minimum of six hours teaching practice plus a minimum of four hours teaching observation. As each approved course centre can set its own syllabus within the prescribed framework, programmes may vary. The minimum required course components are:

- **language awareness (grammar, syntax, lexis, phonetics, phonology and varieties of English**
- language teaching and learning: methods, styles and strategies
- **classroom management and methodology, procedures and techniques**
- using teaching aids: blackboard, white board, tape recorder, overhead projector, etc
- **evaluation of published ELT materials**
- practical instruction in a natural language unknown to the candidates
- **profile of a learner of EFL**
- practical project or materials compilation project
- **needs analysis and lesson planning**

Assessment is carried out first by the course tutor(s) and then moderated by the College Moderator, who also interviews trainees at the end of the course. The assessment normally covers:

- **all course work (continuous)**
- teaching practice
- **examinations/tests set by the institution**
- practical projects or materials compilation projects
- **work on teaching and learning an 'unknown' language**

Outside Europe, other qualifications are offered by a range of private and state institutions. Some of these qualifications are recognised worldwide as evidence of introductory competence. The length of such courses is also around 100 hours or 4 weeks, and areas covered will aim to provide a mix of background information, classroom methodology and as much hands-on, practical experience as possible. While CELTA focuses on teaching English to adults, other courses may broaden the scope of learners to include teaching young learners. In addition, courses may provide specific instruction in foreign languages in order to prepare teachers for work in a specific country, eg survival Korean or basic Japanese; others may include techniques for preparing students for exams such as TOEFL/TOEIC; while others may include more exotic areas such as music in the classroom, cross cultural awareness, or computers in language teaching.

Conclusion

These entry level qualifications provide trainees with the basic skills to teach EFL to adults. The key to continued personal and professional development is, of course, practice and further training. It is recommended that teachers who have completed the CELTA spend the next few years getting as much and as varied (geographical and learners) experience as possible in order to develop their perspective of the profession and their own job prospects. Some of these teachers will return to the classroom for further training, following courses leading to a higher qualification such as a diploma (see page 26).

For more information on Career Development Loans:
DFEE, Sanctuary Buildings, Great Smith Street, London SW1P 3BT
Tel: 0171 925 5000 / Central fax: 0171 925 6000 / Enquiries: 0171 925 5555 / E-mail: info@dfee.gov.uk
or contact your local bank

To search for Centres for UCLES Language Teaching Awards in 47 countries worldwide:
http://www.go-ed.com/ciltsrsa/centres.cfm

For information on training to Teach English as a Second Language in the US:
http://144.96.225.66/esltrain.html
http://www.els.com/intltefl.htm

For information on Teacher Training for English as a Foreign Language in France:
http://www.wfi.fr/volterre/teachtrain.html

---

b.tti
The Bell Teacher Training Institute

RSA/CAMBRIDGE CERTIFICATE AND DIPLOMA COURSES IN TEFLA

The Bell Language Schools have a worldwide reputation for excellence in training teachers in English as a foreign language to adults.
Throughout the year, we offer full-time Certificate and Diploma Courses, with part-time courses also available in Cambridge:

4-week full-time Certificate Courses
• Year round in Cambridge and Norwich

27-week part-time Certificate Course
• October - June in Cambridge

10-week full-time Diploma Courses
• April - June in Norwich • March - May in Saffron Walden

27-week part-time Diploma Course
• October - June in Cambridge

For more information on these courses, please contact:
The Bell Teacher Training Institute (AUTH),
Sales and Registration Department, Hillscross,
Red Cross Lane, Cambridge CB2 2QX, England
Tel: +44 (0)1223 212333 Fax: +44 (0)1223 410282
E-mail: info@bell-schools.ac.uk
Internet: http://www.bell-schools.ac.uk

The *Bell* Educational Trust Ltd   Accredited by The British Council
Registered Charity Number 311585

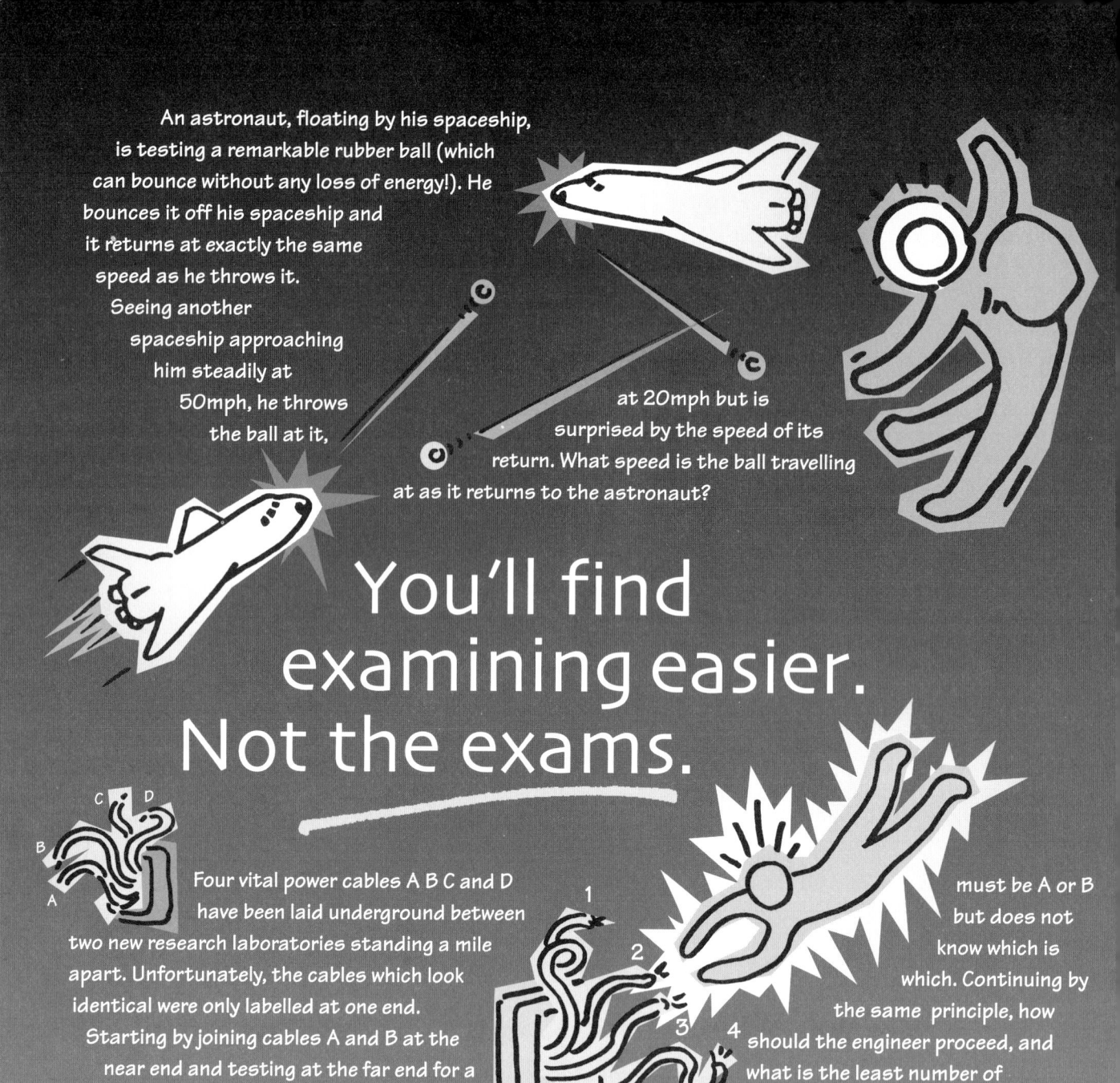

An astronaut, floating by his spaceship, is testing a remarkable rubber ball (which can bounce without any loss of energy!). He bounces it off his spaceship and it returns at exactly the same speed as he throws it. Seeing another spaceship approaching him steadily at 50mph, he throws the ball at it, at 20mph but is surprised by the speed of its return. What speed is the ball travelling at as it returns to the astronaut?

You'll find examining easier. Not the exams.

Four vital power cables A B C and D have been laid underground between two new research laboratories standing a mile apart. Unfortunately, the cables which look identical were only labelled at one end. Starting by joining cables A and B at the near end and testing at the far end for a completed circuit, the engineer can identify the two cables which must be A or B but does not know which is which. Continuing by the same principle, how should the engineer proceed, and what is the least number of trips between labs required, to identify correctly all four cables?

At Pitman Qualifications we believe in providing a simple and highly responsive certification service.

So responsive in fact, that our examinations are available on demand, when you and your candidates want them, and certificates are returned fast, usually within eight weeks. An arrangement that will keep everyone happy.

All of which is particularly relevant when it comes to ESOL. Pitman Qualifications offer five levels of ESOL examinations, which cover both spoken and written English, and cater for all age groups and levels of ability. And with the backing of the Pitman name, it's no wonder that these qualifications command the respect of employers, universities and professional bodies.

As well as examinations on demand, you can also expect
• Competitive pricing
• FEFC funding and SCAA/QCA recognition • The integrity of total external assessment
• Automatic feedback on unsuccessful candidates.

So if you're not already offering our qualifications, finding out more couldn't be easier.

Just complete the coupon and post it back to us in an envelope marked:
FREEPOST Pitman Qualifications
1 Giltspur Street
London EC1B 1RW.
Alternatively, contact Simon Young on 0171 294 2798, fax 0171 294 2418, or E-mail stephenw@city-and-guilds.co.uk

Pitman Qualifications

Please send me further information on
☐ NVQs ☐ Single subjects
Name of organisation

Contact name
Job Title
Address

Tel
Fax   AE/2

Answers. Ball: 120mph. The ball's speed relative to the approaching spaceship is 20mph + 50mph = 70mph. It will bounce back at 70mph relative to the spaceship (still travelling at 50mph towards the spaceman). Relative to the spaceman it will therefore be travelling at 70mph + 50mph = 120mph. Cables: Only one trip to the far end and back is needed, and only two joins of cables! Solution: Connect A to B. At far end label cables 1 2 3 and 4. Suppose 2 and 4 complete the circuit, connect 2 to 3. Return, disconnect A and B, test for new circuit: pair one of which will be C or D (other end of 2), the other will be C or D (other end of 3). Suppose the new pair is A and C, then by deduction A will be 2, B is 4, C is 3, D must be 1.

SECTION **3**

Further Qualifications

In-service qualifications

"Promotion, progression and development are all dependant upon experience and qualification, so we look at in-service qualifications and their value as a leg up"

page 26

University courses

"There are more to Universities than bachelor's degrees, in the UK they provide a wide variety of TEFL related courses from pre-service and in-service qualifications up to post doctoral study"

page 28

Specialisation

"There are as many areas in which a teacher can specialise, from business to leisure. A look at the way forward from General English"

page 33

In-Service qualifications

Promotion, progression and development are all dependant upon experience and qualification, so we look at in-service qualifications and their value as a leg up

In a competitive job market, as ELT has become, a pre-service certificate provides would-be teachers with a marketable qualification which will undoubtedly help them in their job search. After a teaching contract (or two), many teachers will be interested in climbing the job ladder, either by seeking promotion in their current school or getting a post of (greater) responsibility elsewhere. A diploma could be the key. These in-service awards are aimed at those who already have a relevant qualification and experience in TEFL. In general, they aim to develop knowledge of the theoretical background and convert this into effective teaching.

The Cambridge Diploma Awards
The awards offered by Cambridge/RSA are at present undergoing review. DTEFLA (Diploma in Teaching English as a Foreign Language), an award for experienced teachers of English, has been redesignated (as of autumn 1998) DELTA (Diploma in ELT to Adults), though DTEFLA will continue in its present form until June 1999. The DOTE (Diploma for Overseas Teachers of English), designed for experienced teachers who are non-native speakers of English, continues. Three new awards are in preparation:
- *Diploma in ELT to Young Learners (in early stages of piloting)*
- *Endorsements to Diploma awards for those already holding a DTEFLA or DOTE (under consultation)*
- *Diploma in Teaching English for Business (under consultation)*

Finally, the new Advanced Diploma (see below) provides training in management skills for ELT.

Who are they for?
In general, all basic diploma courses are intended for candidates who have a minimum of two years' relevant experience of language teaching to adults, children or teenagers.

Who offers diploma courses?
Approved centres throughout the world as part of a range of EFL teacher training schemes administered by UCLES under the joint title of RSA/Cambridge. In order to offer this course, centres must have their course and programme, staffing and facilities approved by UCLES. At present:
- **DTEFLA is offered by 35 centres worldwide**
- **DELTA is being piloted by some 14 centres in the UK and overseas**
- **more than 250 centres outside the UK offer DOTE (for non-native speakers)**

How long are the courses?
DTEFLA and DELTA courses run for two or three months; part time courses normally for eight or nine months. IH London runs the only accredited distance Diploma training programme, consisting of a compulsory two-week, face-to-face orientation course, usually in London, in July, August or September, followed by a Distance Training Programme, based on correspondence course units DOTE courses are normally one year part time.

What do you need to enrol?
For the DTEFLA and DELTA, candidates should normally have:
- *at least two years' full time experience of teaching English to adults either in the UK or abroad*
- *a first degree or equivalent level of education*
- *educated native speaker proficiency in English (both spoken and written) for candidates whose first language is not English*

Candidates should be at least 21 years old by the date of the examination.

For the DOTE candidates must:
- *be practising teachers with at least 500 hours of relevant classroom experience.*
- **have a minimum standard of English at entry to pass Cambridge First Certificate in English (FCE), Cambridge Examination in English for Language Teachers (CEELT) Level 1 or Certificate in Communicative Skills in English (CCSE), Level 2. (Candidates who have passed CEELT Level 2 are exempt from the language examination of DOTE)**
- *be at least 21 years of age by the date of the examination.*

How much does they cost?
Course fees vary from centre to centre. Individual centres can provide details.

How do I pay for them?
State funding is not available for these courses. However, you may be able to get a Career Development Loan (CDL) from a participating bank to borrow up to £8,000 to study on a vocational course not longer than two years.

About the courses
Syllabus areas
In general DTEFLA, DELTA and DOTE balance theory and practice, and encourage teachers to build on their own experience as well as to learn from the experience and knowledge of others.
The key areas to be covered are:
1. *The English language and its description: grammar, lexis, phonology, discourse; form and function*
2. *The history, practices, principles and theory of teaching and learning in adult language learning*
3. *The process of teaching/learning: managing different learner types and different learning contexts, developing personal effectiveness as a classroom teacher*
4. *From syllabus design to lesson planning*
5. *Lesson delivery: teaching language knowledge and the four skills*
6. *The nature, role and use of teaching and learning*

resources and materials: selection, evaluation and use
7. *Principles and procedures for evaluation, monitoring and assessment of adult learners: from handling errors to preparing for EFL examinations*
8. *Professional development opportunities*
9. *Teaching practice, including observation and feedback, tutor observation and feedback, and formal continuous assessment.*

Methodology
- *Lectures*
- *Seminars*
- *Tutorials*
- *Lesson observation*
- *Teaching practice and feedback*
- *Reading and writing assignments to prepare for the exams*

Assessment
DTEFLA/DELTA
Two written papers and two externally assessed lessons of between 45 minutes and 1 hour. (A partially internally assessed scheme, where written and practical work during the course is taken into account in determining the final result, is operated at some Centres).

DOTE
The assessment is in four parts:
1. *Methodology*
2. *Language*
3. *Project*
4. *Practical test of six assessed lessons*

Results
Candidates are awarded the appropriate diploma (DTEFLA or DELTA), if they satisfactorily fulfil all the requirements of the scheme, based on:
- *course work*
- *teaching practice*
- *exams*

Grades & Certificates
Grades awarded are: pass and distinction.

Other qualifications
The Licentiate Diploma in the Teaching of English to Speakers of Other Languages is offered by Trinity College London. Aimed at native and non-native English speakers (proficient users) with a minimum of two years' full time experience of teaching EFL, candidates must successfully complete a course approved and moderated by the College. Courses leading to the examination are offered at centres in the UK and overseas.

The examination consists of 4 parts:
- *a written paper on the nature and use of English*
- *a written paper concerned with language teaching and learning*
- *an oral interview covering features of spoken English and general aspects of language teaching a sample lesson*

Practical examinations are held on dates agreed by the College with examination centres; written examinations currently take place twice a year. The pass mark in all four parts of the examination is 65%. Candidates failing one, two or three parts may retake the relevant exam(s) within three years.

Pilot courses for a new award, the Advanced Diploma in Language Teaching Management (ADLTM), certificated by RSA/Cambridge, are currently being offered at one UK and two overseas centres. This award, which is higher than DTEFLA and DOTE, is aimed at teachers with substantial experience of working in EFL schools, colleges and departments in the private and/or state sector. It is intended to shift the focus away from the practicalities of the classroom to other more specialised areas where teachers might want to undertake certificated professional development. The aim of ADLTM is to enable language teaching professionals to:

extend their knowledge and awareness of relevant management principles and practices
develop their management skills through the application of this knowledge and awareness to a teaching context
demonstrate these skills in effective practice as language teaching managers

Preparatory programmes will be offered via a variety of course formats with a minimum duration of three months full time and a maximum duration of two years part time. Courses will involve 100 hours of 'contact' time together with approximately 200 hours of work on guided follow up and preparation, with a further 200 hours of work on assignments.

Prospects
In a sector which is characterised by lack of hierarchy, a diploma enhances a teacher's prospects of getting a position of responsibility. Different schools have different hierarchies. Beyond 'teacher' come positions, such as:

- *senior teacher*
- *course co-ordinator*
- *course director*
- *assistant director of studies*
- *director of studies*

Each of these involves responsibilities beyond (and often as well as) classroom teaching; and teachers who have a diploma under their belt can aspire to one such post. Responsibility in the ELT environment includes many areas of pedagogic administration: timetabling, supervision, teacher allocation, course design, materials selection. The list is truly open-ended. So, a word of caution. Exchanging one's customary pedagogic concerns for administrative worries may not necessarily be the golden opportunity that every classroom teacher is cut out for.

For more information on Career Development Loans:
DFEE, Sanctuary Buildings, Great Smith Street, London SW1P 3BT
Tel: 0171 925 5555 / Central fax: 0171 925 6000
E-mail: **info@dfee.gov.uk** or contact your local bank

To search for centres offering UCLES Language Teaching Awards worldwide: **http://www.go-ed.com/ciltsrsa/centres.cfm**

For information on training to Teach English as a Second Language in the US: **http://144.96.225.66/esltrain.html**
http://www.els.com/intltefl.htm

For information on Teacher Training for English as a Foreign Language in France: **http://www.wfi.fr/volterre/teachtrain.html**

For information on the DTEFLA by distance learning:
International House, 106 Piccadilly, London, W1V 9FL
http://www.international-house-london.ac.uk/teacher/rsadelta.html
E-mail: **100733.511@compuserve.com**

University courses

There are more to Universities than bachelor's degrees, in the UK they provide a wide variety of TEFL related courses from pre-service and in-service qualifications up to post doctoral study

University Certificate and Diploma courses

Courses leading to the CELTA award are offered by more than 50 universities and colleges in the UK. (See page 22 for more information about course content). Courses leading to DTEFLA/DELTA and the Trinity Licentiate Diploma in TESOL are run by a smaller number of universities in the UK. So, in this area the universities compete with private organisations in providing preparatory courses. With such a range of options, candidates will need to choose carefully. While course length, entry requirements and basic course content are fairly constant between different organisations, other factors will vary, including:

- *full time, part time or distance-learning basis*
- *fees*
- *start dates*
- *group size*

Finally, the quality of the programme itself needs attention. Organisations which have a dynamic ELT operation are more likely to be abreast of current developments in the profession, which will be carried over into their own teacher training.

In addition, universities and colleges run a wide range of teacher training programmes leading to their own in-house certification. Ranging from one-week introductory programmes to one-year advanced diplomas, these courses compete in an already crowded market. Although most of these programmes are run at fixed dates throughout the year on an open basis, many institutions are happy to tailor-make courses for closed groups of teachers or educationists from specific countries/teaching contexts. Beyond the introductory programmes for those without experience, there are many certificate and diploma programmes aimed at postgraduate teachers with relevant qualifications and experience. Based on lectures, seminars and tutorials, they are unlikely to provide opportunities for teaching practice, which form an integral part of other recognised awards. So, for those teachers looking for an introductory course, the CELTA award will, in general, be a more useful starting point.

One developing market that universities have identified is for 'refresher courses' aimed at giving practising teachers an intensive overview of the latest developments in ELT. So when do teachers have time for such professional development? Usually during the summer holidays when expatriates return to the UK. So tapping into this demand a number of universities are offering 2 - 4 week full or part time (eg mornings only) programmes.

While many university-certificated programmes focus on general ELT methodology for adults and children, other courses are aimed at teachers wishing to specialise in other areas, such as:

- *ESP, including specific ESP areas, e.g. Business or Medicine*
- **materials development**
- *ELT management*

Offered typically at diploma level, these courses are mainly run on a full time, on-site basis at universities with a track record in ESP, including Aston, Essex, Lancaster, Warwick, Liverpool, and College of St Mark and St John.

For those interested in checking the likely quality of what you'll get on a specific university course, a set of league tables were set up in 1996 to evaluate university performance according to the following criteria:

- *Curriculum Design, Content and Organisation*
- *Teaching Learning and Assessment*
- *Student Progression and Achievement*
- **Student Support and Guidance**
- *Learning Resources*
- **Quality Assurance and Enhancement**

The results, which can provide a starting point for checking certain aspects of certificate and diploma courses, can be found at: **http://**

> *"...there are many certificate and diploma programmes aimed at postgraduate teachers with relevant qualifications and experience..."*

www.niss.ac.uk/education/hefce/

PGCE courses

The Post-Graduate Certificate of Education (PGCE) is an introductory teaching award for students who have successfully completed a degree course, usually at a UK university. All TEFL/TESL/TESOL courses which previously led to a PGCE have now been withdrawn except in 9 British universities, where it is offered as a subsidiary subject. TEFL/TESL/TESOL subsidiaries have no formal entry qualifications, though competence in English Language is a pre-requisite (on all PGCE courses).

Secondary PGCE courses prepare candidates to enter the profession to teach a specialist subject. They include modules dealing with:

- *background issues (the educational system, child development, school organisation and curriculum development)*

- *practical teaching issues (school induction, teaching observation and progressive involvement in teaching, including substantial blocks of full time teaching practice)*
- *subject teaching issues (content, teaching approaches and resources)*
- *In addition to the 'first method subject', students are required to follow a subsidiary study, such as TEFL/TESL/TESOL.*

There are no formal requirements as this is an introductory course and no previous experience is required. University schools of education develop their own programmes around key issues including:

- *approaches to teaching EFL/ESL*
- *EFL/ESL in the UK school curriculum*
- *teaching EFL internationally*
- *learner strategies and learning factors*
- *lesson preparation*
- *teaching grammar*
- *teaching vocabulary*
- *teaching pronunciation*
- *teaching the four skills*
- *resources for the EFL/ESL classroom*

Courses are developed through a combination of input sessions and seminars. Teaching practice is not included as standard for subsidiary subjects. Some institutes organise it and others encourage their students to arrange this for themselves if possible.

The teaching profession in the UK has all-graduate entry and it is necessary for new teachers to have professional training in education, as well as a high standard of competence in the subject to be taught. Therefore, if you want to teach in a British maintained (state-run) secondary school, you will need to follow a course leading to the PGCE to achieve qualified teacher status (QTS). In ethnic communities, where English is spoken as a second or foreign language, provision is often made for special teaching or coaching in English. In schools with a small population requiring this type of support, there may be opportunities for part time teaching; in others full time posts may be available. In the British private school sector, the PGCE is also widely recognised. Opportunities for part time and full time work are available in schools which attract non-native pupils who need help with their English. Many Further Education (FE) Colleges also organise EFL and ESL courses, for which the PGCE subsidiary is also a recognised teaching qualification.

In addition, the TEFL/TESL/TESOL subsidiary is recognised as a first qualification for those wishing to work for voluntary agencies, such as VSO and for many private language schools abroad.

Masters degrees

The Masters degrees offered by UK universities cover a wide range of ELT-related subjects. At one end of the spectrum we find those linguistics courses which focus on theoretical issues; at the other, courses that aim to develop practical skills and an understanding of classroom issues. Between these two extremes are programmes specialising in aspects of linguistics, language, language teaching and language teaching management. Linguistics used to be regarded as an arts subject and awards were MA. Now, a course may lead to one of the following postgraduate degrees, according to the orientation of the subject and the tradition of the university:

MA (Master of Arts),
MSc (Master of Science)
MPhil (Master of Philosophy)
MLitt (Master of Letters)
MEd (Master of Education)

MA and MSc programmes are taught courses based on an intensive programme of lectures; MEd, MLitt and MPhil programmes may be taught and/or research based; PhD/DPhil (Doctor of Philosophy) is based on research (see below).

What is linguistics?
Linguistics is the scientific study of human language. The main areas within linguistics are:

Phonetics (physical nature of speech)
Phonology (use of sounds in language)
Morphology (word formation)
Syntax (sentence structure)
Semantics (meaning of words & how they combine into sentences)
Pragmatics (effect of situation on language use)

Together, they provide a picture of the forms and functions of language.
These areas listed above translate into the following academic disciplines:

School of English and American Studies

UNIVERSITY of EXETER

Applied Liguistics, MA/Dip., 1 year full time, 2 years part time. Taught course (6 subjects) + 20,000 word dissertation (supervised).

Lexicography, European MA/Dip., 1 year full time, 2 years part time. Placement with publishers available.

University of Exeter
Queen's Building, Queen's Drive
Exeter EX4 4QH
Tel: +44 (0) 1392 264302 Fax: +44 (0) 1392 264361

- *Theoretical linguistics (how languages work)*
- *Historical linguistics (how languages develop)*
- *Sociolinguistics (language and the structure of society)*
- *Psycholinguistics (how language is implemented in the brain)*
- *Applied linguistics (teaching, translation, etc)*
  Computational linguistics (computer processing of human language)

While all postgraduate degree programmes in linguistics and applied linguistics will introduce the main areas, not all of them will be covered in the same depth, as the precise content of a course will depend on the specialities of the teaching/research staff. In general, pure linguistics is unlikely to be a useful qualification for a practising EFL teaching since it is too far removed from the chalk face.

What is applied linguistics?
Applied linguistics comes closer to the realities of the EFL classroom since it deals with how to apply the insights gained from linguistics study and research. While all course areas are likely to be relevant, some will have more practical orientation to classroom issues than others. In particular:

- *Second Language Acquisition (SLA) deals with how we learn foreign/second languages and proposes models for SLA. This area is useful for examining and considering 'student speak' (the students' linguistic performance) in the classroom*
- *Language Use covers real life topics including verbal vs non-verbal communication (body-language etc); conversational interaction (different styles or levels of speech, politeness, rules for turn-taking in conversation etc)*
- *Techniques for Language Testing deals with methods for measuring language knowledge and linguistic performance*
- *Curriculum and Materials Design covers the role that English plays in the institutional programme and the types of materials that can be used to achieve the learning objectives*
- *Teaching of Language deals with a range of pedagogic issues for managing the learning/teaching process.*

What other Masters programmes are there?
Linguistics and applied linguistics are often combined with other subjects such as:

- *English Language*
- *English Literature*
- *ELT/ESOL*
- *ESP*
- *Bilingualism*
- *Translation*
- *Information Processing*

Other Masters courses focus on specialisations, the most notable being ESP, which is offered by a number of universities, either as an MA, MSc or MPhil programme.

Aimed at those already working in TEFL or TESP, courses typically include modules on:

- *discourse*
- *lexis*
- *functional grammar*
- *second language acquisition*
- *methodology*
- *ESP/EAP*
- *Business English*
- *ESP course design*
- *ESP methodology*

Who are Masters courses for?
There is no standard profile, though course participants are expected to be experienced EFL teachers (minimum 3 years' classroom experience) who have worked at primary, secondary or tertiary levels in different educational systems. Some may have carried out other responsibilities, such as teacher training, course administration, materials and course design, or project work on evaluation and testing, or teaching methodologies. Broadly speaking, these linguistics and linguistics-related courses provide an insight into language so that graduates can pursue a career in language teaching, computing, speech therapy and other less obvious areas such as advertising, publishing as well as translating and interpreting.

How are these courses offered?
Either full time (FT) over 9 months to one year; or part time (PT) over two to five years; or on a distance learning (DL) basis. While full and part time courses follow well-established programme delivery channels, distance education provides a novel mode of

---

MA in Linguistics (TESOL)
and
MSc in English Language Teaching Management
both
by Distance Learning

A choice of distance learning courses for language teaching professionals wishing to upgrade their qualifications and to deepen their knowledge of linguistics.

The Courses
27 months by distance learning (no residency requirements)
October & March intakes

The Content
All modules are written for distance learning courses by language &/or management specialists.
Students take
- 8 Core Modules
- 2 Option Modules
- & write a dissertation on a subject of interest

We also run residential English Language courses for non-native speakers

University of Surrey
Promoting Excellence in Education & Research

For further information please contact:
Mrs T J Hughes
English Language Institute
University of Surrey
Guildford
Surrey, GU2 5XH
United Kingdom
Tel: +44 (0)1483 259910
Fax: +44(0)1483 259507
E-mail: eli@surrey.ac.uk
Internet: http://www.surrey.ac.uk/ELI/eli.html

study, combining the use of self-study printed materials with other kinds of teaching techniques and types of media, eg television, radio, satellite broadcasts, video-cassettes, audio-visual teaching aids, computers etc. In particular, Aston University's well-established modular MSc in TE/TESP has proved very successful with participants and employers, with a reputation for academic depth and practical relevance. The number of universities offering DL programmes is increasing all the time. In addition to Aston, the UK universities of Birmingham, Sheffield, Heriot-Watt, and Leicester have developed or are developing relevant courses.

- *work within one of the examination boards or related organisations, such as UCLES, RSA, LCCI or Trinity College*
- *work within one of the ELT associations, such as IATEFL or TESOL*
- *positions with ELT publishers*

Today's MA's offer a wide range of possibilities and specialisations, in terms of content and delivery. They have moved on from the theoretically-focused approaches of the 70's and many now reflect the service-oriented demands of the vibrant ELT industry. There

> *...applied linguistics will introduce the main areas, not all of them will be covered in the same depth, as the precise content of a course will depend on the specialities of the teaching...*

How are they assessed?

Different criteria are used for assessment - either singly or combined. These include:

- *course work (work submitted and exams taken throughout the year)*
- *assignments during the course*
- *examinations at the end of the course*
- *end-of-course dissertation*
- *research project report*
- *extended essay*

Well, it very much depends on what your professional objectives are. On the personal front, it can be a rewarding and challenging experience to return to university after some years at the chalk face for a period of re-evaluation. In fact, for many mature students the variation in activity, focus and pace can be very satisfying and enriching in itself. However, for a teaching post at a language school, an MA would be something of a luxury. Beyond basic teaching posts, here are some of the doors which may be opened through having an MA:

- *positions of responsibility, such as Assistant Director of Studies or Director of Studies, in language schools in the UK and abroad*
- *positions of responsibility within the UK maintained sector in areas such as curriculum design or inspection*
- *positions of responsibility in-company abroad, where specialist language training is offered to company employees*
- *British Council recruited posts on undergraduate programmes at foreign universities, which may combine English language teaching with some lecturing/teaching in applied linguistics*
- *posts at British universities as tutors on EAP courses or other language courses*
- *posts at foreign universities directly recruited by the institution itself, which may combine ELT with some contribution in applied linguistics*

are plenty of courses on offer. For the intending student, the question is whether the investment of time and money will bring a good return.

PhD degrees

Many of the institutes offering MA's also offer PhD's. PhD's are based on original research and usually take at least three years, and often longer, to complete. Students/researchers admitted on PhD courses are expected to choose a specific research topic. The only limitation is the expertise of the academic supervisor, who needs to support the research project and guide the student. Therefore, in theory, any area relating to linguistic theory or ELT practice could be the basis for investigation leading to a doctorate. However, getting one's PhD is a rigorous undertaking, suited only to the most committed. While TEFL needs research in order to push practice forward, the types of contribution are as likely to come from practical investigation as from applied research.

Information about university courses in ELT, linguistics or related disciplines are available from the British Council's ECCTIS 2000, a national database providing quick and easy access to information on nearly 100,000 courses at over 700 universities and colleges of higher and further education throughout the UK. It gives comprehensive information on course content, entry requirements and institutional data.
Tel: 0171 930 8466 or **0161 957 7755**
E-mail: **education.enquiries@britcoun.org**

More details about postgraduate courses leading to a Masters degree can be found in: **University Courses in Education**, published by:
The Universities Council for the Education of Teachers
58 Gordon Street
London, WC1H 0NT

For more details about postgraduate courses leading to a PGCE contact:
The Graduate Teacher Training Registry
Fulton House
Jessop Avenue
Cheltenham, GL50 3SL

Do you travel as well as the English Language?

British Council Teaching Centres
QUALITY LANGUAGE LEARNING WORLDWIDE

- Europe • Africa • The Middle East
- Latin America • The Far East

The British Council is the largest international ELT employer with an expanding network of over 120 teaching centres worldwide, employing a staff of over 1,600 teachers and managers.

Each year we recruit about 300 teachers through London. These posts offer attractive salaries, airfares, baggage allowance, medical cover and paid leave. For mobile staff a central pension contribution is available. Contracts are usually for a period of 2 years, and are often renewable. Staff are encouraged to transfer to other centres within the network at the end of their contracts, giving the opportunity for career progression for suitably qualified and experienced teachers. Almost all middle and senior managers are recruited from within the network.

Our teaching centres are well equipped and offer excellent resources and support. Staff are encouraged to develop in all areas of interest, such as computer assisted language learning (CALL), teacher training, materials development, young learners and skills through English. Training awards are available to help with further study.

Details of vacancies appear in the *Guardian* and *Guardian International*.

Come and work with us!

For further details and a brochure contact:

*CMDT Recruitment, The British Council,
10 Spring Gardens, London SW1A 2BN.*

Telephone: 0171 389 4931. Fax: 0171 389 4140.

E-Mail:calice.miller@britcoun.org

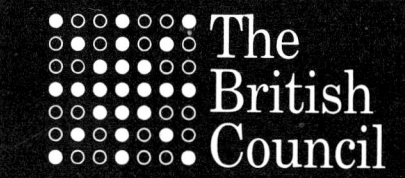

The British Council

The British Council, registered in England as a charity no. 209131, is the United Kingdom's international network for education, culture and development services

The British Council is committed to a policy of equal opportunities.

Specialising In TEFL

There are as many areas in which a teacher can specialise, from business to leisure. A look at the way forward from General English

As the ELT market fragments, reflecting the more diverse and specific demands of language learners, there is an increasing need for specialists. While the term 'general English' can be used to cover the range of courses providing a broad base of language competence, ESP (English for Specific Purposes) includes those programmes satisfying the needs of a special group. Such learner groups may be identified by one (or more) of the following:

- *their divergence from the normal adult learner profile (eg young learners, one-to-one learners, homestay learners, exam preparation learners)*
- *their objectives (academic purposes, professional purposes or leisure purposes)*
- *their professional function (marketing, human resources)*
- *their professional sector (banking, telecomms, insurance, pharmaceuticals)*

For teachers wishing to work in theses areas, there are a few 'developed' teacher training programmes, in particular:

- *young learners (see below and page 22)*
- *ESP (English for Specific Purposes)*
- *Business English*

More often, however, schools offering 'combination' courses or 'options' rely on the earlier training of their teachers, such as English plus Literature (offered by the TEFL teacher who graduated in English Lit), or tap into the trainer's own leisure pursuits as in English plus Golf; alternatively, they may expect trainers to bone up on the essentials of marketing or telecomms in response to varying student needs. There are, however, some notable exceptions:

Some training organisations (rather than language schools) specialise in providing courses to trainees from a particular sector, such as English for Banking, and can therefore invest in training their trainers or recruit from those with a background in the twin disciplines

Others combine familiarity in a number of business sectors or professional functions to run a range of specialist courses

Another exception is in-company trainers, whose employment in a single environment should enable them, in time, to fit together the pieces of the corporate jigsaw so that they can provide training which brings together the mix (sector and function) required by their trainees

The route to working on non-general ELT courses is often circuitous and indirect. Most teachers will have worked in general EFL for a number of years, gaining experience in a range of contexts, before moving on. Some will have found that teaching professionals on a one-to-one basis provides a context for sharing knowledge that is difficult to achieve in a group environment; others grow into an appreciation of the different challenges provided by adult learners in

> *"...Most teachers will have worked in general EFL for a number of years, gaining experience in a range of contexts..."*

Teacher Education & Applied Linguistics

KING'S College LONDON *Founded* 1829
University of London

The English Language Centre at King's College London currently offers two programmes for English Language Teachers wishing to broaden their theoretical knowledge and develop their practical skills.

RSA/Cambridge DipTEFLA

We offer a part-time nine-month course leading to this prestigious postgraduate qualification for experienced teachers of EFL. Trainees who perform well on the course will be eligible for *fast-track* entry to the King's College MA in ELT and Applied Linguistics (below).

MA in ELT and Applied Linguistics

This programme runs on a part-time basis over two academic years. In addition to three core modules providing comprehensive coverage of all key issues, the MA offers a stimulating and practical set of optional courses including British (Cultural) Studies, English for Academic Purposes, Trainer Training and Translation Studies.

For further information, please contact: English Language Centre, King's College London, Campden Hill Road, London W8 7AH. Tel: 0171 333 4075, Fax: 0171 333 4066, E-mail: elc@kcl.ac.uk
WWW:http://www.kcl.ac.uk/kis/schools/hums/ELU/top.html

Promoting excellence in teaching, learning & research
Equality of opportunity is College policy

Section 3 — Further Qualifications

contrast to younger learners. However, for many providing an input on non-general courses is simply an opportunity to vary the daily teaching diet and perhaps pursue a personal interest in a professional environment, as in English plus Golf or English plus Photography.

While general EFL provides a cornerstone for much specialist language teaching, there are certain important characteristics for each of the variants which may place different demands on the teacher

Teaching young learners:
- *learners may need special help with their learning*
- *learners may be away from home for the first time*
- *teacher may have to fulfil social/pastoral duties*
- *teachers may face keen, lively and enthusiastic children*
- *teachers may need to exercise a firm hand to control classes*
- *likely to involve activity and experiential learning*

Teaching one-to-one learners:
- *high expectations of the learner*
- *learner likely to expect tailor-made programme based on his/her needs*
- *teachers will need some materials development expertise*
- *teachers may need to have wide knowledge of business sectors and professional functions*
- *full time programmes, intensive for both learners and teacher; therefore good pacing essential*
- *teacher needs to be flexible to respond to changing learner needs*
- *teacher needs to be attentive at all times*
- *provides opportunities for teacher's own development*
- *variety of teaching contexts*

Running homestay courses:
- *convenience may be offset by unwanted closeness*
- *need to provide both pedagogic and social activities; students expect to be welcomed as one of the family*
- *high expectations, if one-to-one course (see also teaching one-to-one above)*
- *can be a rewarding personal experience*
- *fully under the teacher's control*

Running exam preparation classes:
- *teacher needs familiarity with exam requirements*
- *learners likely be under pressure to achieve results*
- *teacher needs to pace learning programme*
- *exam programmes may be less flexible and less motivating to teach*
- *satisfaction of objectively verifiable results*

Academic purposes courses:
- *familiarity with requirements of academic study in different disciplines*
- *teacher may need to cope with students from different subject specialisations*
- *few teaching materials available*

Professional purposes courses (including professional function and professional sector):
- *high expectations of the learner(s)*
- *learner likely to expect tailor-made programme based on his/her needs*
- *teachers will need some materials development expertise*
- *teachers may need to have knowledge of or at least interest in the world of business and the work of professionals*
- *provides opportunities for teacher's own development*

Students International Ltd

- Certificate in TESOL - six full time courses a year
- Specially designed to instruct in teaching adults and young learners
- Wide range of specialist courses
- Summer Schools in three centres for students aged 8 to adult
- Guardianship scheme for students studying in England

158 Dalby Road, Melton Mowbray, Leicestershire, LE13 0BJ
Tel: (+44) 1664 481997 Fax: (+44) 1664 563332

Leisure activities courses:
- *opportunity to get out of the classroom*
- *balance classwork with outside activities*
- *can provide opportunities for real enjoyment - for learners and teachers*

Specialisation brings with it benefits and drawbacks. At a professional level, as one of an elite group, it makes your knowledge and skills more marketable - but only when they are in demand. Deciding on a specialisation is not easy, as the needs of the market place are constantly shifting. At present, courses for young learners are much in vogue, and having a leisure activity on one's CV is likely to increase the chances of finding work on a summer course in the UK or abroad. Another growth area is Business English - the catch-all term for many kinds of professionally-oriented language courses targeted at both those working in business sectors, as well as those in administrative or technical positions. However, few teachers are likely to have the luxury early in their careers to make a conscious decision about specialising, perhaps with the exception of those wishing to teach young learners. In a profession where flexibility is the key, the more you can offer, the better your chances of trying out the many different ELT contexts. When you've found the one that suits you, then do some more training and stick with it.

Teaching young learners
The Certificate in ELT to Young Learners in Language Schools (CELTYL) is an initial training qualification certificated by the RSA/Cambridge for those with little or no experience of teaching children wishing to specialise in this area. Children are defined in terms of the following age groups 5-10, 8-13 or 11-16. The certificate is available both as a course in its own right and also as a two week extension course for CELTA graduates (see below). As an introductory course, the CELTYL follows a programme similar to CELTA (see page 22 for a fuller description of the course components), but with the emphasis on young learners. The two-week extension course Certificate of Endorsement in ELT to Young Learners in Language Schools (CEELTYLLS) is based around a mix of coursework, written assignments and teaching observation and practice. This extension course is available for those already holding CELTA.

The Trinity College Certificate in the Teaching of English to Young Learners (TEYL)
TEYL prepares those teaching English as a foreign or second language to pupils around 6-12 years both overseas and in the UK. The certificate may be especially useful for those with some teaching experience wishing to add a TESOL qualification to their existing professional expertise.

Teaching one-to-one learners
The ARELS organisation offers a Certificate in Teaching One to One, certified and moderated by Trinity College. This award is designed to enable teachers, normally with an initial TEFL/TESOL qualification and some experience of one-to-one teaching, to understand and apply the principles of one-to-one teaching so that they can emerge as confident practitioners. The current 8 course centres in the UK provide a 25-hour course preparing teachers for a range of different one-to-one contexts - from children to business executives both in the UK and overseas.

Running homestay courses
Homestay courses are an unregulated part of the ELT industry, although some of the larger schools can be found in the ARELS guide. At present it is possible for any individual to provide EFL teaching from home without any certification, though an RSA/Cambridge award or the ARELS Certificate in Teaching One to One (see above) would be an advantage.

Running exam preparation classes
University of Cambridge Local Examinations Syndicate (UCLES) run occasional seminars throughout the UK and at local UCLES centres abroad to help teachers prepare their students more effectively for the range of exams offered by UCLES. These seminars include:

- *background information about the exams*
- *ideas for preparing candidates in the classroom*
- *relating exam preparation to general ELT*
- *insights into testing*

In addition, UCLES provides support through access to past papers and guidelines for candidates. Those interested in becoming more closely involved can sign up as oral examiners and, if in the UK, as examiners of the written papers.

Academic purposes courses
There is no special qualification for teachers wishing to specialise in EAP. The normal practice is for universities to employ people who already have an appropriate higher qualification (MA or equivalent) and then train them up in the skills required to work on their specifics EAP programmes. However, this may change in the future as discussions about an EAP endorsement to a recognised qualification are currently taking place.

Frances King Teacher Training

CAMBRIDGE/RSA CELTA
Four week courses throughout the year.

INTRODUCTION TO TEFL
One week courses throughout the year.

LCCI CERT IN TEACHING ENGLISH FOR BUSINESS
Internationally recognised two week course for qualified teachers. Phone 0171 838 0400 for LCCI course.

5 Grosvenor Gardens, Victoria
London SW1W 0BB
Tel: 0171 630 8055

Professional purposes courses (including professional function and professional sector)

The major area here is Business English, which is a sub-area of ESP (English for Specific Purposes). At present the LCCI (London Chamber of Commerce and Industry) is modifying its range of awards for Business English teachers. The Foundation Certificate for Teachers of Business English (FCTBE), due to be introduced in Autumn 1998, is intended as a qualification for those interesting in teaching Business English. It will be offered either as a course in its own right, or as an add-on to an initial award, such as CELTA. The LCCI is an examining body for the FCTBE and will offer the exam on demand throughout the UK. Centres will be free to offer preparatory courses (30 hours on a full time or part time basis) as well as the exam itself. Three main areas in syllabus:

- *professional areas (needs analysis, tailor-made course design and lesson-planning)*
- **Business English methodologies and materials**
- *knowledge of Business English and the world of business*

Assessment will be by a two-and-a-half hour exam paper. Grades awarded will be: distinction, credit, pass, and fail.

A higher level award, the Certificate in Teaching English for Business (CertTEB), is intended for native-speaker EFL teachers with a first degree, an EFL qualification, and a minimum of 1 year's relevant classroom experience. Course centres, accredited by LCCI, offer a 50-hour programme as preparation for the award. The course develops the areas introduced in the FCTBE above and includes micro-teaching practice. The award is offered to those

> "...*the most important quality is an interest in the leisure activity itself, be it a sport or a self-improvement activity...*"

who complete the course and a follow-up written assignment satisfactorily. Grades awarded are: distinction, pass and fail.

A new award is being developed by UCLES. Currently at the consultation stage, the Diploma in Teaching English for Business is intended for trained teachers (both native and non-native English speakers) who have a minimum of two years' experience of teaching English, largely to Business English learners. Following the other RSA/Cambridge diploma awards, the objectives of the programme will be to provide teachers with an opportunity to:

- *acquire new insights into the principles and practices of teaching English for business*
- *develop an understanding of the business world*
- *examine their current practice and beliefs*
- *apply the results of learning and reflection to their current professional lives and to circumstances beyond present and previous teaching experience*

In addition to these awards, a number of universities offer Masters degrees in ESP. For more information on these, see page 28.

Leisure activities courses

Here, the most important quality is an interest in the leisure activity itself, be it a sport or a self-improvement activity. Those who have completed an ELT teacher training course will already have covered general principles and practices of teaching. These should stand them in good stead when dealing with other areas, as would other training either in the activity itself or in how to teach it to others.

Short courses

A number of organisations offer one-day or weekend programmes on specialist areas. These include the Special Interest Groups (SIGs) of IATEFL as well as private providers.

TEACH ENGLISH AS A FOREIGN LANGUAGE
TEACHER TRAINING COURSES
at the
Bromley School of English

2 Park Road, Bromley, Kent BR1 1HP
Tel: 0181 313 0308 Fax: 0181 313 3957

Cambridge/RSA Certificate in ELTA
4 Week Intensive Courses

The University of Cambridge Local Examinations Syndicate / Royal Society of Arts Certificate in English Language Teaching to Adults is the most widely recognised TEFL qualification worldwide.

ONLY £620 inc. exam fee

... if you are eligible for EU funding. You are eligible if you are a citizen of the UK or of another EU member-state and are not supported by other public or private funding.

NORMAL PRICE £795 (inc. exam fee)

COURSES START ON:
11th May, 27th July, 14th Sept, 2nd Nov & Mar '99

ONE DAY INTRODUCTORY COURSE £50
£20 DISCOUNT IF YOU TAKE BOTH COURSES
in association with West Kent College

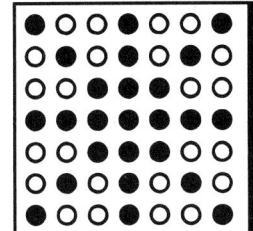

BRITISH COUNCIL INTERNATIONAL SEMINARS

"A CULTURAL AND EDUCATIONAL OPPORTUNITY THAT WILL REMAIN A LIFETIME MEMORY"
(NEW ZEALAND)

"More than fulfilled all expectation"
(SOUTH AFRICA)

"The most stimulating and rewarding professional experience of my career"
(CANADA)

Our 50 years of experience in events management, combined with The British Council's unequalled global network, guarantees top quality events of international acclaim spanning every area of the ELT field.

Why participate in our ELT International Events?

- **Access to a global network within the ELT field**
- **Opportunity for delegate contribution and exchange**
- **Direction by leading experts**
- **Professional Seminar Manager in daily attendance**
- **Lasting personal contacts**
- **Opportunity to enjoy the richness and variety of British Culture**
- **Contributors from leading-edge institutions**
- **Excellent value for money**
- **Exposure to latest developments in ELT**

International Seminars

http://www.britcoun.org/seminars/

The British Council, registered in England as a charity no. 209131, is
The United Kingdom's international network for education, culture and development services.

FOR FULL DETAILS OF THE FORTHCOMING PROGRAMME OF ELT INTERNATIONAL EVENTS PLEASE COMPLETE AND RETURN THIS SLIP TO THE ADDRESS BELOW. (TR)

Name: ....
Address: ....
....
....

International Seminars, The British Council, 1 Beaumont Place, Oxford OX1 2PJ.
Tel: +44(0) 1865 316636.   Fax +44(0) 1865 557368/516590.

International House

You may know us as a teaching and teacher training organisation which employs 300 newly trained and experienced teachers every year for our more than 100 affiliated schools in 27 countries.

Did you know we also have 50-60 senior positions each year for Directors, Directors of Studies, Teacher Trainers, Children's Course Co-ordinators, Business Course Co-ordinators and Assistant Director of Studies?

Did you also know that IH manages the CELTA Job Placement Service? This service is used by employers and teachers worldwide and is free to CELTA qualified teachers.

If you're interested in more information either on working for International House or on the CELTA Job Placement Service please contact the Staffing Unit.

International House

Argentina
Australia
Austria
Belarus
Brazil
Czech Republic
Egypt
England
Estonia
Finland
France
Georgia
Germany
Hungary
Italy
Lithuania
Former Yugoslav Republic of Macedonia
New Zealand
Poland
Portugal
Romania
Singapore
South Africa
Spain
Switzerland
Ukraine
USA

International House
106 Piccadilly London W1V 9FL Telephone: 0171 491 2598 Fax: 0171 491 2679
Website: www.international-house.org

LEARN ABOUT JOBS—YOUR WAY!

Looking for a job?
Whether you're interested in teaching in the hills of China or near the busy streets of Prague, TESOL is the job-listing source for you. A TESOL Placement Services subscription offers the only ESL/EFL job listing available by hard or electronic copy! Now available at new, non-member rates! Published 10 times per year. Subscriptions start at $27.

Ready for your next interview?
Get your next job at the TESOL Employment Clearinghouse where recruiters will be on-site to find their perfect candidate. Why not you? Plan to meet them at the next Clearinghouse at TESOL's 32nd Annual Convention and Exposition in Seattle, Washington, March 17-21, 1998. The TESOL convention is the world's largest ESL/EFL-related exposition, where opportunities for networking and professional growth abound.

TESOL Placement Services
Your job search connection

For more information contact:
Teachers of English to Speakers of Other Languages, Inc.
1600 Cameron Street, Suite 300
Alexandria, Virginia 22314-2751 USA
Tel. 703-836-0774 • Fax 703-836-7864
E-mail place@tesol.edu • http://www.tesol.edu

Careers in TEFL

section 4

Advice for getting work

"Looking for, selecting, and getting the job you want"

page 40

Outline of requirements

"What to expect and what will be expected of you as a teacher"

page 45

Further careers in EFL

"A look at what could lay beyond being a teacher, both in and out of the classroom"

page 48

Advice for getting work

Looking for, selecting and getting the job you want

With the world at your finger tips, you are now ready to embark on a (new) job search. So, where do you start? The answer will depend very much on decisions that you have made about the type of teaching you want to do and where you want to do it. In any and all cases, you should put together a CV which does justice to your qualifications and experience. As your CV is the prospective employer's first view impression of you, you should try to make it look as professional as possible. In these days of easily available word processing power, handwritten CV's just aren't good enough; and make sure that your CV is up-to-date with all relevant details. There are no universal standards for job applications. Some employers will expect a CV plus covering letter; others will provide a standardised form for you to complete. In either case, it is important to tailor your application to the job - stressing your relevant strengths and the qualities that you will bring to the particular job. Be truthful and concise; and sell yourself appropriately for the cultural context in which you are applying.

A second consideration is what type of work you are looking for. Work basically breaks down into contracts and jobs, where a contract is employment for a fixed period of time and a job is open-ended. Contracts can be either short-term (anything from one week to 6 months), medium term (around a year) or long term (from 2 years upwards).

The main channels in which to search for work are:

- *the local, regional and national general press*
- *the specialised press*
- *recruitment agencies*
- *ELT organisations*
- *internal bulletin boards (or Intranets)*
- *telephone directories*

In addition, it is worth mentioning three other avenues:

- *word of mouth*
- *unsolicited mailing*
- *Internet*

Internet provides a low cost method of information transmission. It is therefore being increasingly used as a means of EFL recruitment. Websites range from those dedicated to advertising a school's own vacancies to generalised EFL sites with a 'job shop'. If you have an Internet connection, visiting these sites is a useful exercise, either to look for a specific opening or just to see the range of openings on offer.

Employers may use a variety of channels, depending on the importance of the position. Senior positions and positions of responsibility need to be brought to the attention of the widest possible audience in order to attract the best candidates; junior teaching posts will often warrant little advertising expenditure.

Working in the UK
Private language schools

Work in private language schools fall into two categories - contracts and jobs. The larger language schools will advertise in the national press (e.g. Tuesday's Education Guardian), as well as in specialised journals such as the EL Gazette, the main source of news and views about the profession. Smaller language schools, especially those seeking short-term summer teachers are likely to limit their advertising to the local or regional press. In fact, many summer vacancies are filled by regulars, who swell the ranks of the teaching profession during the boom months of June to September. These may be overseas teachers who return to the UK to visit family, or state school teachers (EFL trained). In either case, their motivation will be to keep their hand in and earn some extra cash, as well.

GROVE HOUSE

Grove House International Language Centre

4 week intensive Trinity College Certificate TESOL Courses throughout the year £795 (+ exam fees)

1 week intensive Introductory courses £195

Weekend intensive Introductory courses £175

Train at our beautiful Victorian residence in a relaxed and friendly atmosphere. Assistance for unemployed, and help with finding jobs.

Take advantage of many years of experience and professionalism.

For further details please contact:
Heather Jeynes,
Grove House,
Carlton Avenue,
Horns Cross,
Nr. Dartford,
Kent DA9 9DR.
Tel: +44 (0) 1322 386826
Fax: +44 (0) 1322 386347

Colleges and universities

Language teaching contracts, for example on pre-sessional EAP courses, are likely to be advertised in the local and regional press; more senior positions, such as Course Director, will be advertised in the national press. Teachers for other contracts, such as summer school programmes, are also likely to be recruited via local or regional press advertising. Part time courses for non-natives - either visitors or residents - are offered at many colleges. Advertisements for trained teachers to staff these courses will appear in national and local press, as well as in specialised professional journals, such as the Times Higher Education Supplement.

State secondary education

Vacancies for ESL teachers to work with children from the ethnic minorities will be advertised in the Times Education Supplement and perhaps also in the Education Guardian. Only teachers with QTS (qualified teacher status) can teach in maintained schools (see Section 3 - PGCE courses).

Private secondary education

Many private schools receive pupils from abroad. In fact, as the private sector becomes more dependent on fee-paying pupils, there is a greater need to recruit pupils from overseas. Some of these need help with their English. This is often provided by withdrawing children from certain lessons in order to coach them in English. These jobs typically require qualified teachers (either QTS or other recognised qualification), and the posts are likely to be advertised in the national, regional and local press, as well as in specialised professional journals, such as the Times Education Supplement.

Working abroad

If you have a particular location in mind, one method would be to search for a teaching job by looking at advertisements in a local newspaper. However, this is not always possible for far-flung destinations; nor are jobs always advertised there. So, as an alternative you could find the details of schools from a Yellow Pages phone directory and contact them directly. A more reliable source of advertised jobs can be found in the EL Gazette (published monthly in the UK), the major newspaper for European-trained EFL teachers. In addition to news and reviews, it provides a listing of vacancies both inside and outside the UK.

For international organisations, such as the British Council or the Centre for British Teachers (CfBT)

The British Council recruits teachers to work at universities and institutes of higher education. These contracts typically involve language teaching plus a contribution to the institute's undergraduate linguistics programme. These posts are advertised in the national press and specialist journals. In addition, the British Council has its own network of more than 120 language schools in some 50 countries, called Direct Teaching Operations (DTO's). These teach general and specialist English, eg Business English, Medical English, EAP, to young and adult learners. Contract teaching positions, as well as positions of responsibility are advertised in the national press and specialist journals, as well as on their website. For teachers already working for the British Council, an internal system provides advance or prioritised information of forthcoming vacancies

The Centre for British Teachers (CfBT) is a registered English charity which employs British teachers abroad. Set up in 1968 it has placed more than 5,000 teachers, mainly in Germany, Malaysia, Morocco, Oman and Brunei. As a major employer within the EFL sector, CfBT advertises widely in the national and specialised press.

International language schools

International language schools include those with their own operations around the world and those with franchise activities. For the prospective teacher, these organisations offer security, professionalism and prospects. They advertise their posts widely using the specialised press and their own websites; senior posts will also be advertised in the national press.

Local language schools

This sector of the market, which ranges from the regulated to the unregulated, may use any or all of the recruitment channels listed above. In unregulated markets, word of mouth is a powerful recruitment channel; in regulated markets, especially where visas and work permits are required, employers are likely to use more formal channels. The rule of thumb is: the smaller the operation, the less they can afford to spend on advertising. Having said that,

---

CELTA

- **We have an excellent reputation for our English courses - validated by BASCELT**
- **Full or Part-time courses available**
- **Pay in instalments**

PART-TIME COURSES
Duration: 16 weeks
Dates: 08/9/97 - 15/01/98
19/01/98 - 21/05/98
Fees: £750
£375 (if you are unemployed and receiving benefit)

FULL-TIME COURSES
Duration: 4 weeks
Dates: 29/06/98 - 24/07/98
27/07/98 - 21/08/98
Fees: £750 (no remission)

Contact: Heather Alcock
Tel: 01484 536521

HUDDERSFIELD TECHNICAL COLLEGE
New North Rd. Huddersfield HD1 5NN
Tel: 01 484 536521 Fax: 01 484 511885
Huddersfield Technical College exists to provide high quality education and training for all.

the EL Gazette provides a comprehensive listing of EFL jobs around the world, many of which are placed by smaller schools. Also for specific destinations, the Yellow Pages will provide a listing of established (and hopefully reputable) language schools together with contact details.

At a local university
University posts tend to be advertised in the national press, both in the UK and in the country where the position is offered. In addition, some adverts are also placed in the Times Higher Education Supplement.

In-company
These positions, for teachers to work on training courses with the company's employees, are typically advertised in the specialised journals and in the national press.

Working for yourself
Of course, you don't need to work for an employer and it is perfectly possible to set yourself up as a self-employed EFL teacher, offering anything from the odd hour at someone's home to running homestay courses from your own home. The shoe is then on the other foot, and you will need to search for customers. Placing advertisements in the world's press to attract students is clearly unrealistic. The key is to find a niche in which to sell your services. This could be a geographical area where you have established contacts or a specialist field, such as Legal English, where you have developed your expertise. In either case, working freelance can be a precarious existence. In a crowded, competitive market, it is not easy to maintain a steady flow of income unless you have a particular market to tap into.

For you to contact
Recruitment agencies, such as English World-wide, ELT Banbury and Saxoncourt, all recruit EFL teachers either for their own or other organisations.

City College Manchester
TESOL Programme 1998

TCL Dip TESOL (part-time)
January and April entry

TCL Cert TESOL (4-week full-time)
February/March — Palma de Mallorca, Spain
April/May — Palma de Mallorca, Spain
June/July — Kalamata, Greece
August — Manchester, England

TCL Cert TESOL (12-week part-time)
January and September starts

TCL Cert TESOL (18-week part-time)
April and November starts

Preliminary Cert TESOL
(12-week part-time)
January and September starts

For further details and an application form please contact:

The Admissions and Guidance Team
City College Manchester
PO Box 40
Manchester M20 0GN
Telephone: 0161 957 1790

City College Manchester - Pursuing excellence in education and training

The Selection Process
For UK-based teachers
Selection itself takes a number of forms. UK-based schools do, of course, run interviews for prospective candidates. For overseas recruitment, practices vary. Some schools visit the UK to assess applicants; others use a local intermediary (based in the UK) to screen candidates; many offer jobs on the basis of your CV and letter of application plus a telephone interview. Whatever form is used for the interview, make sure that you have an opportunity to ask your questions about the work and working conditions (see page 10).

For teachers abroad
If you are already in the country, then you are likely to be invited for some kind of interview, where you will have an opportunity to promote yourself and ask your questions about the work and working conditions (see page 10).

Web sites to view:
http://www.jobs.edunet.com/
http://tefl.com/
http://www.agoralang.com:2410/agora/employment.html
http://www.els.com/intlempl.htm
http://www.pacificnet.net/~speling/jobcenter.html
http://www.tesol.net/tesljob.html
http://www.britcoun.org/ *(for information about job searching)*
http://www.britcoun.org/english/engvacs.htm *(specific vacancies within the British Council)*

National Press in the UK carrying ELT advertising:
The Guardian's Tuesday edition includes an Education Supplement

Specialised Press:
The Times Education Supplement
The Times Higher Education Supplement
    http://www.thesis.co.uk/
The EL Gazette
The SIG (Special Interest Groups of IATEFL) Newsletters carry occasional job adverts

Recruitment services:
English World-wide
ELT Banbury
ILC (International Language Centres) Recruitment
Inlingua Teacher Training and Recruitment
Saxoncourt
World-wide Education Service (WES)

Private UK language schools with international operations:
The Bell Language Schools
Berlitz
EF
inlingua
International House
Linguarama
NordAnglia
Saxoncourt (which owns the Shane schools)

Private US language schools with international operations:
ELS
5761 Buckingham Parkway
Culver, CA 90230-6583
Tel: (310) 642-0988 / Fax: (310) 649-5231
E-mail: international@els.com

Non-profit making organisations with ELT operations:
The British Council
Central Bureau for Educational Visits and Exchanges (CBEVE)
Centre for British Teachers (CfBT)
Voluntary Service Overseas (VSO)

The English Language isn't restricted to the English. Here at the School of Education we recognise that people who are interested in learning to speak and teach English come from many different countries and cultures and learn in many different contexts.

Our courses are designed to suit TESOL professionals from diverse linguistic and cultural backgrounds. As long as you have teaching experience (the length requirement varies according to the course you apply for), we can provide the rest.

Internationally **English.**

World-wide renowned as a centre for excellence in TESOL training and currently involved in a range of extensive research projects, our publications and research are of the highest quality. We have direct experience of TESOL in many countries through our wide-ranging consultancy work, which provides us with up-to-date knowledge of language education contexts around the world. Courses currently on offer are:

BA (Hons) TESOL - designed for trained and experienced TESOL educators at primary or secondary level.

EdD and PhD in TESOL - developing research in a broad range of specialist areas.

MEd TESOL - appropriate for native and non-native speakers. A flexible and learner-centred course with a wide range of options.

GRADUATE DIPLOMA IN TESOL - an opportunity to explore the principles and the context of TESOL professional practice.

GRADUATE CERTIFICATES IN TESOL - providing a substantial introduction to the principles and context of TESOL professional practice.

SHORT COURSES FOR TESOL PROFESSIONALS - a range of options.

And the latest specialist course -

MEd TESOL for Young Learners - we are one of the first institutions to offer a sound introduction to this fast growing area.

For more information, please contact: Jayne Moon, School of Education, University of Leeds, Leeds LS2 9JT.
Tel: 0113 233 4577/4528 Fax: +44 (0) 113 233 4541
E-mail: J.P.Moon@education.leeds.ac.uk
Web site: http://education.leeds.ac.uk/~edu/home.html

T E S O L

The Department of Applied Linguistics
The Institute for Applied Language Studies

Degree, Certificate and Short Courses

MSc in Applied Linguistics
- Core courses in general, descriptive and applied linguistics and a range of 25 options presented by the Department and the Institute. The Department also offers higher degrees in applied linguistics.

Certificated courses at the Institute
- Advanced Certificate in English Language Teaching
- Advanced Certificate in Teaching English for Specific Purposes
- UCLES/RSA Dip TEFLA

Short Summer Courses at the Institute
- Teaching and Learning English
- CEELT Preparation Course
- Teaching English for Specific Purposes
- Teaching English for Medical Purposes
- Teaching English for Business Purposes
- Teaching Literature in EFL
- Grammar and Communicative Teaching
- Drama for TEFL
- Teaching Young Learners
- Pronunciation for Language Teachers

Department of Applied Linguistics 14 Buccleuch Place, EDINBURGH EH8 9LN SCOTLAND UK. Tel 0131 650 3864. Fax 0131 650 6526.	Institute for Applied Language Studies 21 Hill Place, EDINBURGH EH8 9DP SCOTLAND UK. Tel 0131 650 6200. Fax 0131 667 5927.

Email: IALS.enquiries@ed.ac.uk   Website: http://www.ials.ed.ac.uk/

Outline of requirements

What to expect and what will be expected of you as a teacher

There is no doubt that no-one is ever completely prepared for their first overseas contract. It may be that you have not quite finished things back home or that you are not fully ready for the move. So, in this section we will look at some of the many factors which have a marked influence on the overseas experience. These include details to be covered before leaving home, as well as matters to be dealt with in the foreign country.

Essentials before going overseas

Before you go abroad, you will have agreed the basic terms and conditions of your employment. This should cover:

- *who you will be teaching and where the work is to be performed*
- *when you will have to work, ie working days/hours and holidays*
- *how long your contract will be for*
- *how much you will be paid, in what currency, when it will be paid and how it will be paid, as well as any other payments that you may receive, eg airfares at the beginning and end of contract*
- *what help you will receive for accommodation (looking for and paying for)*

In addition, you may need to:
- *obtain visas and/or work permits before you are allowed to enter the country or start work*
- *have a medical check-up in this country to give you a clean bill of health*
- *have vaccinations against certain diseases*

You should make sure that your employer provides all the necessary assistance to handle these administrative matters. At the same time, you may need to wind up/rearrange certain affairs here, including:
- *flat rental*
- *bills for utilities*
- *bank account*
- *other regular payments made by standing order or direct debit*
- *selling your car and other personal effects*

Remember to:
- *check that your passport is valid for the duration of your contract or that it is easy to renew while abroad*
- *make a list of contact addresses abroad in the event of an emergency*
- *make arrangements for mail to be redirected.*

The length of an overseas contract varies from employer to employer, and the normal 'annual' contract may turn out to be only 9 paid months. Based on this type of 'one-year contract', a September start means that you may find yourself free to return to the UK the following summer. However, if you have a two-year contract with airfares only at the beginning and the end, you may choose to use the long vacation to explore the area where you are posted, only returning to the UK after the contract.

Critical factors

Your success overseas depends on many factors, including:
- *realistic expectations*
- *familiarity with the language and culture of the host society*
- *remoteness of the teaching location*
- *single appointment or with family*
- *personal adaptability and flexibility*

Teachers who go abroad with unrealistic expectations run the greatest risk of failure, and those whose sense of adventure leads them to sign innocently on the dotted line may find that their innocent illusions turn into an unrepeatable experience.

---

inlingua®

Teacher Training & Recruitment

Train to teach EFL and get a job ...

- full-time, 5 week Trinity Cert TESOL
- part-time, 9 month Trinity Cert TESOL
- full-time, 2 week inlingua Intro to TEFL

small groups - maximum 10 trainees
high proportion of tutorials
pass-rate consistently over 97%
free recruitment service

Around 200 teaching vacancies worldwide every year

Contact us now at: iTTR, Rodney Lodge, Rodney Road, Cheltenham, GL50 1JF
Tel (01242) 253171

Going to work abroad is not a decision to be taken lightly. Before committing yourself, you should thoroughly research the country that you are going to work in if you have not been there before. Find out as much as you can from books, briefing notes and maps. Familiarise yourself with the politics, the religion, the art, the literature, the present concerns, the past heroes. Find out about the currency and, wherever possible, make contact with teachers who have worked there.

Living in a European city presents its own challenges in terms of lifestyle, but they can be fairly easily researched and anticipated. In fact, the references which are a familiar part of everyday life are a source of security: the advertisements, the buildings, the public transport, the entertainment. For those who choose to work in remoter locations, the absence of these cultural landmarks may come as a severe shock to the system. What may have seemed like an adventure in a job advertisement may prove to be real hardship in reality. Of course, some people relish the isolation and choose the location accordingly. Be sure that you know what you are letting yourself in for. As a rule of thumb, the remoter the location, the greater the isolation, especially if you are the only foreigner in town.

The isolation can, of course, be mitigated in a number of ways. Some organisations have a local co-ordinator with whom teachers can have regular contact to provide support and troubleshoot problems. Even if you don't need their assistance, it is very comforting to know they are there. On the other hand, you may be going out with your family, a ready-made support system. But having a family overseas can also cause problems. While you have a job to go to, your spouse may suffer from dislocation from the familiar home environment. And this may be equally the case whether you are in a European metropolis or an African village. So, again make sure that your whole family knows what they are letting themselves in for.

The key to success is your (and your family's) adaptability to the new environment. Change is always hard. But if everyone approaches the challenge of living and working abroad with a mixture of excitement and trepidation, it indicates that the decision has not been taken lightly.

Contract conditions

Your contract may cover the basics - a monthly payment. It is therefore important that you plan for other eventualities. Some of these are practicalities; others are life's little mishaps. Here is a list of the things you may need to consider for yourself and your family:
- *shipping personal effects*
- *insurance for personal effects in transit and when in the country*
- *life insurance*
- *medical insurance*
- *travel insurance*
- *education for your children*
- *house/flat hunting*
- *driving licence*

Coping with the culture

Coping with the culture typically goes through four predictable stages:

- *The honeymoon phase when the novelty of the new environment makes everything excitingly different*

- *The culture shock phase when problems of housing, transportation, shopping and language begin to intrude.*

- *The initial adjustment phase when people begin to learn, to change and to adapt. This phase is characterised by acceptance of local ways and strategies for handling them.*

> "...the remoter the location, the greater the isolation, especially if you are the only foreigner in town..."

- *The acceptance and integration phase when you come to feel at home and to enjoy the country and the culture.*

Tips for coping with the four phases
- *The best way to handle a new culture is with a mixture of preparedness and openness.*

- *Make sure you have done your homework, but always be ready to learn more.*

- *Try to understand the local culture in its own terms. Talk to the local people to understand better their way of seeing things. Avoid evaluating everything in comparison with 'how things would be done back home'.*

- *Don't deny when things do go wrong; but look for solutions rather than blaming the locals*

- *Make friends with the locals, and try to develop at least one close relationship with someone who can explain and help you understand the local situation.*

- *Avoid expatriates who spend all their time complaining about local conditions*

Use your free time to explore the country:
- *Remember you may never have the opportunity again.*

- *Keep contact with colleagues, friends and family back home*

Returning home

Returning home requires the similar preparation to going out, though the longer the absence, the greater the adjustment needed. Getting ready to leave one's established foreign base may involve the same winding up operations that you needed to do before you left for the foreign posting. Re-entry also requires a similar process of cultural adjustment (especially after longer overseas assignments), though the phases are usually shorter and less intense:

- *The return anxiety phase, when you worry about leaving because friendships will be disrupted.*
- *The return honeymoon phase, when there is a great deal of excitement over renewing friendships.*
- *The re-entry shock phase, when family and friends may not understand the impact that your overseas experience has had on you, and why you have changed*
- *The re-integration phase, when you become fully involved with friends, family and work. At this stage, you are able to see both countries and cultures more objectively and have a more balanced view of your experiences.*

Finances abroad
Basic terms
The remuneration package for a TEFL teacher abroad will be made up of one of more of the following elements:

- *basic pay*
- *additional pay*
- *allowances*

Basic pay will be the contractually agreed terms for the work to be done, based on a fixed number of hours to be taught (or at least a maximum). Additional hours will need to be negotiated with the employer; alternatively, teachers may find further clients on a private basis, giving private lessons outside their normal commitments. In the latter case, teachers should check that the terms of their contract permit them to do this. Allowances are often given for accommodation, usually the most expensive item on a teacher's monthly outgoings.

Method of payment
Most teachers are paid in the local salary, using one of the normal payment methods within the foreign country. Some contracts combine this with a sum of money paid in the UK. Depending on the local norms, teachers may choose to (or have to) open a bank account to manage their financial affairs more effectively.

Local requirements
Local requirements for tax and other deductions are varied and complex. It is, therefore, best to ask your future employer for full details of your local fiscal obligations; at the same time, carry out some local research yourself to check the details for yourself. Some countries have a reciprocal agreement with the UK, defining the social security arrangements for citizens from one country living and working in another. With others there is no agreement, but you may choose to continue paying National Insurance Contributions to help you qualify for benefits when you get back to the UK, or for Retirement Pension or widows' benefits whether you come back or stay abroad. You'll find further details in leaflet NI38, available from the Overseas Branch of the Department of Social Security or available on Internet (http://www.dss.gov.uk/ca/ni38/ni38-con.htm). For countries where no reciprocal agreement exists, you may find yourself liable for local taxes or totally exempt.

The UK requirements
If you are going to be working for a certain period of time in a country with a reciprocal agreement with the UK, you will be subject to the UK tax and social security systems. Some teachers employed abroad have to pay United Kingdom National Insurance contributions; others may choose to, in order to be eligible for benefits. Similarly, if you are going to work abroad for a UK employer, there is a legal requirement for the employer to pay Class 1 National Insurance Contributions on all earnings paid during your first 52 weeks abroad, provided certain conditions are met. Further details are given in leaflet NI38, available from the Overseas Branch of the Department of Social Security or on the Internet (http://www.dss.gov.uk/ca/ni38/ni38-con.htm)

If you are going to work in a country with which no reciprocal agreement exists, then you may avoid paying UK tax on your overseas earnings if you are away for at least 365 days, and your visits to the UK are less than 62 days. However, UK earnings will still be liable to UK tax unless you obtain non-resident status, for which you must work full time abroad for more than a complete UK tax year, and your visits to the UK must be less than three months.

Pension
To qualify for the full basic UK state pension, you must have paid the minimum contribution each year for at least 90% of your whole working life. If you miss payments, you will be reminded by the Department of Social Security and will be able to make up the missing payments, if you wish to do so.

For those who want to make better provision for their old age, a private pension scheme is a better alternative/addition. This has the benefits of being flexible and portable. You can pay in variable amounts at variable times - and choose your own retirement age.

Investments
One of the attractions of TEFL is the opportunities for foreign travel and, while saving money may not be uppermost in a teacher's mind during the early years, the need to 'put something by' becomes more important during the middle period of a TEFLer's career. As with pensions, there are many schemes available to make your money grow, depending on the degree of risk that you are prepared to take. Talk to a reputable independent financial adviser.

Converting money
Not all countries have 'freely convertible' currencies, enabling you to exchange local money for western currencies such as GB pounds or US dollars. Currencies from the former eastern European states (in socialist times) used to fall into this category, so that the only option was to spend the money. Now more and more currencies are freely convertible and can be repatriated for investment in the UK.

Contacts
In the first instance contact your local Social Security office well before you leave the country. You will find the address in the telephone book under Benefits or Contributions Agency, or Social Security, Department of.
Alternatively contact:
Contributions Agency, International Services, Room A2119, Longbenton, Newcastle upon Tyne, NE98 1YX
(The UK Help Line) Tel: 06451 54811 / Fax: 06451 57800
(The overseas Help Line) Tel: 44 -191-22-54811 / Fax: 44 -191-22-57800

Some useful links on a range of subjects relating to living and working overseas can be found at:
http://www.britex.com/links.htm

Details of the range of published titles by Transitions Abroad are at: http://www.transabroad.com/

Looking for effective, easy to use ELT software?

Clarity English software is enjoyable, effective, based on sound teaching principles... and is used by thousands of teachers and students in more than 70 countries worldwide. Easy to install, easy to use!

"Very popular with students, attractive and easy to use."
British Council Network News

Interactive CD-ROM software to help you with

- Grammar at all levels
- English for academic purposes
- Exam practice and instant worksheets
- Report writing
- Authoring self-access courses

Windows disk versions available ✓

FROM £49
Includes full FREE technical support!

Please contact us for a catalogue or see our website for more details.
Clarity Language Consultants Ltd
PO Box 163, Sai Kung, Hong Kong
fax: +852 2791 6484
email: andrew@clarity.com.hk
internet: www.clarity.com.hk

UNIVERSITY OF OXFORD
Delegacy of Local Examinations

Examinations for Your EFL and ESP Needs!

OXFORD-ARELS EXAMINATIONS IN ENGLISH AS A FOREIGN LANGUAGE

- Qualifications in both Written and Spoken English which may be taken separately
- Realistic tasks testing students' ability to communicate internationally
- Two Levels plus Junior Counterpart

OXFORD INTERNATIONAL BUSINESS ENGLISH CERTIFICATE (OIBEC)

- Complete four-skills package
- Assesses use of English in authentic business situations
- Two Levels

Please contact:
David Hodges or Don Malpass, University of Oxford, Delegacy of Local Examinations, Ewert House, Ewert Place, Summertown, OXFORD OX2 7BZ.
United Kingdom Telephone: (+44) (0)1865 554291
Fax: (+44) (0)1865 510085

University of Durham

RSA CELTA COURSES

Four week full-time intensive courses, summer 1998:
June 30th - July 24th
July 27th - August 21st
August 31st - September

Part-time evening course:
October 1998 to March 1999

All courses are £875 (£775 for registered full-time students studying at a Northeast University). Durham is an historic university recognised for academic excellence across the spectrum of subject. The city of Durham is a world heritage, site and the beautiful old town is dominated by its magnificent 11th century cathedral. There are also many museums and other places of interest to visit, as well as shops, modern and traditional pubs, and restaurants for all tastes. Durham is easily reached by a number of different routes. By car, it is just off the A1, and the east coast Inter-city train service makes frequent stops at the mainline station. For people coming from abroad, Newcastle International Airport and Teeside Airport are within easy reach. Self-catering or college accommodation can be arranged during full-time summer CELTA courses.

For further information and an application form, contact:
The Language Centre, University of Durham, Elvet Riverside, New Elvet, Durham, DH1 3JT
Tel: 0191 374 3716 / Fax: 0191 374 7790
E-mail: language.centre@durham.ac.uk / Internet: http://www.dur.ac.uk/~dlc0zz1

Further careers in EFL

A look at what could lay beyond being a teacher, both in and out of the classroom

TEFL is often a stepping stone to other careers and many teachers will leave after some years to move into other professions. However, as the ELT market expands, there are more and more jobs both in the profession itself, as well as in other related areas.

Positions within language schools

Language schools typically have a flat structure, with a principal (often the school owner) and a number of teachers, who teach the classes. However, the larger the organisation, the greater the need for an infrastructure to ensure effective teaching and management. However, though ELT is a business in the service sector, it does not always play by the same rules as other service providers. So, even bigger language schools may operate with a minimal organisational structure. This usually translates into one of two possible scenarios:

- *teachers have great freedom to make choices about materials and methods, or*
- *teachers have no freedom at all to deviate from the prescribed materials and methods*

Where a hierarchy does exist, it may include one or more of the following positions of responsibility:

Senior teacher

This recognition of long service and/or extensive experience is rewarded by fewer classroom lessons and more time for other pedagogic duties, such as materials selection or development, teacher coaching and support or administrative tasks.

Course director /Junior course director

The course director is responsible for some/all of the following:

- *receiving enrolments for a course (usually defined as a programme for a fixed period of time - anything from 2 to 10 weeks)*
- *allocation of students to classes*
- *design of teaching programme*
- *timetable design*
- *allocation of teachers to classes*
- *selection of teaching materials*
- *pedagogic co-ordination during the course*
- *design of social programme*
- *monitoring of students during the course*
- *end-of-course review*

With the right support (teaching, administrative and social), directing a course can be a rewarding experience. However, the greater the number of people (students and teachers), the more people management skills are required to ensure that all the parts of the equation (teaching programme, social programme and accommodation) fit seamlessly together. The course director rarely has time to teach, or if s/he does, it is often to step in for absent colleagues.

Assistant Director of Studies

The Assistant Director of Studies (ADOS) post is found in larger organisations, usually with an established hierarchy. Reporting to the Director of Studies (see below) the ADOS will typically have special responsibility for part of the pedagogic administration. This can include:

- *ongoing activities, as shown in the course director list above*
- *participating in/supervising project work in areas such as:*
    - *materials development*
    - *course design*
    - *computer-assisted learning*
    - *teacher development*
- *teaching on parts of a course*

The University of Reading

CENTRE FOR APPLIED LANGUAGE STUDIES

Long established and highly respected, with thousands of former students throughout the world, CALS offers the following programmes:

- English for Academic Purposes for students entering higher education
- Short Courses for teachers and learners of English
- Diploma in English Language and International Relations
- MA in TEFL *(taught version)*
- MA in TEFL *(distance version)*
- Ph.D. in TEFL *(full and part-time)*.

For further details, contact:
The Secretary (AE)
Centre for Applied Language Studies
The University of Reading
PO Box 241
Reading UK RG6 6WB

TEL: 0118 9 318512 *(UK)*
+44 118 9 318512 *(International)*
FAX: 0118 9 756506 *(UK)*
+44 118 9 756506 *(International)*
E-MAIL: CALS@reading.ac.uk

or visit our Web page: http://www.rdg.ac.uk/AcaDepts/cl/aclsm.html

Director of Studies

The Director of Studies (DOS) is the most senior member of the pedagogic staff. Reporting to the school principal the DOS has ultimate responsibility for all matters relating to the organisation of courses. These can include:

- *ongoing development and implementation of syllabuses*
- *review and development of teaching approaches and other academic projects*
- *supervision of material development projects*
- *teacher recruitment, selection, promotion and appraisal*
- *assistance of teachers through observations and weekly meetings*

In larger schools, the DOS will be supported by one or more ADOS's, to whom some of the above areas may be delegated.

Marketing

Marketing is concerned with increasing awareness of products and services in order, ultimately, to generate (more) sales. In any competitive market place, such as EFL, marketing takes a central position, as schools vie with each other to attract students. The job of the marketing department is to ensure that the school has:

- the right product
- at the right price
- at the right place
- with the right people
- using the right promotion

For those with a mix of commercial acumen and creative flair, marketing can offer a challenging move from the classroom. It is a central position for any school, since the results of the marketing effort will determine the success, or otherwise, of the institution.

> *...For those with a mix of commercial acumen and creative flair, marketing can offer a challenging move...*

Positions within academic institutions

The academic institutions covered in this guide provide a range of teaching programmes:

- *EFL courses for students*
- *EAP courses for students*
- *teacher training courses for pre-service and in-service teachers (see next)*

Teachers of English to Speakers of Other Languages, Inc.

Looking for a job? TESOL can help.

Whether you're interested in teaching in the hills of China or near the busy streets of Prague, TESOL has the job listing for you. TESOL's **Placement Bulletin** offers the only ESL/EFL job listing available by hard or electronic copy and is now available at new, nonmember rates. Published 10 times per year. Subscriptions start at $27.

Career Resources

ELT Guide, 8th edition
Discover thousands of jobs worldwide in more than 100 countries.
$19.95 (+ $3.50 S/H)

More Than a Native Speaker
by Don Snow
This book covers classroom survival skills, lesson planning, and adaptation to life in a new country, with detailed discussions of how to teach listening, speaking, reading, writing, grammar, vocabulary, and culture.
$29.95 (+ $3.50 S/H)

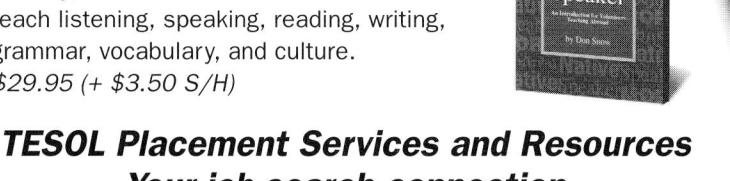

TESOL Placement Services and Resources
Your job search connection

For more information contact:
Teachers of English to Speakers of Other Languages, Inc.
1600 Cameron Street, Suite 300 • Alexandria, Virginia 22314 USA
Tel. 703-836-0774 • Fax 703-836-7864
E-mail tesol@tesol.edu • http://www.tesol.edu/

- applied linguistics courses for undergraduate and postgraduate students

With such a wide range of activities, universities have varied hierarchical structures depending on the service being provided. The structure of the department offering EFL courses is likely to mirror the language school described above. EAP courses are taught either by teachers or trainers or lecturers. Depending on the size of the operation, the EAP department may have a number of layers, including course director, senior teacher/trainer. Responsibilities will cover the areas listed for course director and director of studies above.

As applied linguistics is part of the mainstream activities of a university, rather than the language support provided to non-native speakers to enable them to follow the mainstream activities, here we find the traditional hierarchy of:

- *lecturer*
- *senior lecturer*
- *assistant professor*
- *professor*

While both lecturer and senior lecturer posts involve teaching and running seminars/tutorial, all academic positions require academic research. This is likely to be a major preoccupation, especially for those aspiring to promotion within the academic hierarchy.

Teacher training

For teachers with extensive experience, sharing that experience with others is a natural step in professional development and job progression. Teacher training courses range from:

- *introductory programmes*
- *pre-service recognised programmes*
- *in-service recognised programmes*
- *postgraduate certificate and diploma programmes*
- *specialist programmes*

Each type of programme needs to balance background theory with practical techniques in a context where the course leaders are evaluated according to both their expertise and their teaching skills. So, it is a challenging task. However, in general, teaching teachers is also a very rewarding experience and a valuable way of sharing one's own expertise and developing the expertise of others.

Teacher training is offered by many of the larger language schools as well as universities and colleges. The language schools may have departments devoted to teacher training, with a staff of trainers dedicated to course design and delivery. In the smaller institutions (schools and universities/colleges), teacher trainers may combine this with other teaching duties.

Writing

In every EFL teacher there is a book waiting to come out. The classroom experience usually generates ideas for new materials. Many of these find their way on to paper; some of them are then presented to publishers for consideration; and a few find their way into print (or some other medium). This 'few' has been steadily increasing over the last few years and ELT publishing is now a major industry. Most EFL writers are freelance. The steps in writing EFL material usually involve:

- *submission of concept and sample material to one or more publishers (see below)*
- *acceptance (or rejection) of material*
- *if acceptance, then negotiation of contract*
- *payment of advance payment*
- *writing, writing, writing*
- *submission of manuscript*
- *acceptance of manuscript*
- *payment of remainder of advance*
- *editing of manuscript*
- *publication*

The process can be long, frustrating, and stressful, but the satisfaction of seeing one's name on the front cover of a book is long remembered. Most EFL books sell, but not in great quantities. The payment is normally a royalty based on a percentage of the sales price. These are very welcome contributions to the family finances, but there are few writers who can support themselves simply from their royalties. So don't give up your teaching job just yet.

Jobs in publishing

The other side of 'writing' (see previous paragraph) is publishing. The job of the publisher is to convert ideas for new titles into publications. So, the process may be initiated by:

- *the publisher, who approaches an author which expertise in a specific EFL area, or*
- *the author, who presents an idea to the publisher*

MA IN APPLIED LINGUISTICS & TEFL

School of Languages & Area Studies

Starting towards the end of September
Full-time: One calendar year
Part-time: 24 months (minimum)

Further Details and application forms from:

Admissions Tutor,
MA in Applied Linguistics & TEFL,
School of Languages & Area Studies,
University of Portsmouth, Park Building,
King Henry 1 Street, Portsmouth,
Hants. PO1 2DZ

Telephone:
(01705) 846102
Fax:
(01705) 846040

A centre of excellence for university teaching & research

University of Portsmouth

In either case, the interests of both parties is to take a concept, convert it into a manuscript and then turn it into a best-selling product. To do this, publishers usually have a range of positions, each with its own function. The larger publishers have departments devoted to special areas, such as:

- *course books*
- *Business English*
- *books for teachers*
- *video materials*
- *multimedia media*

Smaller publishers just concentrate on the key functions that need to be carried out.

(Senior) ELT editor

The ELT editor is in charge of publishing strategy within ELT. This involves:

- *managing of the ELT editorial team*
- *developing a strategy for ELT publishing*
- *deciding on priorities for (new) areas to be developed*
- *allocating resources (financial and human) to editorial projects*
- *liaising with other departments, especially production, legal, finance and marketing*

Commissioning editor

The commissioning editor is in charge of a specific writing project. This may be a number of single titles or a series. As such, the work involves:

- *liaising with authors at various stages of the writing*
- *checking the content and consistency of the material delivered*
- *preparing artwork briefs and arranging audio and video recording, where needed*
- *liaising with other departments, especially production, legal, finance and marketing*

Desk editor

The desk editor:

- *checks the manuscript*
- *marks it up - improvement of layout and correction of mistakes*
- *prepares it for publication - integration of text and graphics*

Sales/marketing jobs

The larger ELT publishers have dedicated sales/marketing teams whose job it is to raise awareness of their EFL publications and develop markets for these products. The Marketing Director is usually based at the company's head office, where overall marketing strategy and policies are devised. These policies are then communicated to the marketing managers in individual countries, where they will need to be tailored to local conditions. In general, marketing is concerned with providing in each country:

- *the right product*
- *at the right price*
- *at the right place*
- *at the right time*
- *using the right promotion*

Having raised the customers' awareness of their products, the local sales representatives are then charged with converting this into sales. The customers for EFL books are teachers and students, and so reps need to target both in order to ensure their titles are available to the widest possible audience. Visits to bookshops, schools and other institutes are the core activities, followed by discussions over quantities, price, payment terms and delivery. At the same time, reps will need to maintain contact with head office to ensure regular supplies of titles ordered, as well as dealing with the local bureaucracy to avoid any holdups in delivery to customer.

Setting up a homestay

For those who favour plunging into the commercial world, setting up a homestay is a compromise between working as a freelance teacher and setting up a school. Of

> *...the satisfaction of seeing one's name on the front cover of a book is long remembered...*

course, a homestay is a school, but the scale of the operation is likely to be limited by the physical size of your house, particularly that part to be devoted to your students. Homestay require little infrastructure:

- *a room for teaching*
- *audio/visual equipment*
- *teaching materials*
- *bedroom(s)*
- *other accommodation to be shared between hosts and guests*

However, the success of your homestay lies with the effectiveness of your marketing/sales operation. If you want to go it alone, then you will need to organise your own promotion. The alternative is to join one of the homestay schemes, so that they will market your services for you. For further information, contact:
http://www.homestay-wales.co.uk/
http://www.bitoa.co.uk/scsintl.htm

Setting up a language school

Perhaps the most ambitious move of all is to set up your own language school. The infrastructure needed is minimal, and no official ELT recognition is required; however, the time, effort and money to market and sell your services will be a major drain, especially in the early years as you struggle to establish a market and reputation for yourself. But remember that others have done it before you, so if you have the commitment there are still a lot of people out there who need your services.

References:
For more information on courses to help you develop:
a general EFL teaching career, see page 26
a specialist area within EFL, see page 33
management skills, see page 26 (other qualifications)

If you want to learn English as it's really used ... if you want to teach English as it's really used ... there's only one sensible choice of dictionary.

The Cambridge International Dictionary of English (CIDE) contains a wealth of information to help students understand and use English confidently and accurately.

**Comprehensive
Clear
International**

gob.smacked *only Cambridge will guide you to the real meaning.*

Cambridge University Press,
ELT Marketing,
The Edinburgh Building,
Shaftesbury Road, Cambridge CB2 2RU, UK
Tel: (01223) 325819 Fax: (01223) 325984

GOBSMACKED?

CAMBRIDGE UNIVERSITY PRESS

IH Teacher Training
Hastings, Paris, Prague
The Diploma & CELTA specialists

HASTINGS, England 4-week Cambridge/RSA Certificate (CELTA) courses start every month. 8/9-week RSA/Cambridge Diploma courses start 2 Mar & 28 Sep.
Wide range of other courses and workshops.

PARIS, France 4-week Cambridge/RSA CELTA courses start every month Jan to Nov.

PRAGUE, Czech Republic CELTA courses: Jan-May (part-time in Prague), June (full-time in Prague), July (full-time in Turnov).

All Centres can arrange accommodation.

"an exceptional course" ... "I will recommend it unreservedly" ... "tutors ... empowering and extremely helpful" ... "outshone my expectations" ... "brilliant"

Read our prospectus
International House
White Rock, Hastings
E. Sussex TN34 1JY, UK
Tel +44 (1424) 720104
Fax +44 (1424) 720323
e-mail: 100674.1300@compuserve.com
Web: http://www.ilcgroup.com

*Members of the International House world organisation.
Approved centres for Cambridge/RSA training courses.*

Penguin ELT for...

Vocabulary · Examinations and Tests · Business English and ESP · Photocopiable Resource Books · Penguin Readers · Skills · Language and Literature · Short Stories · Applied Linguistics · Vocabulary · Examinations and Tests · Business English and ESP · Photocopiable Resource Books · Penguin Readers · Skills · Language and Literature · Short Stories · Applied Linguistics · Vocabulary · Examinations and Tests · Business English and ESP · Photocopiable Resource Books · Penguin Readers · Skills · Language and Literature · Short Stories · Applied Linguistics · Vocabulary · Examinations and Tests · Business English and ESP · Photocopiable Resource Books · Penguin Readers · Skills · Language and Literature · Short Stories · Applied Linguistics · Vocabulary · Examinations and Tests · Business English and ESP

| For further details of all Penguin ELT titles |
| please contact |
| Victoria Hamilton |
| Penguin ELT Marketing |
| 27 Wrights Lane, London W8 5TZ |
| Telephone 0171 416 3000 |
| Fax 0171 416 3060 |
| E-mail victoria.hamilton@penguin.co.uk |

SECTION 5

Materials for teaching & learning

Introduction to EFL materials

"Having the right materials can be critical so here is an guide of what to look for"

page 54

Reading List

"There are thousands of EFL books on the market, so here is a small selection to get you started"

page 58

Introduction to EFL materials

Having the right materials can be critical so here is an guide of what to look for

ELT publishing is dominated by three UK-based publishers, Oxford University Press (OUP), Cambridge University Press (CUP) and Longman (now part of the multinational Addison-Wesley group). Between them they produce the majority of best-selling titles, providing teachers with a huge array of classroom materials and pedagogic resources. In addition to these giants, there are a number of other publishers specialising in particular types of materials, e.g. Penguin for Readers, Prentice Hall for Business English, Peter Collin Publishing for Dictionaries, or media for materials, e.g. WIDA for software, International Business Images for video. Beyond the UK publishers, are a host of other companies worldwide, competing for a share in their local market or the international markets.

Such a vast choice can be daunting for the new TEFLer. So, in this section we will establish a framework for categorising ELT materials. Beyond that, teachers will need to browse among the titles, either in a bookshop, on-line or in a catalogue, to see what is available and to make choices about what best suits their needs. Of course, not all schools allow their teachers the luxury of choosing their own materials; many will prescribe what is to be used. This is not necessarily a bad practice as it can help to create a coherent system within which students can move up through the classes, using a book at the appropriate level with each successive move. Schools which pride themselves on providing up-to-date, motivating materials are well-provided for by the ELT publishers. But not all schools come into these categories. Teachers may find themselves saddled with inappropriate, unmotivating or out-of-date materials. The only solution here is to supplement the course book with other materials, either culled from other books or developed oneself. (Remember to keep a copy of all self-made materials for that book that every EFL teacher has up their sleeve).

Course books

These are the cornerstone of every course. As approaches to ELT methodology have changed, writers have responded (or perhaps even initiated) by creating new and ever more comprehensive materials. The organisational characteristics have progressed through the following stages:

- grammatical syllabuses
- communicative syllabuses (including functional/notional syllabuses)
- multi-level syllabuses

> *...As approaches to ELT have changed, writers have responded by creating new and ever more comprehensive materials...*

Grammatical syllabuses are built up around the grammatical forms of the language, as described by applied linguists. The main forms - verbs (and their tenses), nouns, adjectives, adverbs, prepositions, articles, quantifiers etc., are progressively presented. Each level reviews materials covered at an early stage in order to provide an opportunity for consolidation before extension. The focus for the learner is to gain mastery of the forms in order to achieve accuracy in language use.

Communicative syllabuses rebelled against the formal grammatical approach, positing that communicative competence especially competence in speech, could be achieved more effectively by focusing on elements of meaning. These came to be known as language functions and language notions. Throwing accuracy out of the window, most of the early communicative course books provided activities for developing fluency, often at the expense of (the learners') correct language use. A reaction against 'inaccurate fluency' pushed the ELT profession (and writers) to re-evaluate the balance between accuracy and fluency. Later approaches, eclectic in nature, focused on promoting accuracy and fluency, integrating language forms (based on grammar) with language functions (based on meaning). From this, it was only a small step to the multi-level syllabus, which is organised around:

- grammar
- functions
- vocabulary
- pronunciation

Overlaid on this are the 4 skills:

- listening
- speaking
- reading
- writing

This multi-dimensional model covers the range of language knowledge (grammar, vocabulary and the sound system) and communicative skills (listening, speaking, reading and writing) that make up competence.

Obviously, course books need to be developed at different levels; so we find the spectrum divided into:

- beginner
- elementary
- post-elementary/pre-intermediate

- intermediate
- post-intermediate
- advanced

In order to cater for the different interests of learners, we find a further subdivision into:

- children's course books
- general adult course books
- Business English course books

These reflect the interests and concerns of the target group. These are delivered via the content and the activities. Children's books deal with appropriate themes for the age group combined with tasks for activity learning; adult books present other topics suited to the mature learner; and Business English books draw on the world of business.

As the materials have become more sophisticated, so have the media. Today's course book needs to consist of at least a student's book and an audio cassette. To compete in the big league, course books also need:

- a teacher's book
- a work book
- a video

And for the next generation: a multimedia CD-ROM.

Language development materials

In their efforts to provide more materials for the ELT classroom, publishers started to produce supplementary materials. One group of such materials focuses on individual areas within the scope of language. As a result, there are now materials (mostly books) devoted to developing:

- grammar
- vocabulary
- pronunciation

Within grammar, you can find:

- grammar reference books
- grammar practice books
- combined grammar reference plus
- grammar practice

Within vocabulary, you can find:

- dictionaries
- vocabulary practice books (usually thematically based)

Within pronunciation, you can find:

- pronunciation practice materials

Skills development materials

This is the other major category of supplementary materials, covering:

- listening
- speaking
- reading
- writing

These skill areas are often, but not always, handled separately. So, you will find dedicated materials for developing each area, as well as those which combine two or more skills, eg listening and speaking or reading and writing. Further subdivisions are found in terms of content, eg speaking practice activities for young learners, listening practice materials for business English learners, writing skills materials for EAP learners. There are many permutations combining skill area with learner type. There are also different media for these materials: book, audio, video and multimedia CD-ROM. The list of materials is already immense and looks set to continue growing.

Professional development materials

No list of ELT materials would be complete without mentioning books for teachers. As the profession has grown, so have divergent approaches to language teaching methodology. For the new teacher entering the profession, it is important to bear in mind that language teaching is not a science, it is a discipline based on professional skills and personal style. The methodology books are an excellent starting point to help teachers along that path.

Technology in the classroom

Today's technology provides a number of additional dimensions for the resourceful ELT teacher and the committed EFL learner. We are emerging into a world where low-cost international communication is available to everyone with a PC (personal computer), a modem, a telephone and a subscription to an Internet Service Provider (ISP). The explosion in computing power and telecomms connections allows information to flow around the globe

---

COLLINS WORLD CLASS DICTIONARIES ON CD-ROM ... BETTER BY DEFINITION

COBUILD ENGLISH DICTIONARIES FOR TEFL
Helping learners with real English

COBUILD on CD-ROM
CONTAINS Collins COBUILD English Language Dictionary
Collins COBUILD English Grammar
Collins COBUILD English Usage
PLUS a word bank containing 5 million words

£47.00 INC VAT DELIVERY EXTRA

COBUILD English Collocations on CD-ROM
CONTAINS 10,000 headwords
140,000 collocations
2.6 million examples

£47.00 INC VAT DELIVERY EXTRA

COBUILD Student's Dictionary on CD-ROM
CONTAINS 40,000 references
30,000 real examples
More than 50 hours of sound
Activities to record your own voice

£34.08 INC VAT DELIVERY EXTRA

HarperCollins
Electronic Reference

OUT NOW ON WINDOWS CD-ROM

TEL +44 (0)1903 873 555   FAX +44 (0)1903 873 633

rhcc@compuserve.com   www.cobuild.collins.co.uk/rhcc

in ways and at speeds that were unheard of a mere five years ago. This is one dimension of the communication revolution. Another is the availability of ever more sophisticated teaching/learning resources, delivered either via CD-ROM or the Internet. Over time these resources are likely to lead to a radical review of the teaching/learning relationship, through greater student autonomy and increased opportunities for individualised learner-centred programmes. However, it is still early days and to date the new technologies have had hardly any impact on the English teaching classroom. Globally, methods are still conservative, relying on teacher centred learning and traditional frontal teaching. However, things are changing and important contributions have been made to the panoply of ELT resources. So, in our rapid review of the current state of the art, a convenient starting point is the buzzword multimedia.

In technical terms, multimedia is:

the integration of materials in different formats - notably next, graphics, sound, animation and video into...

...a primarily associative system of information storage and retrieval where...

...choices are controlled by the user.

In ELT terms, the first part equates to the familiar mix of materials which includes:

- a course book with text and pictures
- audio materials to develop listening comprehension
- video materials to create a range of contexts for language in use

What the multimedia version offers is no more and no less than what is provided by the traditional media. So, the ELT programme might include video clips, audio passages, animation, charts, tables, different types of texts for exercises and reference, as well as the possibility to record oneself and get feedback on one's performance. But rather than having the elements in different media - book, audio cassette and video cassette - the new format will have all the elements integrated into one programme, stored, for example onto compact disk. The main advantages are:

- **ease of use - no more searching on the audio cassette for unit 16**
- **storage capacity - everything can now fit onto one single disk, complete with teacher's notes, tape and video script and answers.**

The second part of the definition refers to the overall organisation and internal structure of the materials (or computer programme in the multimedia version). Most traditional courses are based around a linear pattern. However, this does not reflect how we learn in reality, which is rather through a cyclical process and by associating linked ideas and concepts. In a traditional course, if the learner encounters a problem which is not part of the core syllabus, there is little chance of resolving it in the course materials themselves. In the multimedia definition, the concept of 'associative information storage and retrieval' means that the learners can branch off from the core syllabus to find answers to questions about non-core areas in other parts of the programme. So, the multimedia version provides a much richer and wider range of possibilities for the committed and enquiring learner.

The final part of the definition refers not to materials, but to the method of use. The ELT classroom has seen some progress in moving from a teacher-centred approach to a learner-participative one. The right classroom balance (including both ends of the spectrum as well as intervening points) can create that rewarding environment where learning takes place in a collaborative atmosphere. The multimedia approach provides a wide range of learning materials and choices which can be (but needn't be) controlled by the learner. In other words, in learner-controlled mode, the learner can be in the driving seat, deciding what to learn and when to learn it; in teacher-controlled mode, the teacher makes the choices. In between is the collaborative ground where learner and teacher work together to define the learning programme and the way of working to progress efficiently through it.

At the heart of multimedia is, of course, the computer. The screen is the text, graphics and video viewer; the sound card and speakers the sound producer. Combined they allow the learner to read, listen and view with one device - exactly as can be done at present with a book, cassette recorder, a video recorder and a TV (four devices). But how much simpler to have all this integrated into one! So, with appropriate multimedia resources and suitable equipment, a new world of language learning opportunities is available to committed learners.

No overview of new technology would be complete without a reference to the Internet. Behind the hype is a network of computers on which are stored vast quantities of information in multimedia formats:

- text
- graphics
- sound
- animation
- video

Through the use of:

- **a browser (Internet Explorer or Netscape Navigator) - a program that searches and retrieves data from the vast Internet databases and delivers it to your computer, and**
- **a search engine - a program that finds the information that matches your requirements**

We have access to a world of English language (as well as other language) material in text, with sound and with graphics and video. This is the passive use

> *"...it is still early days, and to date the new technologies have had hardly any impact on the English teaching classroom."*

of the Internet, from where one can collect resources to add to our teaching programmes, as well as finding out about the world of ELT training, jobs and published materials. Add to that the active elements, through which we can:

- **communicate by e-mail with others**
- **send audio messages to others**
- **send pictures and video clips to others**
- **chat to others by exchanging text messages (Internet Relay Chat) chat to others by exchanging voice messages (Internet Telephony)**
- **videoconference with others combining video images, sound and text/graphics.**

Distance learning is nothing new. It has been used for many years to deliver everything from school lessons and university courses. However, our experience in the area language learning/teaching is quite limited. Freed from the constraints of the physical classroom, open and distance learning (ODL) will open new learning worlds to be tapped into.

However, these brave new worlds need to be put into perspective. A multimedia learning system is about as likely to produce a competent language user as a pair of Nike trainers is likely to produce a world-beating Olympic athlete; and language learning through ODL needs to model itself on the best practices of the ELT classroom. Effective learning will continue to rely on good teachers able to help manage and support the learning process.

Multimedia ELT materials:

All the major ELT publishers have a range of multimedia materials. Contact your local ELT representative or look at the catalogues.

General bookshops on the Web which can supply ELT materials:
http://www.amazon.com

ELT bookshops on the web:

BEBC
http://www.bebc.co.uk

Delta Systems
http://www.delta-systems.com

The English Book Centre
http://www.ebcoxford.co.uk

KELTIC
http://www.keltic.co.uk

Websites with information about Internet-based resources:
http://www.eslcafe.com/search
http://www.linguistic-funland.com/
http://tefl.com/resources/publish.htm
http://agoralang.com/

Links to sites of general interest to ODL:
http://www.man.ac.uk/CELSE/centre/bookmark.html

Websites piloting ODL for ELT:
http://www.hull.ac.uk/merlin/

Bookshops with mail order facilities:
BEBC
Albion Close, Parkstone
Poole BH12 3LL

CIBC
42 Hills Road
Cambridge CB2 2RU

Delta Systems
1400 Miller Parkway
McHenry, IL 60050, USA

The English Book Centre
26 Grove Street,
Oxford

KELTIC
39 Alexandra Road, Addlestone
Surrey KT15 2PQ

The English Language Bookshop
31 George Street
Brighton BN2 1RH

Websites for those interested in finding out about/communicating about materials:
http://www.eslcafe.com/search
http://www.linguistic-funland.com/
http://tefl.com/resources/publish.htm
http://agoralang.com/

NORTHBROOK COLLEGE SUSSEX
Further and Higher Education

Cert TESOL
Full-time: 5 weeks - £477
Part-time: 16 weeks - £377
Contact: Sheri Johnson

LTCL (TESOL) Dip TESOL
Part-time: 9 months - £425
Examination Charge - £182.50
Contact: Theresa Colbeck

Northbrook College Prep TESOL
Full-time: 4 weeks - £138
Part-time: 12 weeks - £77
Contact: Valentina Long

Northbrook College (Sussex), Littlehampton Road,
Goring By Sea, Worthing, West Sussex, BN12 6NU
Tel: 01903 606010 / Fax: 01903 606207
E-mail: enquiries@nbcol.ac.uk

Concessions for Benefit Claimants on all courses. Non-EU charges on application

READING *list*

There are thousands of EFL books on the market, so here is a small selection to get you started

As EFL has matured, the range of materials available to the TEFL teacher has increased enormously. Publishers vie with each other to launch that best-selling title which will be their cash cow for years to come; and nowhere is the market fiercer than for course books, the mainstay of the language classroom. For the novice teacher, the choice can be daunting. So, rather than list the current top course books or resource books, we have decided to focus on books for teachers - those which will provide a solid foundation on which to build. From this, teachers will need to become familiar with what's on offer - by studying the learning objectives, overall structure, internal organisation and appearance of specific materials on the market in order to make their own decisions about what best suits their own teaching style and a particular group's learning objectives and styles. Even in the area of background books for teachers, at any one time there is a wide range of titles and positions. In addition, the practice of ELT is also developing all the time and new books propose new solutions to the old problem of developing the learners' competence. So, teachers should use the following list as a starting point for exploring other publications as well as keeping abreast of new pedagogic developments.

Background Books

The Practice of English Language Teaching
Jeremy Harmer (Longman)
Covers changes in ELT methodology and current practices.
Divided into 3 parts:
- Background theoretical issues
- Practice teaching materials and techniques
- Management and planning: how to organise classrooms and students; lesson preparation

Now accompanied by Internet Worksheets, prepared by Jane Andrews, Patrick Andrews and Charlotte Woods, available from: http://www.awl-elt.com/magazine/pelt.html

How to Teach English
Jeremy Harmer (Longman)
An essential introduction to the teaching of English, emphasising practical issues. The book is suitable for self-study or as a course book for trainee teachers.

Teaching Practice Handbook
Roger Gower (Heinemann)
A reference book for both trainers and trainees, covering the essential skills and techniques involved in language teaching, plus exercises to help trainees master them.

Teaching and Learning Grammar
Jeremy Harmer (Longman)
Advice and techniques to improve the teaching of grammar, while maintaining student motivation

Learning Teaching
Jim Scrivener (Heinemann)
Learning Teaching is a book for teachers starting out in ELT. It is particularly suitable as a coursebook for short initial training courses such as the RSA/UCLES CTEFLA or the Trinity College Certificate. The book offers a range of teaching ideas backed up with a clear rationale - but in a very user friendly and approachable style.

Language Teaching Methodology
Nunan, (Prentice Hall)
A course book in methodology for pre-service language teachers and teacher trainers in language education. The book provides a balanced introduction to theory, research and practice and covers all key areas of language teaching methodology.

The York Associates Teaching Business English Handbook
Nick Brieger (York Associates)
Aimed at new and experienced teachers of Business English, the book covers background issues in Business and Business English, pedagogic issues and language/communication checklists and references.

Activity books
Five-minute Activities
Penny Ur (CUP)
Over 130 short activities to be used immediately in the classroom. They cover a whole range of different skills and activities and encourage teachers to create their own.

Dictionaries for teachers and students

Longman Active Study Dictionary
- For intermediate learners
- Contains 45,000 words
- Uses a defining vocabulary 2,000 core words

Cambridge International Dictionary of English
- For intermediate to advanced learners.
- Contains 100,000 words/phrase arranged under 50,000 headwords; 140 language portraits; 2,000 vocabulary items illustrated.
- Uses a defining vocabulary of 2,000 commonly-used words.

Oxford Advanced Learner's Dictionary
- For upper-intermediate to advanced learners

- **Contains 63,000 references and 65,000 definitions; 90,000 examples**
- **Uses a defining vocabulary of 3,500 commonly-used words**

Grammar books for teachers and students

English Grammar in Use
Raymond Murphy (CUP)
Reference and practice book for intermediate students. Provides comprehensive coverage in simple language of core grammar areas. Contains left-hand page explanations, right-hand page exercises, with key to exercises at back of the book. For self-study or classroom use.

Practical English Usage
Michael Swan (OUP)
An A-Z reference book on English language usage and grammar, but without any grammatical overview.

How English Works
Michael Swan and Catherine Walter (OUP)
Reference and practice book for intermediate to lower-advanced students. Published in full colour and packed with interesting authentic texts, it covers all the important elements in the standard EFL grammar syllabus.

Magazines/Periodicals

Authentically English
Provides teaching ideas and materials drawn from authentic sources. Publishes articles on key language learning issues; informs teachers about the latest publications in ELT; includes photocopiable teaching materials.

Modern English Teacher
Contains a mix of teaching theory and practice and aims to provide professional development and personal help to practising teachers at all levels up-to-date. Includes language focus and good book reviews section

English Teaching Professional
Addresses both the practical and professional aspects of teaching. The former includes materials to photocopy, classroom ideas, checklists and techniques; the latter articles on methodology, pedagogy, technology, language and linguistics.

English Language Teaching Journal
Provides a platform for the discussion of theoretical and practical issues facing teachers. Brings together articles from various disciplines related to ELT, notably education, psychology, sociology and linguistics. Provides information on forthcoming ELT conferences.

EL Gazette
Monthly international newspaper for EFL/ESL teachers, with news and views on both the business and pedagogical aspects in the ELT world. Popular source of press releases, reviews, contact addresses, global conferences and recruitment sections, plus teaching ideas and regular specialist features on specific countries and/or areas of ELT.

Miscellaneous

Dave Sperling's Internet Guide
Dave Sperling (Prentice Hall Regents)
Summary of the best-of-the-best information for English teachers to be found on the Internet. Provides a useful introduction to using the Internet (even how to create your own web page), and lots of advice for finding what you need for ELT. Includes A-Z compendium of hand-picked web sites for articles, dissertations, training, photocopiable worksheets, etc.

The Future of English
Graddol (The British Council)
Assesses the likely world popularity of English in the 21st century by examining global trends in technology, demography, and the economy. With abstracts, summaries, references, charts, and pointers to sources of data on the World Wide Web, this easily navigable text provides the basis for in-house workshops or systematic independent study. A series of double-page spreads display facts and figures at a glance.

Part-time
Language Courses at
ABERDEEN COLLEGE

- **Introduction to TESOL**
  30 hour courses held at regular intervals commencing September 97.
  We also offer an intensive one week **Introduction to TESOL** course commencing 29th June 1998.

- **Trinity College London Certificate**
  Twice weekly over six months commencing 23rd September 1997.

- **Licentiate Diploma**
  (Trinity College London)
  One evening per week over nine months.
  Commences September 1997.

- **Cambridge Examination in English for Language Teachers**
  One afternoon per week over six months, or an intensive two week course for groups of ten. Commences October 1997.

For information on starting dates, fees etc please contact Annne Bain, Team Leader EFL.

Tel **01224 612000**

Aberdeen College, Balgownie Centre, Hutcheon Gardens, Bridge of Don, Aberdeen AB23 8HA.
Fax 01224 612575. Minicom: 01224 612163.
E-mail: abcoll-enquiry@abdn.ac.uk Internet: http://www.abcol.ac.uk/

The first choice for millions of students around the world

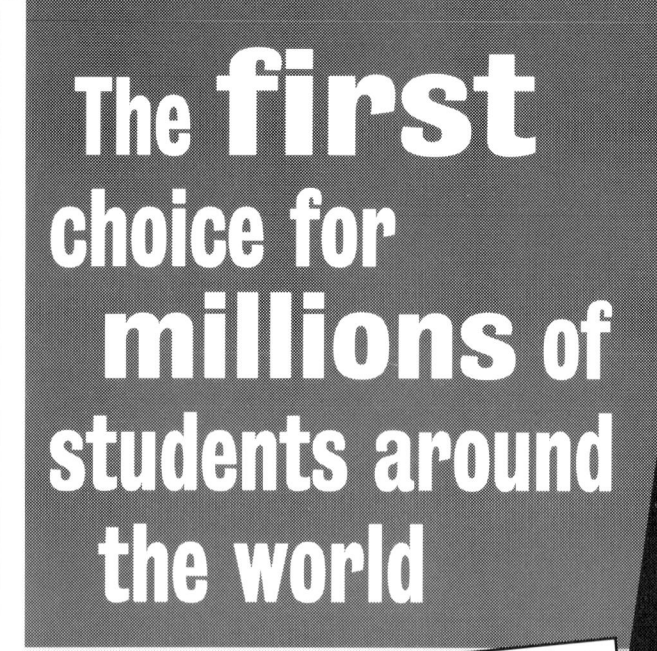

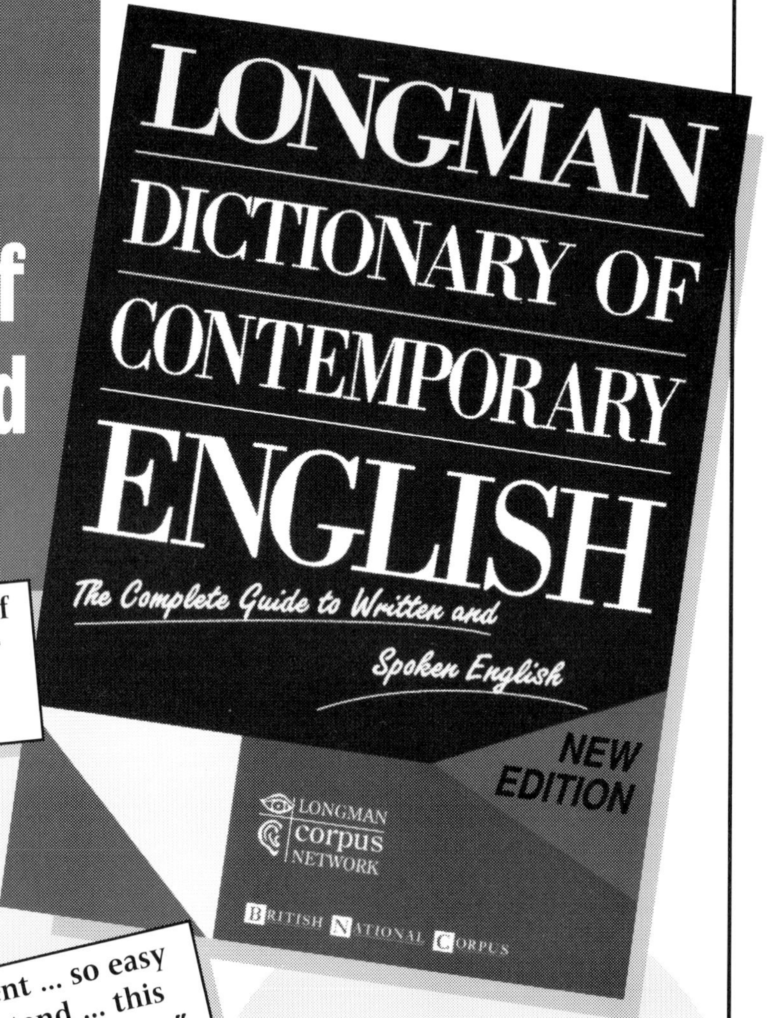

LONGMAN DICTIONARY OF CONTEMPORARY ENGLISH
The Complete Guide to Written and Spoken English

NEW EDITION

LONGMAN corpus NETWORK
BRITISH NATIONAL CORPUS

"... exactly meets the needs of all students - whatever their subject of study."
Professor the Lord Randolph Quirk

"... a remarkable achievement ... more than ever a core item in the English student's library."
Professor David Crystal

"... excellent ... so easy to understand ... this dictionary is my bible."
Trung Do, student, USA

Cased	0 582 23751 3	£18.95
Paper	0 582 23750 5	£12.95
Flexi	0 582 23748 3	£18.95

New Longman ELT dictionaries for 1998:

Longman Active Study Dictionary of English - Third Edition
Paper 0 582 29893 8   August 1998

Longman Dictionary of English Language and Culture - Second Edition
Cased 0 582 30204 8   September 1998   Paper 0 582 30203 X   September 1998

Longman Idioms Dictionary - New!
Cased 0 582 30578 0   June 1998   Paper 0 582 30577 2   June 1998

Longman Interactive English Dictionary - Second Edition
CD-ROM (PC and Macintosh)   0 582 32866 7   November 1998

New FREE Teacher's Resource Pack available now!
For more information, see contact details below

For more information, please contact Maureen Coulson, ELT Marketing, Addison Wesley Longman, Edinburgh Gate, Harlow, Essex CM20 2JE, UK.
Telephone 01279 623623, fax 01279 623426,
e-mail maureen.coulson@awl.co.uk
Visit our website at http://www.awl-elt.com

LONGMAN

Associations in
EFL

Explanation of EFL associations

"Some of the more notable associations with, a brief explanation of their activities."

page 62

Explanation of EFL associations

The following organisations all contribute to EFL. Some are professional organisations which regulate the code of conduct of practitioners, private schools or state institutions; others are larger employers offering job opportunities through their network of schools. The text following each organisation gives a short description of their function and importance in the overall EFL world. For reasons of space, the list leans towards British-based organisations.

ARELS
(Association of Recognised English Language Services)
2 Pontypool Place
Valentine Place
London SE1

Tel: 0171 242 3136
Fax: 0171 928 9378

ARELS is a non-profit making organisation of private English Language Schools in the UK which are inspected and accredited by the British Council, and who conduct courses in English as a Foreign Language. ARELS produce a free annual guide listing member schools and also an information sheet on teaching in their establishments. These are available direct from ARELS. It is advisable for those seeking employment to make direct contact with the ARELS schools.

BALEAP
(British Association of Lecturers in English for Academic Purposes)
Huw Owen Building, OCW
Penglais, Aberyswyth
Dyfed, Wales

BALEAP is a national organisation of centres where EAP (English for Academic Purposes) is taught within British universities. Its aims are to improve the English language provision for international students in institutions of higher education in the UK, and to promote and support the professional development and status of staff in these.

BALEAP offers a service to teachers of EAP looking for work in the UK, particularly on pre-sessional courses. This register constitutes a database of names for BALEAP member universities to use when looking for teaching staff for their courses.

BASELT
(British Association of State English Language Teaching)
Cheltenham and Gloucester College of Higher Education
Francis Close Hall
Swindon Road
Cheltenham GL50 4AZ

Tel: 01242 227099
Fax: 01242 227055

BASELT is an association of nearly eighty state universities and colleges in Britain providing quality English Language courses for overseas students and teachers. An annual free booklet lists all member establishments. It is advisable to contact the institution direct regarding employment.

BATQI
(British Association of TESOL Qualifying Institutions)
School of Education
University of Leeds
Leeds LS2 9AJ

Tel: 0113 233 4528
Fax: 0113 233 4541

BATQI is a voluntary non profit association of UK educational institutions which offer courses leading to ESL/EFL teaching qualifications. It also provides information to those seeking routes to becoming qualified TESOL professionals, maintains

---

LONDON STUDY CENTRE

TRINITY COLLEGE CERTIFICATE IN TESOL

FULL-TIME : 5 WEEKS
PART-TIME: 10/15 WEEKS
THROUGHOUT THE YEAR

- DIPLOMA COURSES BY CORRESPONDENCE
- LARGE COLLEGE
- DEDICATED TO EFL
- VIDEO / AUDIO / OHP IN EVERY CLASSROOM

CONTACT TEACHER TRAINING DEPT.

0171-384 2734

Fax: 0171 731 6060 Tel: 0171 731 3549
E-mail: 106153.2344@compuserve.com
676 Fulham Road, London SW6 5SA

London Study Centre — 20th Anniversary 1975–1995

a code of practice for institutions offering TESOL programs and publishes a register of TESOL courses. Membership includes institutions offering courses ranging from short courses to PhD's.

BC

The British Council
10 Spring Gardens
London SW1A 2BN

Tel: 0171 389 4383
Fax: 0171 3894140

The British Council, registered in England as a charity, is the United Kingdom's international network for education, culture and development services. The Council works to support the British ELT sector as a whole, and is itself a major provider of ELT services overseas through its teaching, examinations and other networks.

C&G

City and Guilds
1 Giltspur Street
London EC1B 1RW

Tel: 0171 294 2798
Fax: 0171 294 2418

C&G is the largest awarding body for National Vocational Qualifications (NVQ) and one of the three awarding bodies for General National Vocational Qualifications (GNVQ). Amongst its awards are two which include an element of training for ESOL teachers:
- **Certificate in Teaching Basic Skills**
- **Teaching Basic Communication Skills**

CfBT

(Centre for British Teachers)
1 The Chambers
East Street
Reading RG1 4JD
Tel: 0118 952 3900
Fax: 0118 952 3924

CfBT Education Services recruits qualified and experienced ELT supervisory staff and teachers for its own projects in Brunei, Oman, and on behalf of Turkish clients. They also manage several aid-funded projects in Africa and S.E. Asia.

CILT

(Centre for Information on Language Teaching and Research)

CILT, a registered educational charity supported by Central Government grants, works to support language teaching and learning in the UK. Through its resources library and information service, publications, training, conferences and professional development, CILT provides a complete range of services for language professionals in every stage and sector of education.

CILTS

(Cambridge Integrated Language Teaching Schemes)
University of Cambridge Local Examinations Syndicate
1 Hills Road
Cambridge CB1 2EU

Tel: 01223 553789
Fax: 01223 553086

CILTS is the name given to the project to develop and extend the range of pre-service and postgraduate awards for teachers of EFL, by drawing on the RSA/Cambridge Certificates and Diplomas in TEFL. (see also UCLES)

TOP QUALITY TEFL COURSES

- Cambridge Diploma — - Part-time
  - Bristol and Cheltenham

- Cambridge CELTA — - Full-time (6 weeks)
  - Unique programme
  - Cheltenham

- Cambridge CEELT — - Cheltenham in July

- Dedicated, experienced team
- Excellent results

Plus
- General and /Business English all year

A centre of excellence for Further Education and Training Courses validated by the British Council

Contact: Paul Burden, Gloscat, 73 The Park, Cheltenham, Glos. GL50 2RR
Tel: 01242 532144   Fax: 01242 532023

Gloscat
GLOUCESTERSHIRE COLLEGE OF ARTS & TECHNOLOGY

Explanation of EFL associations

Some of the more notable associations with a brief explanation of their activities.

EAQUALS
(European Association for Quality Language Services)

EAQUALS is a pan-European Association of language training providers aiming to promote and guarantee quality in modern language teaching institutions. Membership is open to private or state institutions which are involved in the delivery of quality language training or are, in some other way, committed to the achievement of excellence in this area.

EEP
(East European Partnership)
Carlton House
27A Carlton Drive
London, SW15 2BS

Tel: 0171 780 2841
Fax: 0171 780 9592

The EE Partnership is an initiative by Voluntary Services Overseas and places selected graduate volunteers in Central and Eastern Europe and the former Soviet Union. Volunteers must be qualified teachers or have a TEFL qualification with two years' experience and are paid a local salary. (see also VSO)

ESU
English Speaking Union

The ESU is an independent, non-political, educational charity with members throughout the UK, the USA and the world. Its purpose is to promote international understanding and human achievement through the widening use of English as the language of our global village. Many scholarships and exchanges are sponsored by the ESU, providing the opportunity for study both in the UK and overseas.

IATEFL
(International Association of Teachers of English as a Foreign Language)
3 Kingsdown Park, Tankerton
Whitstable,
Kent CT5 2DJ

Tel: 01227 276528
Fax: 01227 274415

IATEFL offers, amongst other services:
- **an annual International Conference**
- **a range of regular publications, including the IATEFL Newsletter**
- **reduced rates for professional journals**
- **special Interest Groups (SIGs) which enable teachers with similar interests to share ideas and make contacts worldwide**

IH
International House
106 Picadilly,
London, W1V 9FL

Tel: 0171 491 2598
Fax: 0171 409 0959

IH is a worldwide network of language schools (over 100 affiliated member schools and centres in 30 countries all over the world) sharing a common commitment to the highest standards of teaching and training.

In particular IH Teacher Training is widely recognised as a leading independent language teacher training organisation. IH Offer courses leading to the RSA/Cambridge Certificate and Diploma, together with a wide range of specialised ELT training and development courses. The IH Staffing Unit arranges the selection and recruitment of teachers and publishes details of IH teaching vacancies around the world.

JALT
Japan Association of Language Teachers
Central Office
Urban Edge Building, 5th Floor 1-37-9 Taito
Taito-ku, Tokyo 110
Japan

Tel: 81 3 3837 1630
Fax: 81 3 3837 1631

JALT is a professional organisation of people interested in promoting excellence in language learning and teaching, with nearly 4,000 members in over 35 Chapters across Japan as well as members abroad.

Amongst other benefits JALT members receive JALT's monthly magazine, 'The Language Teacher', including feature articles, teaching tips, reviews, meeting and conference announcements, and job advertisements;

JET
Japan Exchange and Teaching Programme
Council on International Educational Exchange
52 Poland Street
London W1V 4JQ

Tel: 0171 478 2000

The JET Programme invites young college and university graduates from overseas to participate in international exchange and foreign language education throughout Japan. The programme places participants in schools throughout Japan to act as assistant langauage teachers.

LCCI
London Chamber of Commerce and Industry Examinations Board
112 Station Road
Sidcup
Kent DA15 7BJ

Tel: 0181 302 0261
Fax: 0181 302 4169

LCCI awards a portfolio of business-related NVQs and examinations. For teachers of Business English there is the Foundation Certificate for Teachers of Business English (FCTBE) and the Certificate in Teaching English for Business (CertTEB) See Section 13. LCCI also provide a number of student English exams, these cover specialist topics in business and tourism.

RSA
(Royal Society of Arts)

RSA Examinations Board is firmly established as a leading provider of NVQs in a wide range of vocational areas. The aim of the alliance between RSA and UCLES (see below and Sections 8 and 9) is to provide a 'seamless suite of qualifications across the academic and vocational curriculum'. The range of Cambridge/RSA Certificates and Diplomas for Teachers of English as a Foreign Language are the most valuable professional qualifications for EFL teaching, both in the United Kingdom and elsewhere in the world.

SIETAR
Society of International English Training and Research

SIETAR International is an interdisciplinary professional and service organisation whose purpose is to implement and promote cooperative interactions and effective communication among peoples of diverse cultures, races, and ethnic groups. Its objective is to encourage the development and application of knowledge, values, and skills which enable effective intercultural, interracial, and interethnic actions at the individual, group, organisation, and community levels.

TESOL
The Association for (Teachers of English to Speakers of Other Languages)
1600 Cameron Street
Suite 300, Alexandria
Virginia VA22314
USA

Tel: 00 1 703 836 0774
Fax: 001 703 836 7864

TESOL is an international education association of almost 18,000 members with headquarters in Alexandria, Virginia, USA. The association promotes scholarship, disseminates information, and advocates for credentialed instruction and quality programming.

TESOL publishes books, materials and publications on a wide range of theoretical and practical topics as well as position papers and resources for newcomers to the field. Its premier program is the annual convention, usually held in March in the continental United States, which attracts 7-8,500 participants. In addition to the international association, there are over 88 worldwide affiliated organisations representing another 50,000 members.

UCLES
(University of Cambridge Local Examinations Syndicate)
University of Cambridge Local Examinations Syndicate
1 Hills Road
Cambridge CB1 2EU

Tel: 01223 553789
Fax: 01223 553086

UCLES is a world leader in the provision of educational assessment services, with schools and colleges in more than 150 countries. The range of Cambridge/RSA Certificates and Diplomas for Teachers of English as a Foreign Language are the most valuable professional qualifications for EFL teaching, both in the UK and elsewhere in the world.

USIS
(United States Information Service)

With a wide variety of activities, the English Language Programs Division supports English teaching programs and activities outside the United States, serving USIS posts in more than 140 countries. Activities include the development of English teaching curricula, textbooks, and teacher training workshops. The Washington office staff provide academic expertise, advisory and consultative assistance, and materials resources worldwide. They also stimulate and reinforce academic exchange programs between the United States and other countries and help to interpret American life and institutions to the world.

VSO
(Voluntary Services Overseas)
Enquiries
317 Putney Bridge Road
London, SW15 2PN

Tel: 0181 780 7500

Voluntary Service Overseas (VSO) is a charity that sends aid to developing countries - not in the form of money, food, clothing or equipment, but in the form of expert volunteers, including ELT.

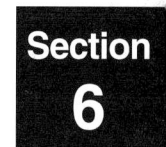

English Language Teaching

Books, Cassettes, Videos, Software...
from KELTIC : Specialist ELT booksellers

- Fast mail order service UK & worldwide
- Specialists in ELT
- FREE Guide to ELT Materials
- All publishers, British prices
- Non-ELT titles available on request
- Competitive discounts and postal rates

Methodology
Language Games
Coursebooks
Exams
Grammar
Dictionaries
Vocabulary
Skills
Pronunciation
Testing
Linguistics
Business English
EAP & Study Skills
Readers
Video
Software

KELTIC INTERNATIONAL

39 Alexandra Road, Addlestone, Surrey KT15 2PQ, England
Tel +44 (0)1932 820485   Fax +44 (0)1932 854320
E-mail keltic@keltic.co.uk   http://www.keltic.co.uk

OXFORD BOOKWORMS

Now more than 100 titles to choose from!

Send off today for your free copy of the latest Oxford Bookworms catalogue

New titles include *Goodbye Mr Hollywood, Death in the Freezer, The Mystery of Allegra, Lord Jim,* and *Matty Doolin*

Plus...

Free poster with picture quiz!

OXFORD BOOKWORMS FACTFILES

An eye-catching new series of non-fiction readers with exercises and glossaries. Illustrated in lavish full colour.

New titles published: *Seasons and Celebrations, Kings and Queens of Britain,* and *The Cinema*.

For your new Oxford Bookworms catalogue and free Factfiles poster with picture quiz, please contact:
ELT Promotions Department, Oxford University Press,
Great Clarendon Street, Oxford OX2 6DP
E-mail: elt.enquiry@oup.co.uk
http://www.oup.co.uk/elt

OXFORD UNIVERSITY PRESS

Directory of centres

Section 7

Course providers Grid

"Listings of courses by area"

page 68

Directory of centres

"Certificate and Diploma providers in the UK"

page 70

Teacher Training Certificate & Diploma COURSE

Directory of centres — Section 7

Avon	CELTA	Cert. TESOL	Dip. TESOL	Dip. TEFLA	Page
Bath College, City of	◆				71
Bristol College, City of	◆				72
English Language		◆			75
Filton College	◆				75
The Language Project		◆	◆		79
University of the West of England		◆			87

Bedfordshire					
Bedford College	◆				71
University of Luton		◆	◆		87

Berkshire					
Bracknell and Wokingham College		◆			73
East Berkshire College		◆	◆		74
Reading College			◆		82
Windsor Schools TEFL		◆			88

Buckinghamshire					
Amersham & Wycombe College	◆				70

Birmingham					
Brasshouse Centre	◆				72
Handsworth College	◆				77
Solihull College	◆				84

Cambridgeshire					
Anglia Polytechnic University	◆				70
Bell Language School (Cambridge)	◆				71
Newnham Language Centre	◆			◆	80
Studio School of English	◆				85

Cheshire					
Mid Cheshire College of Further Education	◆			◆	80

Cleveland					
Middlesborough College of F.E.		◆	◆		80

Devon					
College of St Mark & St John	◆				73
Mayflower College		◆			80
Plymouth College of F.E.		◆			82
Sidmouth International School		◆			84
South Devon College	◆				84
Torbay Language Centre	◆				86

Dorset					
Anglo-Continental	◆				70
Bournemouth & Poole College of F.E.	◆				71
Harrow House	◆				77
International Teaching and Training Centre	◆			◆	78
International Training Network		◆			78

County Durham					
Darlington College of Technology		◆			74
Gateshead College		◆			75
New College Durham		◆			80
University of Durham	◆				86

Essex	CELTA	Cert. TESOL	Dip. TESOL	Dip. TEFLA	Page
Bell Language School (Saffron Walden)				◆	71
Colchester Institute		◆		◆	73
S.E. Essex College of Arts & Technology		◆			84
Thurrock College		◆			86

Gloucestershire					
Cheltenham & Gloucester College of H.E.	◆				73
GLOSCAT	◆			◆	76
inlingua Teacher Training & Recruitment		◆			77

Greater Manchester					
City College Manchester		◆	◆		73
Hopwood Hall College		◆			77
Manchester College of Arts and Technology		◆			80
Stockport College		◆			85

Hampshire					
Basingstoke College of Technology		◆			70
Eastleigh College	◆				75
Farnborough College of Technology		◆	◆		75
Harts Villages Centre		◆			77

Hertfordshire					
Barnet College	◆				70
Oaklands College		◆	◆		81

Humberside					
The Hull College		◆			77
University of Hull	◆				87

Kent					
Bromley School of English	◆				72
Canterbury College		◆			72
Cicero Languages International		◆			73
Concorde International Study Centre	◆				73
Grove House Language Centre		◆			76
Hilderstone College	◆			◆	77
Kent School of English		◆			79
Medway Adult Education Centre		◆			80
Pilgrims English Language Courses	◆				82
Regency School of English		◆	◆		82
West Kent College	◆				88

Lancashire					
Blackpool & The Fylde College		◆			71
Bolton College		◆			71
Bury College		◆			72
Wigan & Leigh College	◆				88

Leicestershire					
Loughborough College	◆				80
Loughborough University		◆			80
Students International Ltd.		◆			85
Wigston College of Further Education	◆				88

London					
Angloschool	◆				70

Page 68

Teacher Training
Certificate & Diploma

London Continued

	CELTA	Cert. TESOL	Dip. TESOL	Dip. TEFLA	Page
Croydon English Language Scheme	◆				74
English Worldwide			◆		75
Frances King Teacher Training Centre	◆				75
Golders Green College		◆			76
Greenhill College	◆				76
Hammersmith & West London College	◆			◆	76
International House (London)	◆			◆	78
King's College English Language Centre				◆	79
Kingsway College	◆				79
Language Link Training		◆			79
London Study Centre		◆			79
Oxford House College		◆	◆		81
Polyglot Language Services		◆			82
Regent Language Training (London)	◆				82
Saint George International		◆	◆		83
St. Giles College London	◆				83
School of Oriental & African Studies	◆				83
Skola Teacher Training	◆				84
South Thames College	◆				84
Southwark College		◆			84
Stanton Teacher Training	◆				84
Thames Valley University	◆				85
University of Westminster		◆			87
Waltham Forest College		◆		◆	87
Westminster College	◆				88

Midlands

	CELTA	Cert. TESOL	Dip. TESOL	Dip. TEFLA	Page
Coventry Technical College		◆	◆		74
Sandwell College		◆			83
University of Wolverhampton		◆			88

Newcastle-Upon-Tyne

	CELTA	Cert. TESOL	Dip. TESOL	Dip. TEFLA	Page
International House (Newcastle)	◆				78

Norfolk

	CELTA	Cert. TESOL	Dip. TESOL	Dip. TEFLA	Page
Bell Language School Norwich	◆			◆	71
University of East Anglia	◆				86

Nottinghamshire

	CELTA	Cert. TESOL	Dip. TESOL	Dip. TEFLA	Page
Clarendon College	◆			◆	73
South Nottingham College		◆			84

Oxfordshire

	CELTA	Cert. TESOL	Dip. TESOL	Dip. TEFLA	Page
ELT Banbury	◆				75
Godmer House Teacher Training	◆				76
Oxford Brookes University	◆				81
Oxford College of Further Education	◆				81
Oxford English Centre				◆	81

Staffordshire

	CELTA	Cert. TESOL	Dip. TESOL	Dip. TEFLA	Page
Stoke-on-Trent College	◆				85

Surrey

	CELTA	Cert. TESOL	Dip. TESOL	Dip. TEFLA	Page
Brooklands College	◆				72
Richmond Adult and Community College		◆			82
Surrey Language Centre		◆			85
Surrey Youth & Adult Education Services		◆		◆	86

Surrey Continued

	CELTA	Cert. TESOL	Dip. TESOL	Dip. TEFLA	Page
Sutton College of Liberal Arts		◆			85
Universal Language Training		◆			86

Sussex

	CELTA	Cert. TESOL	Dip. TESOL	Dip. TEFLA	Page
Chichester College of Arts	◆				73
Eastbourne College of Arts & Technology	◆			◆	74
Eastbourne School of English	◆			◆	74
Friends Centre	◆				75
GEOS English Academy Brighton & Hove	◆				76
International House (Hastings)	◆			◆	77
ITS English School		◆	◆		78
Northbrook College		◆			81
St. Giles College (Brighton)	◆				83

Yorkshire

	CELTA	Cert. TESOL	Dip. TESOL	Dip. TEFLA	Page
Bradford and Ilkley Community College		◆			72
Calderdale College		◆			72
Huddersfield Technical College	◆				77
International Language Institute (Leeds)	◆		◆		78
Joseph Priestly College		◆			78
Leeds Metropolitan University	◆	◆			79
Park Lane College		◆			81
The Sheffield College		◆			83
Sheffield Hallam University		◆	◆		83

Channel Islands

	CELTA	Cert. TESOL	Dip. TESOL	Dip. TEFLA	Page
St. Brelade's College		◆	◆		83

Wales

	CELTA	Cert. TESOL	Dip. TESOL	Dip. TEFLA	Page
University of Glamorgan	◆				86
University of Wales, Swansea				◆	87

Scotland

	CELTA	Cert. TESOL	Dip. TESOL	Dip. TEFLA	Page
Aberdeen College		◆	◆		70
Basil Paterson/ Edinburgh Language Foundation	◆				70
Dundee College	◆			◆	74
Langside College, Glasgow		◆			79
Regent Edinburgh		◆			82
Stevenson College	◆				85
University of Edinburgh				◆	86
University of Glasgow	◆				86
University of St. Andrews		◆			87
University of Strathclyde	◆				87

Northern Ireland

	CELTA	Cert. TESOL	Dip. TESOL	Dip. TEFLA	Page
Queens Universty of Belfast		◆			82

PROVIDERS

Section 7

Directory of centres

Page 69

Aberdeen College
Ellon Road
Bridge of Don
ABERDEEN AB23 8LQ
Tel: (01224) 612506
Fax: (01224) 612500
E mail:
abcoll-enquiry@abdn.ac.uk

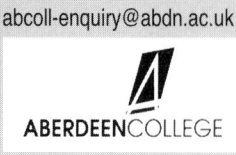

Cert. TESOL
Part Time 6 mths £330
Max. Trainees per course 10
Contact: Anne Bain
Start Dates: 2 courses per year Sept. to Mar.

LTCL (TESOL) (Dip. TESOL)
Part Time 18 wks £300 per module (2 modules)
Max. Trainees per course 10
Contact: Anne Bain
Start Dates: 1 course per year Sept.

The Cert. TESOL course runs 2 afternoons or evenings per week.

Aberdeen College is the largest further education college in Scotland with an intake of approximately 500 foreign EFL students. Trainees also have the opportunity to teach young learners at French and Dutch schools locally.

Aberdeen also runs a 1 week introduction to TESOL course at £85.

Amersham & Wycombe College
Amersham Campus
Stanely Hill, Amersham
BUCKS HP7 9HN
Tel: (01494) 735555
Fax: (01494) 735566
E-Mail: info@amerwyc.ac.uk

CELTA
Part Time 10 wks £200
Max. Trainees per course 12
Contact: Sheila Tracey
Start Dates: 2 courses per year June and Sept.

Amersham & Wycombe College has a high national profile and recently scored in the top 25% in a inspection report of further education colleges in England and Wales. The college is able to offer some of the best resources in the region.

Admission is available for some students, please contact the college for further details of eligibility.

All students are invited to join the Student Union and are welcome to use college facilities.

Anglia Polytechnic University
East Road
CAMBRIDGE CB1 1PT
Tel: (01223) 363271
Fax: (01223) 352973
E-Mail: a.m.m.shea@anglia.ac.uk

CELTA
Full Time 4 wks £950
Max. Trainees per course 15
Contact: Anna Shea
Start Dates: 2 courses per year June and Aug.

Applicants have to attend an interview for the courses and complete a pre-interview task consisting of an elementary English exercise and short essay question on approaches to learning and teaching English.

Anglo-Continental
33 Wimborne Road
BOURNEMOUTH BH2 6NA
Tel: (01202) 557414
Fax: (01202) 556156
E-Mail: 100065,2523@compuserve.com

CELTA
Full Time 4 wks £925
Max. Trainees per course 10
Contact: J. Manwaring
Start Dates: 2 courses per year May and Aug.

Anglo Continental was established 1950 and has gained a strong international reputation for teaching English. Help can be given with accommodation. Anglo Continental is a recognised school and offers employment to successful candidates whenever possible.

Angloschool
146 Church Road
Crystal Palace
LONDON SE19 2NT
Tel: (0181) 653 7285
Fax: (0181) 653 9667
E-Mail: english@angloschool.co.uk

CELTA
Full Time 4 wks £820
Max. Trainees per course 8
Contact: Administration
Start Dates: F/T 4 courses per year Apr, May, Aug, Nov.

Angloschool Teacher Training Institute has been providing teacher training courses since 1978. The Institute is part of Angloschool which was founded in 1960 and is recognised by the British Council.

On the CELTA programme, mornings are primarily theoretical with lectures, seminars and afternoons practical.

Help with accommodation and finding a first post is available.

Barnet College
Wood Street
Barnet
HERTFORDSHIRE
EN5 4AZ
Tel: (0181) 440 6321
Fax: (0181) 441 5236
E-Mail: cso2@barnet.ac.uk

CELTA
Full Time 4 wks £721
Part Time 9 mths £721
Max. Trainees per course 15
Contact: Lesley Shaperio
Start Dates: 1 P/T course per year Sept. 4 F/T courses per year Sept, Jan, Apr, June.

The P/T course runs on Wednesday evenings from Sept to June.

Basil Paterson/Edinburgh Language Foundation
22/23 Abercromby Place
EDINBURGH EH3 6QE
Tel: (0131) 556 7695
Fax: (0131) 557 8503
E-Mail: courses@bp-coll.demon.co.uk

CELTA
Full Time 4 wks £999
Max. Trainees per course 12
Contact: Mary Beresford-Peirse
Start Dates: 12 courses per year, monthly.

During the course help will be given on how to find employment.

Basingstoke College of Technology
Worting Road
Basingstoke
HAMPSHIRE
RG21 8TN
Tel: (01256) 354141
Fax: (01256) 306444
E-Mail: peterdickinson@bcot.ac.uk

Cert. TESOL
Full Time 4 wks £500 + £50 registration fee + £50 exam fee
Part Time 24 wks £500 + £50 registration fee + £50 exam fee
Max. Trainees per course 12
Contact: John Rogers
Start Dates: 1 F/T course per year July. 2 P/T course per year Sept and Dec.

Bath College, City of
Avon Street
Bath
AVON BA1 1UP
Tel: (01225) 312191
Fax: (01225) 444213
E-Mail: bulld@eng.citybathcoll.ac.uk

CELTA
Full Time 4 wks £950 (provisional)
Part Time 6 mths £950 (provisional)
Max. Trainees per course P/T 15, F/T 12
Contact: David Bull
Start Dates: 1 P/T course per year Sept. 3 F/T courses per year Mar, July, Aug.

Bedford College
Enterprise House
Queens Park
BEDFORDSHIRE
MK40 4PF
Tel: (01234) 271492
Fax: (01234) 324674
E-Mail: fnapthine@bedford.ac.uk

CELTA
Part Time 6 mths £695 including fees
Max. Trainees per course 14
Contact: Frances Napthine
Start Dates: 2 P/T courses per year July and Oct.

Bell Language School
(Cambridge)
1 Red Cross Lane
CAMBRIDGE
CB2 2QX
Tel: (01223) 247242
Fax: (01223) 412410
E-Mail: info@bell-lang.ac.uk

CELTA
Full Time 4 wks £930 +£66.50 exam fee
Part Time 30 wks £895 +£66.50 exam fee
Max. Trainees per course 15
Contact: Judith Giles
Start Dates: 1 P/T course per year Oct. 6 F/T courses per year Feb, May, July, Sept (early), Sept (late) and Oct.

DTEFLA
Part Time 27 wks £990 + £165 exam fee. Max. Trainees per course 15. Contact: Judith Giles. Start Dates: 1 course per year Oct.

For details see below.

Bell Language School
(Norwich)
Bowthorpe Hall
NORWICH
NR5 9AA
Tel: (01603) 745615
Fax: (01603) 747669
E-Mail: info@bell-lang.ac.uk

CELTA
Full Time 4 wks £930 + £66.50 exam fee
Max. Trainees per course 15
Contact: Sarah Knights
Start Dates: 6 courses per year Mar, June, July, Aug, Sept, Oct.

DTEFLA
Full Time 10 wks £1355 + £165 exam fee
Max. Trainees per course 12
Contact: Sarah Knights
Start Dates: 1 course per year April.

For details see below.

Bell Language School
(Saffron Walden)
South Road
Saffron Walden
ESSEX CB11 3DP
Tel: (01799) 522918
Fax: (01799) 526949
E-Mail: info@bell-lang.ac.uk

DTEFLA
Full Time 10 wks £1355 + £165 exam fee
Max. Trainees per course 12
Contact: Bruce Milne
Start Dates: 1 course per year Mar.

The first Bell school was opened by Frank Bell in 1955 with the aim of furthering international understanding through language learning. There are now 6 Bell Language Schools in the U.K.. The Bell Schools offer a wide range of English courses for adults over 17 years of age and operate 10 summer schools for young learners between 8 and 17.

Every Bell School offers fully equipped classrooms, video equipment, computer aided language learning facilities, language laboratories and an extensive teacher resource library.

The Bell Courses include more tuition and supervision than the minimum required by RSA/UCLES. All course tutors are qualified and experienced teacher trainers.

The Bell Schools are recognised by the British Council.

Blackpool & The Fylde College
Ashfield Road
Bispham, Blackpool
LANCASHIRE FY2 0HB
Tel: (01253) 352352
Fax: (01253) 356127
E-Mail: bma@blckpool.ac.uk

Cert. TESOL
Part time course pending, subject to approval. For further details, please contact Barbara McDougal.

Bolton College
Manchester Road
Bolton
LANCASHIRE
BL2 1ER
Tel: (01204) 531411
Fax: (01204) 380774

Cert. TESOL
Part Time 36 wks £450
Max. Trainees per course 12
Contact: Nicky Salmon
Start Dates: 1 course per year Sept.

Bournemouth & Poole College of F.E.
Landsdowne Centre
BOURNEMOUTH
BH1 3JJ
Tel: (01202) 747600
Fax: (01202) 205790

CELTA
Part Time 2 terms £660
Max. Trainees per course 12
Contact: Felicity Bond
Start Dates: 1 course per year Sept.

The CELTA course is run on 1 afternoon and 1 evening per week.
The College provides trainees with reference books, study space and word processing materials.

Section 7

Page 71

Bracknell and Wokingham College
Broad Street
Wokingham
BERKSHIRE RG40 1AU
Tel: (0118) 978 2728
Fax: (0118) 989 4315
E-Mail: study@bracknell.ac.uk

Cert. TESOL
Part Time 9 mths £600 + £20 fee
Max. Trainees per course 16
Contact: Colette Galloway
Start Dates: 1 course per year Sept to June.

The course runs on two evenings a week over one academic year; as well as one Saturday per term. It also requires 8 hours of teaching observation and 6 hours of teaching practice.

Bradford and Ilkley Community College
8 Westbrook
Great Horton Road
BRADFORD BD7 1AY
Tel: (01274) 753207
Fax: (01274) 741553
E-Mail: elainet@billc.ac.uk

Cert. TESOL
Full Time 4 wks £650
Part Time 30 wks £650
Max. Trainees per course 16
Contact: Nancy Hall
Start Dates: 1 P/T course per year Oct. 4 F/T courses per year Sept, Jan, Apr.

The English Language Centre offers 11 full time EFL courses at all levels. These cover general English, EAP and ESP topics. The college attracts students from over 50 countries so there is plenty of opportunity for teaching practice and access to a wide range of international students.

The Cert. TESOL course has a strong emphasis on practical teaching. Other areas covered include syllabus planning, development of teaching materials, evaluating course books and classroom management.

Brasshouse Centre
50 Sheepcote Street
BIRMINGHAM B16 8AJ
Tel: (0121) 643 0114
Fax: (0121) 633 4782
E-Mail: brasshouse@easynet.co.uk

CELTA
Part Time 10 wks £900
Max. Trainees per course 12
Contact: Deborah Cobbett
Start Dates: 3 courses per year Sept, Jan, Apr.

The Brasshouse Centre is Birmingham City Council's specialist languages centre, providing courses in 25 languages. The centre offers a wide range of general and specific English courses to a varied audience of students. This provides many opportunities for teacher trainees to observe and gain teaching practice. The centre offers excellent teaching resources and has an extensive course library. There is also an on site book shop that stocks relevant texts.

The CELTA course is instructed on Mondays and Wednesdays, with extra days throughout the course to allow teaching observation.

The centre also run a 1 week introductory courses at £110.

Bromley School of English
2 Park Road
Bromley
KENT BR1 1HP
Tel: (0181) 313 0308
Fax: (0181) 313 3957

CELTA
Full Time 4 wks £795 (£620 if eligible for EU funding)
Max. Trainees per course 12
Contact: Robin Summers
Start Dates: 5 courses per year Mar, May, July, Sept, Nov.

The Bromley School of English offer the CELTA course at the lower cost of £620 for candidates who are eligible for E.U. funding.

To be eligible for E.U. funding, candidates must be a citizen of the UK or of another E.U. member state and not supported by other public or private funding.

The School also offers a one day introductory course at £50.

Brooklands College
Faculty of Education
Heath Road
Weybridge
SURREY KT13 8TT
Tel: (01932) 853300
Fax: (01932) 821713

CELTA
Full Time 1 mth £695 (including fees)
Part Time 4 mths £695 (including fees)
Max. Trainees per course P/T 12 F/T 18
Contact: Janet Drysdale
Start Dates: 1 F/T course per year starting June. 2 P/T courses per year starting Feb, Sept.

Bristol College, City of
Ashley Down
BRISTOL BS7 9BU
Tel: (0117) 904 5000
Fax: (0117) 904 5180
E-Mail: cbc@bristol.tcom.co.uk

CELTA
Part Time 10 wks £825 + £65 examination fee
Max. Trainees per course 8
Contact: Sue Scott
Start Dates: 1 course per year Jan, others pending.

Bury College
Market Street
BURY BL9 0BG
Tel: (0161) 280 8280
Fax: (0161) 280 8228

Cert. TESOL
Part Time 2 & 3 terms £320 + £70 Trinity Fee.
Max. Trainees per course 15
Contact: David Mars
Start Dates: 2 courses per year - 3 term course starts Sept, 2 term in Jan.

Calderdale College
Francis Street
HALIFAX HX1 3UZ
Tel: (01422) 399327 ext. 9319
Fax: (01422) 399320

Cert. TESOL
Part Time 1 academic year £600
Max. Trainees per course 14
Contact: Rita Naughton de Sierra
Start Dates: 1 course per year Sept.

The Cert. TESOL course at Calderdale runs on Tuesday afternoons 1-4, and evenings 6-9, as well as one Saturday per term. Monolingual, Multilingual and ESL students are available for teaching practice. The course contains an ESP element which goes beyond that of the Trinity Syllabus.

The College is located about ten minutes walk from central Halifax.

Canterbury College
New Dover Road
CANTERBURY CT1 3AJ
Tel: (01227) 811111
Fax: (01227) 811101

Cert. TESOL
Part Time 10 wks £610 + exam fee
Max. Trainees per course 10
Contact: Scilla Brumfit
Start Dates: 2 courses per year Jan, Sept.

Cheltenham & Gloucester College of H.E.
Cheltenham International Language Centre
Francis Close Hall
Swindon Road
GLOS. GL50 4AZ
Tel: (01242) 532925
Fax: (01242) 532926
E-Mail: tcook@chelt.ac.uk

CELTA
Full Time 5 wks £850
Max. Trainees per course 12
Contact: Piers Wall
Start Dates: Jan, Apr, June, July, Nov.

Cheltenham International Language Centre (CILC) is a unit of International Education at Cheltenham & Gloucester College of Higher Education. CILC provides a range of EFL programmes for adults and teenagers. CILC has a good and long standing reputation for quality and professionalism.

Chichester College of Arts Science & Technology
Westgate Fields
WEST SUSSEX PO19 1SB
Tel: (01243) 536294
Fax: (01243) 775783
E-Mail: intunit@inetgw.chichester.ac.uk

CELTA
Part Time 2 terms £350 + £66.50 UCLES fee
Max. Trainees per course 12
Contact: Brenda Pike
Start Dates: 1 course per year Jan.

Cicero Languages International
42 Upper Grosvenor Road
Tunbridge Wells
KENT TN1 2ET
Tel: (01892) 547077
Fax: (01892) 522749
E-Mail: cicero@pavilion.co.uk

Cert. TESOL
Full Time 4 wks £780 + £70 Trinity fee. With half board accommodation, £1220 + £70 Trinity fee.
Max. Trainees per course 12
Contact: Administration
Start Dates: 7 courses per year Jan, Feb, Mar, May, Sept (beginning), Sept (end of), Nov.

Cicero have been running the TESOL course since 1990 and offer modules on teaching young learners. Cicero is situated in the attractive 17th century town of Tunbridge Wells.

City College Manchester
141 Barlow Moor Road
MANCHESTER M20 2PQ
Tel: (0161) 957 1660
Fax: (0161) 434 0443
E-Mail: aspencer@manchester-citycollege.ac.uk

Cert. TESOL
Part Time 12/18 wks £620
Max. Trainees per course 15
Contact: Arnold Spencer
Start Dates: 2 courses per year Nov, and Jan.

LTCL (TESOL) (Dip. TESOL)
Part Time 1 or 2 years £270 per year + exam fee
Max. Trainees per course 18
Contact: Arnold Spencer
Start Dates: 1 course per year Sept.

City College Manchester also run CELTA courses in Spain.
Course content for the Cert. TESOL includes language learning skills, management of learning and assessed teaching practice.
The College is close to both Manchester International Airport and Manchester City Airport.

The College also has a well equipped learning resources centre.

Clarendon College
Nottingham Corporation
Clarendon Language Centre
11 Queen Street
NOTTINGHAM NG1 2BL
Tel: (0115) 9553110
Fax: (0115) 9506546
E-Mail: enquiries@clarendon.ac.uk

CELTA
Full time 4 wks £718
Part Time 3 terms £718
Max. Trainees per course 16
Contact: Jenny Gee
Start Dates: 2 P/T courses per year day time and evening both starting Sept. 1 F/T course per year July.

LTCL (TESOL) (Dip. TESOL)
Part Time 6 mths £700
Max. Trainees per course 12
Contact: John Watson
Start Dates: 1 course per year Sept.

Colchester Institute
Sheepen Road
Colchester
ESSEX CO3 3LL
Tel: (01206) 718000
Fax: (01206) 763041
E-Mail: efl2@colch-inst.ac.uk

Cert. TESOL
Full Time 8-10 wks £675
Max. Trainees per course 10
Contact: Barbara Stewart
Start Dates: 2 courses per year Mar and Sept.

DTEFLA
Part Time 10 wks approx. £800 + £170 exam fee
Max. Trainees per course 12
Contact: Barbara Stewart
Start Dates: 1 course per year Jan.

The Cert. TESOL course offered by the institute is a 10 week course with an alternative 8 week course including a 5 week distance learning component. The course includes English grammar, phonology, language awareness, lexis skills, class management and materials evaluation. Trainees teach and observe multilingual classes from elementary to intermediate levels.

College of St. Mark & St. John
Derriford Road
PLYMOUTH PL6 8BH
Tel: (01752) 636700
Fax: (01752) 686820
E-Mail: intec@lib.marjon.ac.uk

CELTA
Full Time 4 wks £1100
Max. Trainees per course 12
Contact: Ross Lynn
Start Dates: 3 courses per year Mar, Aug, Oct.

Concorde International Study Centre
22-24 Cheriton Gardens
Folkestone
KENT CT20 2AT
Tel: (01303) 256752
Fax: (01303) 220538
E-Mail: concorde@dial.pipex.com

CELTA
Part Time 1 term £850-£900
Max. Trainees per course 10
Contact: Pamela Aboshiha
Start Dates: 3 courses per year Jan, Apr, Sept.

Section 7

Directory of centres

Coventry Technical College
Butts
COVENTRY CV1 3GD
Tel: (01203) 526742
Fax: (01203) 526743
E-Mail: info@covcollege.ac.uk

Cert. TESOL
Full Time 4 wks £695
Part Time 36 wks £325
Max. Trainees per course 12
Contact: Christopher Fry
Start Dates: 1 P/T course per year Sept. 8 F/T courses per year Jan, Feb, Mar, Apr, June, Sept, Oct, Nov.

LTCL (TESOL) (Dip. TESOL)
Part Time distance learning £950. This course is for candidates teaching within the Midlands only, flexible start/finish dates, 1 seminar per month, contact Christopher Fry.

The College is one of the largest F. E. colleges in the Midlands.

Croydon English Language Scheme
Sandown Road
LONDON SE25 4XE
Tel: (0181) 656 6620
Fax: (0181) 662 1828

CELTA
Part Time 25 wks £650
Max. Trainees per course 16
Contact: Janet Ott
Start Dates: 1 course per year Sept.

Applicants are given a personal interview with a pre-interview task. The success rate of candidates is high. Candidates attend two half-day sessions per week: one, for input, the other for teaching practice. The course offers training in both TESL and TEFL.

Darlington College
Cleveland Avenue
DARLINGTON DL3 7BB
Tel: (01325) 503050
Fax: (01325) 503000
E-Mail: enquire@darlington.ac.uk

Cert. TESOL
Part Time 36 wks £199
Max. Trainees per course 15
Contact: Claire Mann
Start Dates: 1 course per year Jan.

The course runs for 3 terms. It combines an active social programme for students and teachers with the ESOL summer school. This gives trainees extra time with students.

Dundee College
Blackness Road
DUNDEE
DD1 5UA
Tel: (01382) 834898
Fax: (01382) 322286
E-mail: enquiry@dundeecoll.ac.uk

CELTA
Full Time 4 wks £795
Part Time 4 mths £795
Max. Trainees per course 12
Contact: Liz Turner
Start Dates: 1 P/T course per year Jan. 2 F/T courses Jan, May.

DTEFLA
Dundee College offer a distance learning DTEFLA course in conjunction with IITI (International House). This allows teachers to follow the DTEFLA course at Dundee College. Please contact Mr. Edwards for further details.

Dundee College is one of the largest and best resourced in Scotland, offering a wide range of nationally and internationally recognised qualifications and a friendly environment in which to study.

East Berkshire College
Langley Centre
Station Road
Langley
Slough
BERKSHIRE SL3 8BY
Tel: (01753) 793000
Fax: (01753) 793316

Cert. TESOL
Part Time 23 wks £595
Max. Trainees per course 12
Contact: Chris Hammonds
Start Dates: 1 course per year Sept.

LTCL (TESOL) (Dip. TESOL)
Part Time 36 wks £495
Max. Trainees per course 12
Contact: Chris Hammonds
Start Dates: 1 course per year Sept.

East Berkshire College is one of the largest Further Education colleges in South East England, serving over 25,000 people each year. It has an extensive library, a resource centre and a comprehensive selection of computers and educational software, as well as open learning and self access material.

Trainees also have access to the College fitness centre and other sports facilities.

Eastbourne College of Arts & Technology
St. Anne's Road
Eastbourne
EAST SUSSEX BN21 2HS
Tel: (01323) 644711
Fax: (01323) 412239
E-Mail: ecat@fastnet.co.uk

CELTA
Full Time 5 wks £528 + £72 registration fee
Part Time 24/8 wks £370 + £72 registration fee
Max. Trainees per course 18
Contact: Carol Clack
Start Dates: 2 P/T courses per year P/T 24 wks Sept. P/T 8 wks Apr. 1 F/T course per year June.

DTEFLA
Part Time 8 mths £558 + £172 registration fee.
Max. Trainees per course 16. Contact: Carol Clack Start Dates: 1 P/T course per year Oct.

Eastbourne College of Arts and Technology (ECAT) aims to provide teacher training courses at the same high standard as other centres, while maintaining substantially lower fees than many other providers.

Eastbourne School of English
8 Trinity Trees
EAST SUSSEX BN21 3LD
Tel: (01323) 721759
Fax: (01323) 639271
E-Mail: english@escoe.co.uk

CELTA
Full Time 4 wks £900
Part Time 5 mths £560
Max. Trainees per course 12
Contact: Dorothy Rippon
Start Dates: 1 P/T course per year Oct. 3 F/T courses per year July, Aug, Sept.

DTEFLA
Full Time 9 wks £1200
Part Time 7 mths £800
Max. Trainees per course 12
Contact: Dorothy Rippon
Start Dates: 1 P/T course per year Oct. 1 F/T course per year Mar.

The Eastbourne School of English is recognised by the British Council and is a member of ARELS. As such, it is committed to raising the standard of teaching English and they have a strong tutorial team of practising English teachers.

The school has 22 well equipped classrooms, a multimedia learning centre and an extensive range of graded materials.

Accommodation can be arranged for full time trainees.

Eastleigh College
Chestnut Avenue
Eastleigh
HAMPSHIRE S050 5HT
Tel: (01703) 326326
Fax: (01703) 322131
E-Mail: goplaces@eastleigh.ac.uk

CELTA
Part Time 18 wks £500 + £77.50 exam fee and £30 for course books
Max. Trainees per course 12
Contact: Elaine Secluna
Start Dates: 1 course per year Oct.

Eastleigh College also run 2 introduction to TEFL courses in September and April at £55.

ELT Banbury
49 Oxford Road
Banbury
OXFORDSHIRE
OX16 9AH
Tel: (01295) 263480/263502
Fax: (01295) 271658
E-Mail: 100760.2247@compuserve.com

CELTA
Full Time 4 wks £950
Max. Trainees per course 12
Contact: Dr. Gerighty
Start Dates: 2 courses per year Mar, Nov.

English Language Centre Bristol Incorporating Abon Language School
44 Pembroke Road
Clifton
BRISTOL BS8 3DT
Tel: (0117) 973 7216
Fax: (0117) 923 9638
E-Mail: elcbristol@compuserve.com

Cert. TESOL
Part Time 9 mths £750
Max. Trainees per course 12
Contact: Erica McCarthy
Start Dates: 1 course per year Sept.

With the merger of the English Language Centre and Abon Language School, resources and opportunities for teaching and observation are considerably increased. Assessment is continuous with teaching practice and written assignments. The written assignments are designed to be practical, and are based around producing teaching materials and ideas which can be used in the classroom.

The centre is recognised by the British Council and provides courses for foreign students between 17 and 25 years old throughout the year. Trainees are able to use the school facilities and participate in its social programme.

The centre regularly runs a 1 week introductory course at £140.

English Worldwide
The Italian Building
Dockhead
LONDON SE1 2BS
Tel: (0171) 252 1402
Fax: (0171) 231 8002
E-Mail: alan.eww@pop3.hiway.co.uk

LTCL (TESOL) (Dip. TESOL)
English Worldwide offer a distance learning preparation for the Trinity Dip. English Worldwide also provide support for the practical exam through visits to observe candidates in his/her school by a tutor. The examiner can come to the candidates school for the practical exam. For further details, please contact Alan Whitehead.

English Worldwide (EWW) was established in 1984 and has become a leader in the field of services for education and training. EWW offers a range of services which include teacher training courses, recruitment and educational consultancy.

EWW also offer training for the London Chamber of Commerce and industry certificate in Teaching of English for Business.

Farnborough College of Technology
Manor Park Centre
Manor Walk
ALDERSHOT GU12 4JN
Tel: (01252) 407300
Fax: (01252) 407302
E-Mail: info@farn-ct.ac.uk

Cert. TESOL
Full Time 4 wks £650
Part Time 30 wks £650
Max. Trainees per course 15
Contact: David Constable
Start Dates: 1 course per year Sept.

LTCL (TESOL) (Dip. TESOL)
Part Time 30 wks £650
Max. Trainees per course 15
Contact: David Constable
Dates: 1 course per year Sept.

Filton College
Filton Avenue
BRISTOL BS12 7AT
Tel: (01179) 312121
Fax No: (01179) 312233

CELTA
Part Time 30 wks £750
Max. Trainees per course 12
Contact: Jenny Hall
Start Dates: 1 course per year Sept.

Filton also offer weekend introductory courses at £80

Frances King
5 Grosvenor Gardens
LONDON SW1W 0BB
Tel: (0171) 630 8055
Fax: (0171) 630 8077
E-Mail: sean@fkse.ac.uk

CELTA
Full Time 4 wks £799
Max. Trainees per course 15
Contact: Sean Leahy
Start Dates: 8 F/T courses per year Mar, Apr, May, June, Aug, Sept, Oct, Nov.

Friends Centre
Ship Street
BRIGHTON BN1 1AF
Tel: (01273) 327835
Fax: (01273) 747546

CELTA
Part Time 2 terms £500 + £65 UCLES fee
Max. Trainees per course 12
Contact: Chris Edge
Start Dates: 1 course per year Oct.

The course fee can be paid in instalments by arrangement.

Gateshead College
Durham Road
GATESHEAD NE9 5BN
Tel: (0191) 490 0300
Fax: (0191) 490 2313
E-Mail: bill.elliott@post.gateshead.ac.uk

Cert. TESOL
Part Time 8 mths £250
Max. Trainees per course 12
Contact: Bill Elliott
Start Dates: 1 course per year Sept to May.

The Cert. TESOL is run as an evening course, with teaching practice in the local area.

The college gives trainees access to the library computer centre and a modern language laboratory.

It is recommended that trainees live within easy reach of the college.

GEOS English Academy
Brighton & Hove
55-61 Portland Road
Hove
EAST SUSSEX BN3 5DQ
Tel: (01273) 735975
Fax: (01273) 732884
E-Mail: info@geos2.demon.co.uk

CELTA
Full Time 4 wks £870
Max. Trainees per course 15
Contact: Elaine Langstaff
Start Dates: 9 courses per year Jan, Mar, Apr, June, July, Aug, Sept, Sept (end), Oct.

GEOS is a recognised English Language School and a member of ARELS. The academy runs courses throughout the year and has over 100 students from over 15 countries at any one time. This gives teacher trainees a varied and international atmosphere in which to learn and study.

GEOS has a well stocked resource room, language laboratory and a self access centre.

Accommodation can be arranged with a host family or in a guest house.

GLOSCAT
Park Campus
73 The Park
Cheltenham
GLOUCESTERSHIRE
GL50 2RR
Tel: (01242) 532144
Fax: (01242) 532023
E-Mail: postman@gloscat.demon.ac.uk

CELTA
Full Time 6 wks £840 + registration fee
Part Time 20 wks £840 + registration fee
Max. Trainees per course 12
Contact: Paul Burden
Start Dates: 1 P/T course per year Jan. 3 F/T courses per year Jan, Apr, Oct.

DTEFLA
Part Time 32 wks £895 + exam fee
Max. Trainees per course 12
Contact: Paul Burden
Start Dates: 1 course per year Sept.

Godmer House Teacher Training - Regent Oxford School of English
90 Banbury Road
OXFORD
OX2 6JT
Tel: (01865) 515566
Fax: (01865) 512538
E-Mail: email@regoxford.demon.co.uk

CELTA
Full Time 4 wks £978 + V.A.T. (£1149.15) + registration fee £66.50
Max. Trainees per course 14
Contact: Debbie Smith
Start Dates: 12 courses per year monthly.

Godmer House is a recognised English school that was established in 1953. The School has been providing teacher training courses since 1985.

The School runs full time English language courses throughout the year and normally has 40-70 students from as many as 20 countries studying at any one time.

Godmer House has well equipped classrooms. The school has a language laboratory, computers, video equipment and a variety of resource materials and a teacher training library.

The school also run a one week introduction to TEFL course at £150. Facilities and help with finding a first teaching position are available.

Accommodation can be arranged at £65 per week self catering and £110 homestay half board.

Golders Green College
11 Golders Green Road
LONDON NW11 8DE
Tel: (0181) 905 5467
Fax: (0181) 455 6528
E-Mail: ggcol@easynet.co.uk

Cert. TESOL
Full Time 5 wks £595 + £68 moderation fee
Max. Trainees per course 14
Contact: Rosalind Tricker
Start Dates: 8 courses per year Jan, Mar, Apr, May, July, Aug, Sept, Nov.

The College offers a 5 week course rather than a 4 week course to allow candidates time to adjust and prepare for classroom teaching which starts in the second week of the course. The College is aware that many courses are expensive and have tried to offer a high quality course at the lowest possible price - up to 33% below that of many other institutes.

The College and other associated schools select a large number of trainees who wish to remain in the UK.

College accommodation can be arranged for approx. £65 per week.

Greenhill College
Lowlands Road
MIDDLESEX HA1 3AQ
Tel: (0181) 869 8805
Fax: (0181) 427 9201
E-Mail: enquiries@harrow.greenhill.ac.uk

CELTA
Part Time 5 mths £507 + registration fee
Max. Trainees per course 12
Contact: Liz Koten
Start Dates: 2 courses per year Jan, Oct.

Grove House Language Centre
Carlton Avenue
Horns Cross
KENT DA9 9DR
Tel: (01322) 386826
Fax: (01322) 386347

Cert. TESOL
Full Time 4 wks £795
Max. Trainees per course 14
Contact: Heather Jeynes
Start Dates: 8/9 courses per year

Trainees study for two to three weeks at the Grove House centre. Teaching practice is done with business and government English language students from the former Soviet Union.

Courses are overseen by the principle, and trainees will benefit from the experienced and well qualified teaching staff.

The College offers guidance in finding suitable teaching posts for qualified trainees and continues to offer assistance during the first teaching post.

The College also run introductory courses.

Hammersmith & West London College
Gliddon Road
LONDON W14 9BL
Tel: (0181) 563 0063
Fax: (0181) 563 8247
E-Mail: cic@hwlc.ac.uk

CELTA
Full Time 4 wks £595 + £67 exam fee
Part Time 20 wks £595+£67 exam fee
Max. Trainees per course 18
Contact: College Information Centre
Start Dates: 2 P/T courses per year Sept. to March. 7 F/T courses per year June, July, Sept, Nov, Jan, Mar, Apr.

DTEFLA
Part Time 9 mths £575+£150 exam fee
Max. Trainees per course 15
Contact: College Information Centre. Start Dates: 1 course per year Sept to June

Handsworth College
Soho Road
Handsworth
BIRMINGHAM B21 9DP
Tel: (0121) 551 6031
Fax: (0121) 523 4447

CELTA
Part Time 9 mths £350
Max. Trainees per course 10
Contact: Brigit Bird
Start Dates: 2 courses per year both starting Sept.

Harrow House
Harrow Drive
Swanage
DORSET BH19 1PE
Tel: (01929) 424421
Fax: (01929) 427175
E-Mail: harrowhouse@mailhost.lds.co.uk

CELTA
Full Time 4 wks £824
Max. Trainees per course 10
Contact: Eileen Hyslop
Start Dates: 6 courses per year Feb, Apr, May, Sept, Oct, Nov.

Full board host family accommodation can be arranged, from £70 per week.

The College also provides a 1 week introductory course throughout the year. This course costs £195.

Harts Villages Centre
Robert May's School
West Street
ODIHAM RG29 1NA
Tel: (01256) 703808
Fax: (01256) 703012

Cert. TESOL
Part Time 33 wks £450
Max. Trainees per course 15
Contact: Anita Taylor
Start Dates: 1 course per year Sept.

The course at the Mayhill School in Odiham runs on Fridays between 09.15 and 13.15. Teaching practice begins in the Autumn term until the end of the Summer term.

Hilderstone College
St. Peter's Road
Broadstairs
KENT CT10 2AQ
Tel: (01843) 869171
Fax: (01843) 603877
E-Mail: info@hilderstone.ac.uk

CELTA
Full Time 4 wks £860 + £68.65 exam fee
Max. Trainees per course 12
Contact: Teacher Training
Start Dates: 3 courses per year Jan, Apr, Oct.

DTEFLA
Part Time 8 mths £1025 + exam fee
Max. Trainees per course 12
Contact: Teacher Training Dept.
Start Dates: 1 course per year Oct.

Hilderstone College also provide a 6 day preliminary course at £199.

Hopwood Hall College
Rochdale Campus
St. Mary's Gate
ROCHDALE OL12 6RY
Tel: (01706) 345346 or Freephone 0800 834297
Fax: (01706) 41426
E-Mail: enquiries@hopwood.ac.uk

Cert. TESOL
Part Time 3 terms £540
Max. Trainees per course 16
Contact: Maria Lowther
Start Dates: 1 course per year Sept.

Cert. TEYL
Part Time 3 terms £540
Max. Trainees per course 16
Contact: Maria Lowther
Start Dates: 1 course per year Sept.

The College offers comprehensive study facilities including a computer network. Trainees can obtain reduced membership to the Bobby Charlton International Health and Fitness Suite and have access to social and crèche facilities.

Both courses are run on one day a week (Mon). There is also a 10% discount for early enrolment.

Huddersfield Technical College
New North Road
WEST YORKSHIRE HD1 5NL
Tel: (01484) 536521 ext.402
Fax: (01484) 511885
E-Mail: info@huddcoll.ac.uk

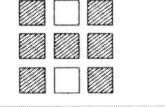

CELTA
Part Time 4 mths £750
Max. Trainees per course 12
Contact: Heather Alcock
Start Dates: 2 courses per year Sept and Jan.

Hull College
School of Languages & EFL
Hull College
Park Street Centre
Park Street
HULL HU2 8RR
Tel: (01482) 329943
Fax: (01482) 598989

Cert. TESOL
Part Time 10 contact weeks + 1 reading week £223
Max. Trainees per course 12
Contact: Howard Jopp
Start Dates: 3 courses per year Jan, Apr, Sept.

Hull College has been providing the Cert. TESOL course for 4 years. The emphasis is on teaching practice usually with multilingual classes. The College has well equipped facilities, including a language laboratory and computer rooms.

The Certificate course takes approximately 150 hours of college time with a number of assignments to complete. Students have to complete a minimum of 6 hours assessed teaching practice.

inlingua Teacher Training & Recruitment
Rodney Lodge
Rodney Road
CHELTENHAM GL50 1JF
Tel: (01242) 253171
Fax: (01242) 253181
E-Mail: 101367.156@compuserve.com

Cert. TESOL
Full Time 5 wks £840 + moderation fee
Part Time 3 terms £890 + moderation fee
Max. Trainees per course 10
Contact: Dagmar Lewis
Start Dates: 1 P/T course per year Sept. 8 F/T courses per year Feb, Apr, June, July, July (end), Aug, Sept, Oct.

inlingua Teacher Training & Recruitment, has trained and placed teachers for over 25 years.

International House
(Hastings)
White Rock
EAST SUSSEX TN34 1JY
Tel: (01424) 720100
Fax: (01424) 720323
E-Mail: ilc@compuserve.com

CELTA
Full Time 4 wks £835 + exam fee
Part Time 22 wks £549 + exam fee
Max. Trainees per course 18
Contact: Teacher Training Dept.
Start Dates: 1 P/T course per year Jan. 12 F/T courses per year monthly.

DTEFLA
Full Time 8 wks £1470 + exam fee
9 wks £1570 + exam fee
Max. Trainees per course 8

Contact: Teacher Training Dept. Start Dates: 2 F/T courses per year 9 wks Mar. 8 wks Sept.

International House Hastings has an international reputation for the practical and innovative nature of it's training programmes. Teacher trainers are selected for their breadth of experience, their practical skill and knowledge in teaching and training.

Accommodation can be provided along with access to internal recruitment for successful candidates.

International House
(London)
106 Piccadilly
LONDON W1V 9FL
Tel: (0171) 491 2598
Fax: (0171) 495 0689
E-Mail:
teacher@dial.pipex.com

CELTA
Full Time 4 wks £917
Part Time 8 wks £1062
Max. Trainees per course 15
Contact: Teacher Training Dept.
Start Dates: 6 P/T courses per year Jan(2), May(2), Aug, Sept. 12 F/T courses per year monthly.

DTEFLA
Full Time 8 wks £1395 + exam fee
Max. Trainees per course 14
Contact: Teacher Training Dept.
Start Dates: 3 F/T courses per year Jan, Mar, Sept.

International House Teacher Training was established in 1962 and is widely known for training teachers of English as a foreign language. Its original introductory course provided the model for what is now the Cambridge/RSA Certificate. During 1995/96, courses were attended by over a thousand participants, many of whom are now teaching in schools all over the world. With a tradition of innovation and development, the range of courses offered by IH Teacher Training in London and abroad increases every year.

Accommodation can be arranged on request.

International House
(Newcastle-upon-Tyne)
14-18 Stowell Street
NEWCASTLE-UPON-TYNE
NE1 4XQ
Tel: (0191) 232 9551
Fax: (0191) 232 1126
E-Mail:
101606.2123@compuserve.com

CELTA
Full Time 4 wks £895
Max. Trainees per course 12
Contact: Teacher Training Dept.
Start Dates: 8 courses per year Jan, Mar, Apr, June, July, Aug, Sept, Nov.

Accommodation can be arranged on request.

International Language Institute *(Leeds)*
County House
Vicar Lane
LEEDS
LS1 7JH
Tel: (0113) 2428893
Fax: (0113) 2347543
E-Mail:
101322.1376@compuserve.com

CELTA
Full Time 4 wks £874 (£970 June 1998)
Max. Trainees per course 12
Contact: Nigel McEwen
Start Dates: 6 courses per year Sept, Nov, Feb, Mar, Apr, June.

LTCL (TESOL) (Dip. TESOL)
Part Time 32 wks £982
Max. Trainees per course 10
Contact: Nigel McEwen
Dates: 1 course per year Oct.

International Language Institute (Leeds) has an experienced teacher training team, drawing from skills gained working abroad and in a diverse range of language institutions. The institute also provides a 1 week introductory course at £164.

International Teaching and Training Centre (ITTC)
674 Wimborne Road
BOURNEMOUTH BH9 2EG
Tel: (01202) 531355
Fax: (01202) 538838
E-Mail:
enquiries@ittc.co.uk

CELTA
Full Time £851 (inc. VAT) + £66.50 assessment fee
Max. Trainees per course 18
Contact: Miss Pillar Tiazcaneja
Start Dates: 12 courses per year monthly

DTEFLA
Full Time 8 wks £1306 + £169 exam fee
Part Time 8 mths £1306 + £169 exam fee
Max. Trainees per course 15.
Contact: Miss Pillar Tiazcaneja
Start Dates: 1 P/T course per year Sept. 3 F/T courses per year Feb, Apr, Sept.

International Training Network
Upper Hinton Road
BOURNEMOUTH BH1 2HH
Tel/Fax: (01202) 789089
E-Mail: itnet@globalnet.co.uk

Cert. TESOL
Full Time 5 wks £780 + £70 moderation fee
Max. Trainees per course 15
Contact: Eileen Hobby
Start Dates: 7 courses per year

International Training Network is a non-denominational Christian organisation and provides training for candidates preparing for Christian service either in this country or overseas.

ITS English School
43-45 Cambridge Gardens
HASTINGS TN34 1EN
Tel: (01424) 438025
Fax: (01424) 438050
E-Mail:
itsbest@its-hastings.co.uk

Cert. TESOL
Part Time 16 wks £360 + £75 moderation fee
Full time 4 or 5 wks £450 + max £150 moderation fee
Max. Trainees per course 12
Contact: John Palim
Start Dates: P/T Jan. F/T Feb Apr, July, Sept.

LTCL (TESOL) (Dip. TESOL)
Full Time distance learning + 6 wks £695 + exam fee approx. £190
Part Time distance training + 36 wks £695 + exam fee approx. £190 by arrangement D/T + TP sessions £695 + exam fee approx. £190
D/T+ TP off site + tutorials £695 + exam fee approx. £190
Max. Trainees per course 12. Contact: John Palim/John Power
Dates: P/T 36 wks Mar. 1 F/T course per year Nov. Other courses by arrangement, D/T starts on acceptance and receipt of fees.

Joseph Priestly College
71 Queen Street
Morley
LEEDS LS27 8DZ
Tel: (0113) 253 3749
Fax: (0113) 252 8654
E-Mail: tesol@jpc.ac.uk

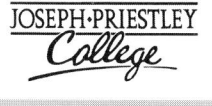

Cert. TESOL
Part Time 20 wks £495 + Trinity registration fee
Max. Trainees per course 15
Contact: Carolyn Wright
Start Dates: 3 courses per year Mar, July, Sept.

All courses begin with one week intensive.

Kent School of English
3 Granville Road
BROADSTAIRS CT10 1QD
Tel: (01843) 868207
Fax: (01843) 860418
E-Mail: kse@adept.co.uk

Cert. TESOL
Full Time 4 weeks £650
Max. Trainees per course 10
Contact: Chris McDermott
Start Dates: 3 courses per year Jan, June, Sept.

King's College
English Language Centre
Atkins Building
Kensington Campus
Campden Hill Road
LONDON W8 7AH
Tel: (0171) 333 4075
Fax: (0171) 333 4066
E-Mail: jennifer.jenkins@kcl.ac.uk

DTEFLA
Part Time 9 mths £800 + £150 exam fee
Max. Trainees per course 13
Contact: Jennifer Jenkins
Start Dates: 1 course per year Sept.

Candidates who perform well on the course, and who wish to expand their theoretical knowledge, will also be eligible for fast track entry to the College's part time MA in ELT & Applied Linguistics.

Kingsway College
Vernon Square
Penton Rise
LONDON WC1X 9EL
Tel: (0171) 306 5880
Fax: (0171) 306 5800
E-Mail: enquiries@kingsway.ac.uk

CELTA
Full Time 5 wks £750
Max. Trainees per course 18
Contact: Will Rowe
Start Dates: 2 courses per year Jan, May.

Langside College, Glasgow
50 Prospecthill Road
GLASGOW G42 9LB
Tel: (0141) 649 4991
Fax: (0141) 632 5252
E-Mail: langside@dial.pipex.com

Cert. TESOL
Part Time 36 weeks
Max. Trainees per course 18
Contact: Tony Foster
Start Dates: 1 course per year Sept. to June

Language Link Training
45 High Street Kensington
LONDON W8 5EB
Tel: (0171) 938 1225
Fax: (0171) 938 1227
E-Mail: 100643.657@compuserve.com

Cert. TESOL
Full Time 4 weeks £650 + Trinity Fee
Max. Trainees per course 15
Contact: Marilyn McPherson
Start Dates: 11 courses per year, Jan, Feb, Mar, Apr, May, June, July, Aug, Sept, Oct, Nov.

Language Link offer a guaranteed pass scheme whereby if a candidate fails the Cert. course a free place will be offered on a subsequent course within 6 months, provided the candidate has completed the course and assignments set.

Language Link operates in various countries including Russia, Poland, the Czech Republic and Germany. It also has associations with other language schools in Europe. This means it is able to offer employment opportunities and career guidance to successful candidates.

Language Link also offer 1 week introductory courses every month at £160. 50% of the fee can be refunded if the subsequent Cert. TESOL course is taken.

The Language Project
78-80 Colston Street
BRISTOL BS1 5BB
Tel/Fax: (0117) 927 3993
E-Mail: administration@langproj.demon.co.uk

Cert. TESOL
Full Time 4 wks
Contact: John Wright - Dr. Val Hennessay
For further details please contact The Language Project.

LTCL (TESOL) (Dip. TESOL)
Full Time 10 wks £900 + exam fee
Max. Trainees per course 12
Contact: John Wright
Dates: 2 courses per year Mar, Oct.

The Language Project also run introductory courses.

Leeds Metropolitan University
Beckett Park Campus
LEEDS LS6 3QS
Tel: (0113) 283 7440
Fax: (0113) 274 5966
E-Mail: cls@lmu.ac.uk

Cert. TESOL
Part Time 32 wks £457 (pre-payment discount £419.80)
Max. Trainees per course 20
Contact: David Killick
Start Dates: 1 course per year Oct.

CELTA
Full Time 4 wks £740 (Spring) £840 (Summer) £770 (Autumn) £670 (Winter) + Cambridge exam fee
Max. Trainees per course 18
Contact: David Killick
Start Dates: 9 courses per year (Spring) Apr, May (Summer) June, July (Autumn) Sept, Oct, Nov. (Winter) Jan, Feb.

Trainees have access to a well stocked resource library.
Help with accommodation can be given.
Assistance with finding employment for successful candidates is given. The part time Cert. TESOL course is run over one academic year on 1 evening per week.
Leeds Metropolitan University also runs a number of post graduate courses.

London Study Centre
Munster House
676 Fulham Road
LONDON SW6 5SA
Tel: (0171) 731 3549
Fax: (0171) 731 6060
E-Mail: 106153.2344@compuserve.com

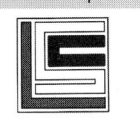

Cert. TESOL
Full Time 5 wks £750 + £70 moderation fee
Part Time 15 wks £750 + £70 moderation fee
Max. Trainees per course 16
Contact: Teacher Training Department
Start Dates: 4 Full Time courses per year June, July, Sept, Nov. 2 Part Time courses per year May, Sept.

The London Study Centre was established in 1975 and has been training teachers since 1991. The centre is a recognised school and normally has over 850 EFL students enrolled at any given time. This provides a good opportunity for teaching practice with an enormous diversity of students.

The centre has well equipped teaching facilities with contemporary teaching aids and materials.

Help with accommodation can be given.

The part time cert. is offered on 2 evenings per week plus 5 Saturdays throughout the ten week course. This makes it ideal for people in full time employment.

Loughborough College
Radmoor Road
Loughborough
LEICESTERSHIRE LE11 3BT
Tel: (01509) 215831
Fax: (01509) 232310
E-Mail: 106010,3207@compuserve.com.uk

CELTA
Part Time 5 mths £395
Max. Trainees per course 15
Contact: Hilary Hale
Start Dates: 2 courses per year Sept to Feb and Feb to June

Loughborough College run their part time CELTA course on Monday and Tuesday of each week for the duration of the course. Attendance is necessary from 9.00 to 17.00 each day.

Pre-courses interviews normally take place in groups. Candidates are expected to participate in shared and individual activities.

Loughborough University
English language Study Unit
Ashley Road
LOUGHBOROUGH LE11 3TU
Tel: (01509) 222058
Fax: (01509) 223919
E-Mail: j.e.mee@lboro.ac.uk

Cert. TESOL
Full Time 4 wks
Max. Trainees per course 10
Contact: Jane Mee
Start Dates: 1 course per year July to Aug.

Manchester College of Arts and Technology (MANCAT)
Dept.of Language Studies
Lower Hardman Street
MANCHESTER M3 3ER
Tel: (0161) 953 5995
Fax: (0161) 953 2259
E-Mail: efl-unit@mancat.ac.uk

Cert. TESOL
Part Time 34 wks £560
Max. Trainees per course 12
Contact: Judith Porter
Start Dates: 1 course per year Sept.

Manchester College of Arts and Technology (MANCAT) is one of the UK's largest further education colleges with 44,000 student enrolments in 1996.

The College provides a high-tech learning environment as well as classroom teaching.

Mayflower College
36 Pier Street
The Hoe
PLYMOUTH PL1 3BT
Tel: (01752) 673784
Fax: (01752) 671537
E-Mail: english@mayflowr.zynet.co.uk

Cert. TESOL
Part Time £900
Max. Trainees per course 10
Contact: Jon Salisbury
Start Dates: 1 course per year Sept.

Medway Adult Education Centre
Eastgate
ROCHESTER ME1 1EW
Tel: (01634) 845359
Fax: (01634) 405673

Cert. TESOL
Part Time 25 wks approx. £750
Max. Trainees per course 16
Contact: Theresa Cambell
Start Dates: 1 course per year Sept.

Mid Cheshire College of Further Education
Hartford Campus
Northwich
CHESHIRE CW8 1LJ
Tel: (01606) 74444
Fax: (01606) 75101
E-Mail: admin@midchesh.u-net.com

CELTA
Part Time 1 academic year £450
Max. Trainees per course 12
Contact: Barbara Murphy
Start Dates: 1 course per year Sept.

DTEFLA
Part Time 1 academic year £850 + £165 exam fee
Max. Trainees per course 12
Contact: Barbara Murphy
Start Dates: 1 course per year Sept.

Middlesbrough College of Further Education
Roman Road
Linthorpe
MIDDLESBROUGH TS5 5PJ
Tel: (01642) 333246
Fax: (01642) 333310
E-Mail: courseinfo@middlesbrough.ac.uk

Cert. TESOL
Part Time 9 mths approx. £400
Max. Trainees per course 12
Contact: Rosemary Smith
Start Dates: 1 course per year Sept.

LTCL (TESOL) (Dip. TESOL)
Part Time 9 mths approx. £450
Max. Trainees per course 12
Contact: Rosemary Smith
Dates: 1 course per year Sept.

New College Durham
Framwellgate Moor Centre
DURHAM DH1 5ES
Tel: (0191) 375 4380
Fax: (0191) 375 4222
E-Mail: jean.ryan@newdur.ac.uk

Cert. TESOL
Part Time 9 mths approx. £180
Max. Trainees per course 12
Contact: Jo Fayram
Start Dates: 1 course per year Sept.

Newnham Language Centre
8 Grange Road
CAMBRIDGE CB3 9DU
Tel: (01223) 311344
Fax: (01223) 461411
E-Mail: nlc@dial.pipex.com

CELTA
Full Time 4 wks £908 + £67 assessment fee
Max. Trainees per course 16
Contact: Marie-Louise Banning
Start Dates: 7 courses per year Jan, Mar, Apr, June, July, Aug, Oct.

Newnham Language Centre has been providing an UCLES TEFL Certificate course since 1987 and successfully train over 100 teachers per year. The Centre provides well over the minimum suggested hours for the CELTA, normally reaching 125 hours, 25 more than the requirement.

Cambridge is a beautiful and historic university city. The centre is located in a residential district close to the river and only 15 minutes from the city centre.

Help and advice are given for finding a first teaching post. Also accommodation can be arranged if necessary.

Northbrook College
Littlehampton Road
Goring-by-Sea
WORTHING BN12 6NU
Tel: (01903) 606010
Fax: (01903) 606207
E-Mail: enquiries@nbcol.ac.uk

NORTHBROOK COLLEGE SUSSEX
Further and Higher Education

Cert. TESOL
Full Time 4 wks £477
Part Time 16 wks £377
Max. Trainees per course 12
Contact: Sheila Brady
Start Dates: 3 P/T courses per year Jan, Apr, Sept. 5 F/T courses per year Jan, Apr, June, Sept, Nov.

Oaklands College
St. Albans City Campus
St. Peters Road
St. Albans
HERTFORDSHIRE AL1 3RX
Tel: (01727) 847070
Fax: (01727) 847071

Cert. TESOL
Full Time 5 wks £595
Part Time 10-12 wks £595
Part Time 36 wks £595
Max. Trainees per course 14
Contact: TESOL Course Director
Start Dates: 1 P/T 36 week course per year Sept. 2 P/T semi intensive 10-12 week courses per year Jan and Sept. 1 F/T 5 week course per year July.

LTCL (TESOL) (Dip. TESOL)
Part Time 30 wks £450. Max. Trainees per course 14. Contact: TESOL Course Director. Dates: 1 course per year Oct.

Oaklands College is one of the largest colleges in the UK with both Trinity Validated Cert. TESOL and Diploma course offered.

The teacher training takes place at the St. Albans City campus, about 20 minutes by train from London. The site has a well equipped study centre with CALL, word-processing and Internet facilities.

Trainees are offered assistance with finding work after completion of the course. An information base is maintained regarding employment for trainees. Some successful candidates have gone in to do some work for the College.

Oxford Brookes University
Gipsy Lane Campus
Headington
OXFORD OX3 0BP
Tel: (01865) 483874/483725
Fax: (01865) 483791
E-Mail: icels@soi.brookes.ac.uk

OXFORD BROOKES UNIVERSITY

CELTA
Part Time 10 wks £1100
Max. Trainees per course 16
Contact: ICELS Secretary
Start Dates: 2 courses per year Sept, April.

Oxford College of Further Education
Oxpens Road
OXFORD OX1 1SA
Tel: (01865) 245871
Fax: (01865) 248871

OXFORD COLLEGE of Further Education

CELTA
Full 4 wks (contact College for cost).
Part Time 20 wks £863.65
Max. Trainees per course 15
Contact: Jane Tomlinson
Start Dates: 2 P/T courses per year Jan, Oct. 1 F/T course per year July

Oxford English Centre
Wolsey Hall
66 Banbury Road
OXFORD OX2 6PR
Tel: (01865) 516162
Fax: (01865) 310910
E-Mail: info@utsoxford.co.uk

THE OXFORD English Centre

DTEFLA
Part Time 8 mths £1200 + exam fee
Max. Trainees per course 16
Contact: Mark Bartram
Start Dates: 1 course per year Oct.

Oxford English Centre (formally UTS Oxford Centre) is a British Council accredited language school in a beautiful Victorian building near Oxford town centre. We usually have 50-120 EFL students.

Our part time DTEFLA course runs from October to June, with input sessions every Wednesday evening and occasional Saturdays. The course is best suited to teachers already in employment in Oxford or the surrounding area. (Teaching practice generally takes place in the Trainee's own school).

All the trainers are very experienced in the DTEFLA course, having run the course in various schools and colleges. trainees are welcome to use the school's own academic and social facilities.

Oxford House College
3 Oxford Street
LONDON W1R 1RF
Tel: (0171) 580 9785
Fax: (0171) 323 4582
E-Mail: oxhc@easynet.co.uk

OXFORD HOUSE COLLEGE

Cert. TESOL
Full Time 4 wks £650 approx.
Part Time 13 or 22 wks £750
Max. Trainees per course 16
Contact: Chris Polatch
Start Dates: P/T courses every 3 months. F/T courses monthly.

LTCL (TESOL) (Dip. TESOL)
Part Time 13 wks £700 approx.
Distance Learning £900 approx.
Max. Trainees per course 16.
Contact: Chris Polatch.
Start Dates: Distance start any time. P/T every 3 months.

Oxford House College is one of the largest teacher-training centres in the world, offering Trinity College validated Certificate and Diploma courses, as well as courses in teaching English for Business (TEFIC). Trainees stand an excellent chance of finding post-course work as we have a regularly updated jobs board in the College in London. All courses include sessions and individual counselling on job hunting. Our centres overseas regularly recruit teachers straight off course.

Park Lane College
Park Lane
LEEDS LS3 1AA
Tel: (0113) 216 2000
Fax: (0113) 216 2020

PARK LANE COLLEGE

Cert. TESOL
Part Time 9 months
Max. Trainees per course 15
Contact: Anita Taylor
Start Dates: 1 course per year Sept. to Jul.

Situated in Leeds city centre, Park Lane College is one of the largest FE colleges in the country. It has the latest facilities and offers year-round courses in English taught by well qualified and dedicated staff. The College has been awarded the Charter Mark for excellence.

Pilgrims
Pilgrims House
Orchard Street, Canterbury
KENT CT2 2AP
Tel: (01227) 762111
Fax: (01227) 746542
E-Mail: mariannecarter@pilgrims.co.uk

CELTA
Full Time 4 wks £1085
Max. Trainees per course 12
Contact: Marianne Carter
Start Dates: 3 courses per year June, July, Aug.

Plymouth College of F.E.
Kings Road, Devonport
PLYMOUTH PL1 5QG
Tel: (01752) 385300
Fax: (01752) 385343
E-Mail: jgodfrey@pcfe.plymouth.ac.uk

Cert. TESOL
Part Time 1 year £995
Max. Trainees per course 15
Contact: Jill Godfrey
Start Dates: 1 course per year Sept.

Polyglot Language Services
214 Trinity Road
LONDON SW17 7HP
Tel: (0181) 767 9113
Fax: (0181) 767 9104
E-Mail: 100517.2313@compuserve.com

Cert. TESOL
Full Time 4 wks £790 + £80 exam fee
Max. Trainees per course 8
Contact: John Carmichael
Start Dates: 7 courses per year Jan, Mar, June, July, Aug, Sept, Nov.

Queens University of Belfast
BELFAST BT7 1NN
Tel: (01232) 335373
Fax: (01232) 335379
E-Mail: tefl@qub.ac.uk

Cert. TESOL
Full Time 5 wks £735
Part Time 8 mths £735
Max. Trainees per course 20
Contact: Deirdre Duffy
Start Dates: 1 P/T course per year Sept. 2 F/T courses per year June, July.

Successful candidates also receive a certificate from the university.

Reading College
Crescent Road
RG1 5RQ
Tel: (0118) 967 5000
Fax: (0118) 967 5301

LTCL (TESOL) (Dip. TESOL)
Part Time 30 wks £560 + £220 exam fees
Max. Trainees per course 15
Contact: Catherine Spargo
Start Dates: 1 per year Sept.

Regency School of English
Royal Crescent
Ramsgate
KENT CT11 9PE
Tel: (01843) 591212
Fax: (01843) 850035
E-Mail: regency@btinternet.com

Cert. TESOL
Full Time 4 wks £700
Max. Trainees per course 12
Contact: The Director of Teacher Training
Start Dates: 2 courses per year Apr, Nov

LTCL (TESOL) (Dip. TESOL)
Part Time 9 mths Please contact the school for costs.
Max. Trainees per course 12
Contact: The Director of Teacher Training. Start Dates: 1 course per year Oct.

Regent Edinburgh
29 Chester Street
EDINBURGH EH3 7EN
Tel: (0131) 225 9888
Fax: (0131) 225 2133
E-Mail: regentedin@compuserve.com

Cert. TESOL
Full Time 4 wks £795
Max. Trainees per course 12
Contact: Stuart Swanston
Start Dates: 10 courses per year

The Cert. TESOL course includes Methodology, phonology, language analysis and 6 hours of assessed teaching practice. Trainees have the opportunity to take classes without assessment to build confidence.
The college is located in the centre of Edinburgh, and only a short walk away from the attractions of this historic Capital city.

Regent London
12 Buckingham Street
LONDON WC2N 6DF
Tel: (0171) 872 6620
Fax: (0171) 872 6630
E-Mail: 100545.76@compuserve.com

CELTA
Full Time 4 wks £795
Max. Trainees per course 12
Contact: Tessa Ryall
Start Dates: 7 courses per year Jan, Apr, June, June (end), July, Sept, Nov.

Regent London was established in 1964 and offers General English courses to overseas adults.
Advice on finding employment is given. Also Regent Summer Schools have a large number of temporary post available.

Richmond Adult and Community College
Clifden Centre, Clifden Road
TWICKENHAM TW1 4LT
Tel: (0181) 891 5907
Fax: (0181) 892 6354
E-Mail: richmond_a_cedu@msn.com

Cert. TESOL
Full Time 4 wks £795 + exam fee
Part Time 12 mths £795 + exam fee
Max. Trainees per course 12
Contact: Hugh Burnie
Start Dates: 1 P/T course per year Jan. 1 F/T course per year June.

St. Brelade's College
Mont Les Vaux
St. Brelade
JERSEY JE3 8AF
Tel: (01534) 41305
Fax: (01534) 41159
E-Mail: sbc@itl.net

Cert. TESOL
Full Time 4 weeks £700 + £75 exam fee
Max. Trainees per course 12
Contact: Brian Le Marquand
Start Dates: 2 courses per year Mar, Sept.

LTCL (TESOL) (Dip. TESOL)
Part Time 4 wks F/T preceded by 5 mths D/T £900 + £150 exam fee
Max. Trainees per course 12
Contact: Brian Le Marquand. Start Dates: D/T section starts March F/T section starts Sept.

The Certificate course is run primarily to train teachers for St. Brelade's summer school. The course has a preparatory distance learning component to cover basic theory. The course has a practical bias.
Trainees seeking work after qualification are often offered positions at the College or through College contacts in the Czech Republic, Italy and Spain.

Saint George International
76 Mortimer Street
LONDON W1N 7DE
Tel: (0171) 299 1700
Fax: (0171) 299 1711
E-Mail: teflenq@stgeorges.co.uk

Cert. TESOL
Full Time 4 wks £830 + £72 Trinity fee
Part Time 20 wks £830 + £72 Trinity fee
Max. Trainees per course 12
Contact: Max Loach
Start Dates: 2 P/T courses per year Jan, Aug. 6 F/T courses per year Mar, May, June, July, Aug, Sept.

LTCL (TESOL) (Dip. TESOL)
Distance Training Programme £945 or by instalments. Contact: Max Loach. Dates: Start any time but written papers have to be taken in Jan, May, July or Aug, Dec.

St. Giles College
3 Marlborough Place
Brighton
EAST SUSSEX BN1 1UB
Tel: (01273) 682747
Fax: (01273) 689808
E-Mail: stgiles@pavilion

CELTA
Full Time 4 wks £920
Max. Trainees per course 15
Contact: The Principal
Start Dates: 9 courses per year Jan, Feb, Mar, Apr, May, June, July, Aug, Sept.

St. Giles College
51 Shepherds Hill
Highgate
LONDON N6 4QP
Tel: (0181) 340 0828
Fax: (0181) 348 9389
E-Mail: lonhigh@stgiles.u-net.com

CELTA
Full Time 4 wks £920
Max. Trainees per course 12
Contact: Teacher Training
Start Dates: 10 courses per year monthly except July and Dec.

St. Giles was founded in 1955 and has been providing short pre-service courses for TEFL since 1961. St. Giles was one of the first schools to run the RSA CTEFLA (now CELTA).

Sandwell College
Crocketts Lane
Smethick
WEST MIDLANDS B66 3BU
Tel: (0121) 556 6000
Fax: (0121) 253 6322
E-Mail: gill.gibbons@sandcis.demon.uk

Cert. TESOL
Part Time 1 yr £700
Max. Trainees per course 12
Contact: Gillian Gibbins
Start Dates: 1 course per year Sept.

Sandwell College has a large number of ESOL students drawn from the local community.
The College also offers an introductory course and a City & Guilds Certificate teaching basic skills for ESOL.

School of Oriental & African Studies (SOAS)
University of London
4 Gower Street
LONDON WC1E 6HA
Tel: (0171) 580 8272
Fax: (0171) 631 3043
E-Mail: english@soas.ac.uk

CELTA
Full Time 4 wks £860
Max. Trainees per course 12
Contact: Fiona English
Start Dates: 1 course per year June

The Sheffield College
Stradbrooke Centre
Spinkhill Drive
SHEFFIELD S13 8FD
Tel: (0114) 260 2100
Fax: (0114) 260 2101

Cert. TESOL
Part Time 9 mths £690
Max. Trainees per course 16
Contact: Suzanne Dinsdale
Start Dates: 1 course per year Sept.

Sheffield Hallam University
TESOL Centre
Totley Hall Lane
SHEFFIELD S17 4AB
Tel: (0114) 253 2816
Fax: (0114) 253 2832
E-Mail: tesol@shu.ac.uk

Cert. TESOL
Full Time 4 wks preceded by 12 wks distance learning £910 + £75 Trinity fee
Part Time 22 wks £910 + Trinity fee
Max. Trainees per course 15
Contact: The TESOL Centre
Start Dates: 1 P/T course per year Jan. 4 F/T courses per year Mar, Apr, May, Aug.

LTCL (TESOL) (Dip. TESOL)
Full Time 4 wks preceded by 9 mths distance learning £1400 + £185 Trinity fee. Max. Trainees per course 20. Contact: The TESOL Centre. Dates: 2 courses per year June, Oct.

The Certificate and Diploma courses are offered as a dual award with study toward the Postgraduate Certificate and Diplomas respectively. The University awards require further study and completion of a researched assignment.

Sidmouth International School
May Cottage
DEVON EX10 8EN
Tel: (01395) 516754
Fax: (01395) 579270
E-Mail: sdmthint@mail.zynet.co.uk

Cert. TESOL
Full Time 4 wks £795
Max. Trainees per course 12
Contact: Rosanne Morgan
Start Dates: 2 courses per year
Mar, Nov.

Homestay or guest house accommodation can be arranged for those who live outside the area.

South East Essex College of Arts & Technology
Carnarvon Road
SOUTHEND-ON-SEA SS2 6LS
Tel: (01702) 220400
Fax: (01702) 432320
E-Mail: marketing@se-essex-college.ac.uk

Cert. TESOL
Part Time 8 mths £385 (+£70 fees)
Max. Trainees per course 30
Contact: Richard Hopkins
Start Dates: 1 course per year
Sept.

Skola Teacher Training
21 Star Street
LONDON W2 1QB
Tel: (0171) 724 2217
Fax: (0171) 724 2219

CELTA
Full Time £850 4wks
Max. Trainees per course 12
Contact: Lyndel Sayle
Start Dates: 5 courses per year
June, Aug, Sept, Oct, Nov.

Skola Teacher Training is a medium sized college and shares facilities with Marble Arch Intensive English, a recognised English language school. Teacher trainees can benefit from informal contact with overseas students and also are welcome to join in with the schools full social programme.

Skola offer a two week extension to the CELTA course, which gives instruction on how to teach young learners.. This can lead to a Cambridge endorsement for teaching young learners.

Help with accommodation can be given. Also, Skola operate a recruitment agency for English language teachers. Toward the end of their course, trainees will be made aware of employment opportunities in a variety of countries.

Skola also run a 2-day Grammar for TEFL course which costs £65 if taken in conjunction with a CELTA course (normal fee £85).

South Nottingham College
Greythorn Drive
West Bridford
NOTTINGHAM NG2 7GA
Tel: (0115) 914 6400
Fax: (0115) 914 6444
E-Mail: enquiries@south-nottingham.ac.uk

Cert. TESOL
Part Time 6 wks distance learning 1 evening per wks and 4 wks intensive. £500
Max. Trainees per course 16
Contact: Kate Preston
Start Dates: 1 course per year
Sept.

South Thames College
50-52 Putney Hill
LONDON SW15 6QX
Tel: (0181) 918 7000
Fax: (0181) 918 7347

CELTA
Part Time 20 wks approx. £600 + exam fee
Max. Trainees per course 18
Contact: Susan Weir
Start Dates: 2 courses per year
Sept, Apr.

Solihull College
Language & Communications
Blossomfield Road
Solihull
BIRMINGHAM B91 1SB
Tel: (0121) 678 7172
Fax: (0121) 711 2316
E-Mail: pmorris@staff.solihull.ac.uk

CELTA
Full Time 4 wks £600
Part Time 8 wks £600
Max. Trainees per course 12
Contact: Pat Morris
Start Dates: Please contact the college for details.

A concessionary course fee of £200 is available for those claiming benefit.

Southwark College
EFL Section
Waterloo Centre, The Cut
LONDON SE1 8LE
Tel: (0171) 815 2109
Fax: (0171) 261 1301

Cert. TESOL
Full Time 5 wks £540 + moderation £80 + registration £10
Part Time 20 wks £350 + moderation £80 + registration £10
Max. Trainees per course 14
Contact: Philip Jakes
Start Dates: 1 P/T course per year Jan. 1 F/T course per year Feb.

The Cert. TESOL at Southwark also includes a pre-course distance learning element.

South Devon College
Language Department
Newton Road
TORQUAY TQ2 5BY
Tel: (01803) 386338
Fax: (01803) 383333
E-Mail: 04100360.furve@dialnet.co.uk

CELTA
Part Time 6 mths £880
Max. Trainees per course 12
Contact: Diane Davies
Start Dates: 1 course per year
Sept.

The course will be taught by very experienced tutors who currently teach English as a Foreign Language and Overseas Teachers' Courses.

Stanton Teacher Training
167 Queensway
LONDON W2 4SB
Tel: (0171) 221 7259
Fax: (0171) 792 9047
E-Mail: study@stanton-school.co.uk

CELTA
Full Time 4 wks £645
Max. Trainees per course 12-18
Contact: The Principle
Start Dates: 8 courses per year
Jan, Feb, June, July, Aug, Sept, Oct, Nov.

Stevenson College
Bankhead Avenue, Sighthill
EDINBURGH EH11 4DE
Tel: (0131) 535 4600
Fax: (0131) 535 4666

CELTA
Full Time 4 wks £750
Part Time 2 terms £750
Max. Trainees per course 12
Contact: David Gibson
Start Dates: 1 P/T course per year Sept. 1 F/T per year Aug.

Stevenson College also run a introduction to TESOL course on one evening a week for 10 weeks.

Stockport College
EFL Department
Wellington Road South
STOCKPORT SK1 3UQ
Tel: (0161) 958 3100
Fax: (0161) 480 6636
E-Mail: stockcoll@cs.stockport.ac.uk

Cert. TESOL
Part Time 6 mths £740
Max. Trainees per course 12
Contact: Pat Coull
Start Dates: 1 course per year Sept. March course pending.

Stoke-on-Trent College
Stoke Road, Shelton
STOKE-ON-TRENT ST4 2DG
Tel: (01782) 208208
Fax: (01782) 603504

CELTA
Full Time 5 wks £800
Part Time 12 wks £800
Max. Trainees per course 15
Contact: Dot Stone
Start Dates: 3 P/T courses per year Jan, Apr, Sept. 1 F/T course per year Apr.

Students International Ltd.
158 Dalby Road
MELTON MOWBRAY LE13 0BJ
Tel: (01664) 481997
Fax: (01664) 563332
E-Mail: 106474.2225@compuserve.com

Cert. TESOL
Full Time 4 wks £795
Max. Trainees per course 16
Contact: Mrs. Blyth
Start Dates: 5 F/T courses per year Jul, Aug, Sept, Nov, Jan.

The Studio School of English
Station Road
CAMBRIDGE CB1 2JF
Tel: (01223) 369701
Fax: (01223) 324605
E-Mail: studio-cambridge@dial.pipex.com

CELTA
Full Time 4 wks £870 + £66.50 assessment fee
Max. Trainees per course 12
Contact: Lucy J. Purvey
Start Dates: 5 courses per year Feb, Mar, Apr, May, Sept.

The Studio School was founded in 1954. It is a recognised English language school and, each year, in excess of 3,000 foreign students attend EFL courses. The School is able to provide teaching observation in both internationaland monolingual groups. Accommodation can be arranged either self catering or homestay. The Studio school is registered centre for NVQ and as such the CELTA course qualifies for Vocational Training Relief (VTR). This means that students who qualify for VTR can claim back 23% of their course fees.

Surrey Language Centre
Standford House
39 West Street
FARNHAM GU9 7DR
Tel: (01252) 723494
Fax: (01252) 717692
E-Mail: stb.ltd@highfield.sprint.com

Cert. TESOL
Full Time 4 wks £650
Max. Trainees per course 10
Contact: Trudy Kitabayashi/ Director of Admissions
Start Dates: 10 courses per year Jan, Feb, Mar, Apr, June, July, Aug, Sept, Oct, Nov.

Surrey Language Centre is based in Sandford House. This is one of the finest historical 18th century houses in Surrey and has a large and beautiful garden. The school's location, facilities and relaxed atmosphere provide the trainee with an ideal environment in which to develop the skills of a modern-day EFL teacher. The centre also runs a wide range of general and specific Purpose English courses for overseas students, as well as teacher training courses.

Surrey Youth & Adult Education Services (Esher Green Centre)
19 Esher Green
Esher
SURREY KT10 8AA
Tel: (01372) 465374
Fax: (01372) 463019

Cert. TESOL
Part Time 22 wks £595
Max. Trainees per course 14
Contact: Ursula Over
Start Dates: 1 course per year Nov.

LTCL (TESOL) (Dip. TESOL)
Part Time 30 wks £465
Max. trainees per course 14
Contact: Ursula Over
Dates: 1 course per year Oct.

Sutton College of Liberal Arts
St. Nicholas Way, Sutton
SURREY SM1 1EA
Tel: (0181) 770 6901
Fax: (0181) 770 6933

Cert. TESOL
Part Time £500.20
Max. Trainees per course 12
Contact: Caroline O'Reilly
Start Dates: 1 course per year Sept.

Thames Valley University
ELT Department
Walpole House
18-22 Bond Street
LONDON W5 5AA
Tel: (0181) 231 2958
Fax: (0181) 231 2900
E-Mail: celtaenq@tvu.ac.uk

CELTA
Full Time 4 wks £890
Part Time 9 mths £890
Max. Trainees per course 10
Contact: John Waterman
Start Dates: 1 P/T course per year Oct. 2 F/T courses per year Apr, June.

The School of ELT has always been at the forefront of research and development in its field. It has a very strong reputation in the field of research in ELT and ESOL, and in 1995 the centre for Applied Linguistic Research was founded. The School's work also includes Direct Language teaching to students from all over the world. On average, over 600 students attend courses each year.

The faculty is also involved with teacher training at undergraduate and postgraduate level. The University offers extensive facilities for learning and teaching EFL including video, computers, language laboratories, a student self access centre and well equipped classrooms.

Thurrock College
Woodview
Grays
Essex RM16 2YR
Tel: (01375) 391199
Fax: (01375) 373356
E-Mail: thurrock@rmplc.co.uk

Cert. TESOL
Full Time 4 wks £595
Max. Trainees per course 10
Contact: John Saunders
Start Dates: 2 courses per year Nov, Feb.

Torbay Language Centre
Conway Road
Paignton
Torbay
DEVON TQ4 5LH
Tel: (01803) 558555
Fax: (01803) 559606
E-Mail: tlc.lal@dial.pipex.com

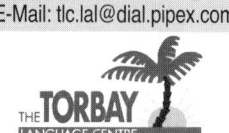

CELTA
Full Time £799 + £66.50 exam fee
Max. Trainees per course 12
Contact: Val Lynas
Start Dates: 2 courses per year May, Oct.

Universal Language Training
The Old Forge
Ockham Lane
Ockham
SURREY GU23 6NP
Tel: (01483) 210083
Fax: (01483) 211185

Cert. TESOL
Full Time 4 wks £695 + £73 moderation fee
Part Time 4 mths £695 + £73 moderation fee
Max. Trainees per course 8-20
Contact: Elaine Stafford
Start Dates: 1 P/T course per year Oct. 8 F/T courses per year Jan, Mar, May, June, July, Sept, Oct, Nov.

Universal Language Training (ULT) is well established and specilises in the training of teachers to teach EFL. ULT provide a pre-course training package which covers key areas of course.

University of Durham
The Language Centre
Elvet Riverside, New Elvet
DURHAM DH1 3JT
Tel: (0191) 374 3716
Fax: (0191) 374 7790
E-Mail: A.C.Pugh@durham.ac.uk

CELTA
Full Time 4 wks £875
Part Time 5 mths £875
Max. Trainees per course 12
Contact: Chris Anderson
Start Dates: 1 P/T course per year Oct. 4 F/T courses per year Mar, June, July, Aug.

The University is recognised for academic excellence and offers a wide variety of educational, sporting and social facilities for students.

University of East Anglia
School of Modern Languages & European History
NORWICH NR4 7TJ
Tel: (01603) 456161
Fax: (01603) 593718
E-Mail: graduate.enquiries@uea.ac.uk

CELTA
This course is available as part of the UEA masters programme. For further details please contact Richard Francis.

University of Edinburgh
Institute for Applied Language Studies
21 Hill Place
EDINBURGH EH8 9DP
Tel: (0131) 650 6200
Fax: (0131) 667 5927
E-Mail: s.lawson@ed.ac.uk

DTEFLA
Full Time 11 wks £1450
Max. Trainees per course 8
Contact: Course Director
Start Dates: 1 course per year March

The Institute for Applied Language Studies at Edinburgh University was founded in 1979 as a research and development centre for language teaching.

The DTEFLA course lasts for 11 weeks one of which is a reading week. Help with finding accommodation is available.

University of Glamorgan
Pontypridd
Mid Glamorgan
WALES CF37 1DL
Tel: (01443) 480480
Fax: (01443) 480558
E-Mail: mmcnorto@glamorgan.ac.uk

CELTA
Full Time and Part Time Courses pending
Contact: Maggy McNorton

University of Glasgow
EFL Unit
Dept. of Adult & Continuing Education
Hetherington Building
Bute Gardens
GLASGOW G12 8RS
Tel: (0141) 339 8855
Fax: (0141) 339 1119
E-Mail: E.Dunbar@arts.gla.ac.uk

CELTA
Part Time 4 mths £900 approx.
Max. Trainees per course 15
Contact: Esther Dunbar
Start Dates: 1 course per year Dec.

University of Hull
Language Centre
Cottingham Rd
HULL HU6 7RX
Tel: (01482) 465900
Fax: (01482) 466180
E-Mail: langc@hull.ac.uk

THE UNIVERSITY OF HULL

CELTA
Full Time 4 wks £800 + RSA fee
Part Time 20 wks £800 + RSA fee
Max. Trainees per course 12
Contact: Deborah Marsh
Start Dates: 1 P/T course per year Oct. 1 F/T course per year summer.

University of Luton
Department of Linguistics
Faculty of Humanities
Castle Street
LUTON LU1 3JU
Tel: (01582) 489019
Fax: (01582) 489014
E-Mail: andrew.russell@luton.ac.uk

Cert. TESOL
Part Time 2 yrs £780 (6 modules at £130 each)
Max. Trainees per course 15
Contact: Course Administrator
Start Dates: 1 course per year Oct.

LTCL (TESOL) (Dip. TESOL)
Starting in Oct. 1999 Contact the college for further details

University of St. Andrews
English Language Teaching
Butts Wynd
St. ANDREWS KY16 9AL
Tel: (01334) 462255
Fax: (01334) 462270
E-Mail: amm3@st-andrews.ac.uk

Cert. TESOL
Full 4-5 wks £805
Max. Trainees per course 12
Contact: Alison Malcolm-Smith
Start Dates: 3 courses per year Jan, Apr, June.

University of Strathclyde
English Language Teaching Division
Department of Modern Languages
Livingston Tower
26 Richmond Street
GLASGOW G1 1XH
Tel: (0141) 548 3065
Fax: (0141) 553 4122
E-Mail: eltd.les@strath.ac.uk

CELTA
Full Time 4 wks £890
Part Time 13 wks £890
Max. Trainees per course 12
Contact: The Secretary
Start Dates: 1 F/T course per year Feb. 1 P/T course per year Oct.

University of the West of England
Faculty of Languages and European Studies
Coldharbour Lane
Bristol BS16 1QY
Tel: (0117) 976 3914
Fax: (0117) 976 3843
E-Mail: g-mann@uwe.ac.uk

Cert. TESOL
Full Time 5 weeks £840
Max. Trainees per course 15
Contact: George Mann
Start Dates: 5 courses per year Jan, Feb, Apr, Nov, Oct.

The University of the West of England also offer introductory courses.

University of Wales, Swansea
The Centre for Applied Language Studies
SWANSEA SA2 8PP
Tel: (01792) 295391
Fax: (01792) 295641
E-Mail: cals@swansea.ac.uk

DTEFLA
Courses are pending. For confirmation, please contact the college.

University of Westminster
9-18 Euston Centre
LONDON NW1 3ET
Tel: (0171) 911 5000 ext. 4361
Fax: (0171) 911 5001
E Mail: efl@wmin.ac.uk

Cert. TESOL
Full Time 5 wks £760
Max. Trainees per course 18
Contact: Elaine Dacosta
Start Dates: 5 courses per year Feb, Apr, June, Aug, Oct.

Suitable applicants will be invited for interview.

University of Wolverhampton
School of Education
Gorway Road
WEST MIDLANDS WS1 3BD
Tel: (01902) 323131
Fax: (01902) 323177

Cert. TESOL
Part Time 9 mths £ 790
Max. Trainees per course 16
Contact: Tony Shannon-Little
Start Dates: 1 course per year Sept.

Waltham Forest College
Forest Road
Wathamstow
LONDON E17 4JB
Tel: (0181) 527 2311
Fax: (0181) 523 2376
E-Mail: lowesr@waltham.ac.uk

Cert. TESOL
Full Time 4 wks £650 inclusive
Part Time 6 mths £650 inclusive
Max. Trainees per course 14
Contact: Nicole Delalouviere
Start Dates: 1 P/T course per year Sept. 2 F/T courses per year June, July.

DTEFLA
Part Time £650 + £150 exam fee
Max. Trainees per course 14
Contact: Nicole Delalouvier
Start Dates: 1 course per year Sept.

Section 7

Directory of centres

Page 87

West Kent College
Brook Street
Tonbridge
KENT TN9 2PW
Tel: (01732) 358101
Fax:(01732) 771415

wkc
West Kent College

CELTA
Part Time 13 wks £495 inclusive
Max. Trainees per course 14
Contact: Admission Office
Start Dates: 4 courses per year
Nov, Feb, Mar, June.

Westminster College
Peter Street
LONDON W1V 4HS
Tel: (0171) 437 8536
Fax: (0171) 287 0711

WESTMINSTER COLLEGE

CELTA
Full Time 5 wks £750
Max. Trainees per course 14
Contact: Katrina Francis
Start Dates: 6 courses per year Jan, Feb, Apr, June, Sept, Nov.

Wigan & Leigh College
Wigan Campus
PO Box 53
Parsons Walk, Wigan
LANCASHIRE WNI 1RS
Tel: (01942) 761600
Fax: (01942) 761563

WIGAN & LEIGH COLLEGE

CELTA
Part Time £500 + exam fee
Max. Trainees per course 12
Contact: Lucy Hale
Start Dates: 2 courses per year Sept, Jan.

Wigston College of F. E.
Language Centre
Station Road
Wigston
LEICESTERSHIRE
LE18 2DW
Tel: (0116) 2885051
Fax: (0116) 288 0823

WIGSTON COLLEGE

CELTA
Part Time 36 wks £500
Max. Trainees per course 12
Contact: David Harris
Start Dates: 1 course per year Sept.

Windsor Schools TEFL
89 Arthur Road
WINDSOR SL4 1RU
Tel: (01753) 858995
Fax: (01753) 831726

Windsor Schools TEFL

Cert. TESOL
Full Time 4 wks £799
Part Time 4 mths £799
Max. Trainees per course 15
Contact: Paul Lowe
Start Dates: 12 courses per year

The School is located in central Windsor and has well equipped facilities. The Windsor School offers assistance with finding a first teaching post through the sister school in Barcelona and agents in Italy.

SECTION 8

Directory of university courses

University courses

"UK universities offering TEFL and TEFL related courses"

page 90

Aston University
Language Studies Unit
Aston Triangle
BIRMINGHAM
B4 7ET
Tel: (0121) 359 3611 ext. 4242
Fax: (0121) 359 2725
E Mail: lsu@aston.ac.uk

ASTON UNIVERSITY
Birmingham UK

Advanced Cert. Principles of TEFL
Full Time £1200 (non E.U. £6180)
Contact: Course Secretary
Entry requirements: A teaching certificate and/or a degree. A minimum of 2 years classroom teaching experience.

The course is designed for experienced teachers who may be considering a change of direction or who wish to develop their skills in ELT. The course aims to train such teachers to an advanced level of professional competence in TEFL and prepare them for careers throughout the world.

The course consists of 6 distance learning modules and a teaching performance profile either by submission of video recordings of teaching practice or attending a 1 week teaching practice programme at Aston.

MSc in TESOL/TESP
Full Time £2540 (non E.U. £6180)
Distance Learning minimum of £5000 for 100 credits or £500 per module with a supplement for students outside of Europe. If the course is completed within 2 years, this will allow reduction of the dissertation fee of £600
Contact: Sue Morton
Entry requirements: Normally 3 years relevant professional experience and a good bachelor's degree.

The course is available in-house at Aston over one calendar year or by distance learning.

Canterbury Christ Church College
International Programmes Office
CANTERBURY CT1 1QU
Tel: (01227) 458459
Fax: (01227) 470442
E Mail: ipo@canterbury.ac.uk

MA/Diploma English Language Education (University of Kent)
Full Time £2570 (non E.U. £6200)
Contact: Richard Cullen
Entry requirements: Normally 3 years relevant professional experience and a good bachelor's degree.

The MA and Diploma ELE are University of Kent awards designed to cater for the needs of educators with relevant experience who wish to develop their skills and knowledge in wider aspects of English Language education. The programme begins with issues related to the classroom and the moves beyond to the design, management and evaluation of both language teaching and teacher education curricula.

The Post Graduate Diploma comprises ten 30 hour modules, including two on methodology. The MA can be taken on successful completion of the Diploma plus a dissertation of 12,000 words.

MA/Diploma TEFL (University of Kent)
Full Time £2570 (non E.U. £6200)
Part Time £585 per year
Contact: Richard Cullen
Entry requirements: Normally 1 years relevant teaching experience plus a relevant bachelors degree or teaching certificate.

The MA and Dip TEFL are University of Kent awards designed for practising teachers who wish to further their professional competence and develop their understanding of the theoretical implications of teaching. They focus on the classroom in the first instance, explore all key aspects of classroom dynamics and practice, and also investigate the key issues which underlie good teaching practice in EFL.

The Postgraduate Diploma comprises ten 30 hour modules, including four modules in methodology. The MA TEFL can be taken on successful completion of the Postgraduate Diploma TEFL plus a further module in Research methods and a dissertation of 12,000 words.

Chichester Institute of Higher Education
The Dome
Upper Bognor Road
Bognor Regis
WEST SUSSEX PO21 1HR
Tel: (01243) 829291
Fax: (01243) 841458
E-mail: ciem@dial.pipex.com

CHICHESTER INSTITUTE of HIGHER EDUCATION

Cert./Dip Advanced Educational Studies (ELT Administration)
Full Time 5-6 wks per certificate £510 (non E.U. £1310)
Full Time 5 months all 4 certificates for the Diploma £2040 (non E.U. £5240)
Contact: Angela Karlsson
Entry requirements: Normally a qualified teacher with at least 3 years experience.

The course is structured with four component certificates. If all four are completed successfully, this will lead to the Diploma award.

Each of the four certificates offers an award framework for short, professional training courses for ELT personnel who intend or are involved in teacher training, course design and implementation, testing, and the management of resources for learners and teachers. The certificates aim to provide practical know-how and skills to bring about various aspects of professional change and development related to the participants' work situation.

MA ELT Management
Full Time 1 year £2350 (non E.U. £6300)
Part Time (3 modules in 10 wks) £350 per module (non E.U. £900)
Part Time (1 module in 10 wks) £350 per module (non E.U. £900)
Contact: Angela Karlsson
Entry requirements: Normally a good honours degree and at least 3 years experience.

The aim of the course is to provide those who are already, or intending to be, involved in ELT management, with an understanding of the process of management. The route focuses on management issues through the experiences of the course members, relating their work situation to various paradigms.

The course consists of 6 modules plus a dissertation equivalent to 4 modules. The modules may be followed consecutively, with intervals between awards, or as individual modules.

College of St Mark and St John
International Education Centre
Derriford Road
PLYMOUTH
PL6 8BH
Tel: (01752) 777188
Fax: (01752) 761120

BPhil (Ed)/MEd (Exon) in English Language Teaching
Full Time 1 year £3050 (non E.U. £5900)
Contact: The Director
Entry requirements: A good first degree and 3 years teaching experience.

This course is offered under the auspices of the University of Exeter, and is designed for those concerned with English Language teaching at secondary and tertiary levels, from both Britain and overseas. The BPhil Ed/MEd ELT is a broad based ELT course, which emphasises the practical application of current theories and approaches set within the wider developmental education context. Course participants come from a variety of ELT situations to update their skills and knowledge, and so have the opportunity of exchanging experiences derived from many different settings. The course is normally taken over one year but can be taken in modules (1 term each) or part time.

BPhil Ed/MEd (Exon) in Teacher Training for ELT
Full Time 1 year £3050 (non E.U. £5900)
Contact: The Director
Entry requirements: A good first degree, a teaching qualification and 3 years teaching experience.

The course is offered under the auspices of the University of Exeter. The course is designed for teachers already involved in training or those who wish to make the move from classroom teaching to teacher training. The course is normally taken over one year but can be taken in modules (1 term each) or part time.

BPhil Ed/MEd (Exon) in Teaching English for Specific Purposes
Full Time 1 year £3050 (non E.U. £5900)
Contact: The Director
Entry requirements: A good first degree, a qualified teacher and 3 years teaching experience with experience in TESP.

The course is offered under the auspices of the University of Exeter. The course is intended for teachers, lecturers, administrators etc. who wish to acquire a stronger professional base or wish to specialise in TESP. The course is normally taken over one year but can be taken in modules (1 term each) or part time.

Institute of Education
University of London
20 Bedford Way
LONDON WC1H 0AL
Tel: (0171) 580 1122
Fax: (0171) 612 6097

TESOL MA
Full Time 1 year £2540 (non E.U. £6711)
Part Time 2 years £1269 per year
Contact: John Norish
Entry requirements: A good honours degree a professional qualification in TESOL or professional experience of TESOL.

The compulsory modules of the course introduce basic aspects of the subject. The optional modules cover a variety of topics, allowing students to emphasise different aspects of enquiry. Students seeking a practical orientation to high-level professional education, can choose modules which enable them to analyse practice and, to subject to critical appraisal new developments in language teaching pedagogy. Students seeking a more theoretical applied linguistic orientation can choose modules which provide for the consideration of more conceptual problems in the development and teaching of English to speakers of other languages.

In addition to the course studied at the Institute, there is an Internet route. This is taught largely by computer conferencing on the Internet and with regular meetings at the Institute.

King's College London
The English Centre
Kensington Campus
Campden Hill Road
London W8 7AH
Tel: (0171) 333 4650
Fax: (0171) 333 4066
E-mail: jennifer.jenkins@kcl.ac.uk

MA in ELT and Applied Linguistics
Full Time 1 year £1270 (non E.U. £3765)
Part Time: Contact college
Contact: Jennifer Jenkins
Entry requirements: A good honours degree and 3 years teaching experience.

The MA course in ELT & Applied Linguistics has been designed specifically with the idea of providing an opportunity for experienced languages teachers to reflect upon and further develop their understanding of the various theoretical and practical issues that impact upon the field of language teaching. It places particular emphasis on the notion of informed teaching practice and the need for teachers to mediate between theory and practice in constructing pedagogies according to specific teaching-learning contexts.

The MA has a DTEFLA fast track option. This allows teachers who have obtained the DTEFLA qualification within 3 years prior to entry, or who elect to register initially for the DTEFLA at King's to by-pass the whole of the methodology and half of the linguistic analysis module.

Leeds Metropolitan University
Beckett Campus
LEEDS LS6 3QS
Tel: (0113) 283 7440
Fax: (0113) 274 5966
E-mail: cls@lmu.ac.uk

PG Cert/PG Dip/MA Language Teaching
Full Time 1 year £2610
Part Time 1-5 years £217 per module (12 modules)
Contact: Ivor Timmis
Entry requirements: A good first degree.

The programme is designed for teachers of adults whether in the UK or overseas. Participants need have no experience of teaching languages. The programme is practically oriented, focusing on the synthesis of theory, reflective practice, and applied research or curriculum/materials development. The programme aims to provide participants with a critical understanding of their own professional practice, a framework for reflective analysis, and the capabilities for professional development.

There are three levels of award available, Post Graduate Certificate, Post Graduate Diploma and MA. The MA component is assessed through an extended project, usually involving applied research, materials/curriculum development, and/or reflective practice.

There are opportunities for applicants with appropriate experience or professional qualifications to claim accreditation for prior learning for up to 50% of the programme.

Moray House Institute of Education
Holyrood Road
EDINBURGH EH8 8AQ
Tel: (0131) 556 8455
Fax: (0131) 557 5138

MA TESOL
Full Time 1 year £1800 (non E.U. £5400)
Part Time £150 per module (non E.U. £450)
Contact: The Administrator
Entry requirements: Applicants will normally have a first degree and at least 3 years TESOL experience.

The course is designed as a flexible modular programme which allows freedom of choice of specialisation in TESOL. The course aims to give participants an opportunity to develop their knowledge and expertise in all aspects of TESOL.

The programme consists of a taught course normally lasting from October to June, followed by preparation of a 20,000 word dissertation. The MA is awarded on the basis of the taught course plus a dissertation.

Norwich Institute for Language Education (NILE)
P.O. Box 2000
NORWICH NR2 2EY
Tel: (01603) 451450
Fax: (01603) 451452
E-mail: nile_uk@compuserve.com

MA in Education and Professional Development for TEFL
in collaboration with The University of East Anglia.
Modular course. Please contact the Institute for costs.
Contact: Penny Miller
Entry requirements: Applicants will normally have a first degree and at least teaching qualification.

The Masters award requires candidates to complete 3 units and a dissertation. There are 5 units, which on completion have a 30 point value. The topics covered are: from key principles to good practice, evaluation, assessment and testing in TEFL, new contexts for language learning, researched based professional development and educational evaluation for senior teachers and management. At any stage during the course, candidates can 'cash in' their points for an academic award - 30 points for an Advanced Certificate, 60 points for a Diploma, 90 for an Advanced diploma and, on successful completion of a dissertation (30 points), a Masters degree. NILE also offer a number short specialist teacher development courses.

Ripon & York St John College
College Road
Ripon
HG4 2QX
Tel: (01765) 602691
Fax: (01765) 600516

MA Linguistics and Modern Languages

This course is available as a 1 year full time and 2 year part time course and also as a PgDip if taken without a dissertation. For further information, please contact the college directly.

Sheffield and Hallam University
TESOL Centre
Totley Campus
Totley Hall Lane
SHEFFIELD S17 4AB
Tel: (0114) 253 2816
Fax: (0114) 253 2832
E-mail: TESOL@shu.ac.uk

MA /PgDip TESOL
Full Time 1 year £2500 (non E.U. £2800)
Contact: TESOL Centre
Entry requirements: Applicants must have a first degree or hold a recognised teaching qualification, or relevant experience.

The Teacher Education programme has three stages covering; the needs of new entrants to the profession (Postgraduate Certificate); experienced teachers seeking to progress by adding an in-service qualification to their experience; (Postgraduate Diploma); and those wishing to pursue their career development through specialised research (MA).

The design of the courses also allows the University's Credit Accumulation and Transfer Scheme to be used, so that each stage of the programme gains a credit for the next stage.

The University has pioneered extensive use of distance learning allowing a high degree of flexibility.

St Mary's University College
Waldegrave Road
Strawberry Hill
Twickenham TW1 4SX
Tel: (0181) 240 4000
Fax: (0181) 240 4255

MA Applied Linguistics and ELT and MA Linguistics in Education
Full Time per year £2400 (non E.U. £5400)
Part Time £180 per module
Contact: Dr. Michael Connelly F/T courses. Peter Dewar P/T courses.
Entry requirements: Please contact the college.

St. Mary's University College offers both part-time and full-time programmes leading to a Masters Degree in Applied Linguistics and English Language Teaching or a Masters Degree in Linguistics Education.

The degrees consist of 12 modules covering aspects of applied linguistics, language teaching and the management of language teaching processes. A 15,000 word dissertation counts as four modules.

Thames Valley University
St. Mary's Road
LONDON
W5 5RF
Tel: (0181) 579 5000
Fax: (0181) 566 1353

Cert/Dip/MA/English Language Teaching - MPhil/PhD
Full Time 1 year £1960 (non E.U. £5750)
Part Time 2-5 years £245 per module
Contact: School of English Language Teaching
Entry requirements: A degree or professional teacher qualification and normally over 3 years relevant professional experience.

The programme focuses on the needs of ELT practitioners in the classroom and at all levels of English Language Education. The core modules explore theory and practice in ELT and combine with the choice of practical studies in specialist areas. The MA consists of six taught modules (four core and two options) plus a 10,000 to 12,000 word dissertation (double module). The Postgraduate Diploma requires the successful completion of six modules. The Postgraduate Certificate requires three taught modules (one core).

The University encourages applications from those wishing to pursue research degrees.

University of Brighton
The Language Centre
Brighton
EAST SUSSEX
BN1 9PH
Tel: (01273) 643337
Fax: (01273) 690710

Diploma TEFL
Full Time 1 year £900 (non E.U. £5700)
Part Time 2 years £350 per year
Contact: Angela Pickering
Entry requirements: Normally a first degree and TEFL experience.

The course aims to consolidate and evaluate practical teaching while, at the same time, enabling students to explore related theory and to develop key areas of expertise within the field of TEFL, such as teaching young learners and syllabus design.

MA TEFL
Full Time 1 year £2350 (non E.U. £5700)
Part Time 2 years £900 per year
Contact: Geofrey Pullen
Entry requirements: TEFL experience and preferably already at diploma level.

The emphasis of the course is on bringing together theory and practice and enabling students to build on their professional experience, while extending conceptual and teaching skills.

MA Media-Assisted Language Teaching and Learning
Full Time 1 year £2200 (non E.U. £5200)
Part Time 2 years £1100 per year
Contact: Elspeth Broady
Entry requirements: Normally an honours degree, plus at least three years teaching experience in EFL or Foreign Languages.

The MA aims to provide experienced EFL or foreign language teachers with a comprehensive framework for the evaluation and development of media assisted language teaching and learning. The course examines the use of video, audio, computers, new transmission technologies, as well as print- based support materials.

University of Bristol
School of Education
35 Berkeley Square
BRISTOL BS8 1JA
Tel: (0117) 928 7046
Fax: (0117) 925 1537

MEd TEFL
Full Time 1 year £2490 (non E.U. £6470)
Part Time £208 per unit
Contact: Jaqui Upcott
Entry requirements: UK honours degree and 1 years experience.

The course is designed to meet the needs of practitioners in TEFL and provide opportunities for theoretical development to equip them for senior positions. The course allows students to construct a programme with particular focus to suit their interests where appropriate. Selections of other options may also be made from other areas of study within the school.

University of Central Lancashire
Department of Languages
Preston PR1 2HE
Tel: (01772) 893137
Fax: (01772) 892413
E-mail: c.barwood@uclan.ac.uk

MA in Teaching English for International Business
Full Time 1 year, Part Time 2 years
Contact the University for fee details.
Contact: Chris Barwood
Entry requirements: Normally a good first degree, a certificate in TEFL or equivalent, and two years relevant teaching experience.

The aims of the course are; to offer a clear and unrivalled career advantage in this developing field; to develop expertise as a Business English teaching professional; to develop awareness of current trends in the field in practice and research, and to gain a high degree of familiarity with the business, management and linguistic foundations of Teaching English for International Business.

University of Durham
School of English
Elvet Riverside
2 New Elvet
DURHAM
DH1 3JT
Tel: (0191) 374 2641
Fax: (0191) 374 2685
E-mail: durham.linguistics@durham.ac.uk

MA Applied Linguistics with reference to ESOL
MA Applied Linguistics with reference to ELT
MA Applied Linguistics with reference to ESP
MA Applied Linguistics with reference to ELT and Materials development
MA Applied Linguistics with English Language
Full Time 1 year £2540 (non E.U. £6415)
Part Time 2 or 3 years £715 per year (non E.U. £1800)
Contact: Martha Young-Schulton
Entry requirements: Normally a good first degree, and three years teaching experience.

The MA at Durham is based around a core linguistics course which then allows specialisation into various fields. The courses are offered on a modular basis allowing full time or part time study. The full time course can be taken as 8 taught modules and a 15,000 word dissertation or 10 taught modules and 8,000 words.

University of East Anglia
School of Modern Languages
NORWICH
NR4 7TJ
Tel: (01603) 592750
Fax: (01603) 250599

ELT and Applied Linguistics MA MPhil/PhD
Full Time 1 year £2540 (non E.U. £6100)
Contact: Keith Harvey
Entry requirements: Normally an honours degree and three years teaching experience.

The MA consists of 3 core taught units with options of further relevant units followed by a 15,000 word dissertation.

ELT and Applied Linguistics MPhil/PhD
The department welcomes applications from intending research students who wish to study for a higher degree.

University of Edinburgh
Department of Applied Linguistics
14 Buccleuch Place
EDINBURGH EH8 9LN
Tel: (0131) 650 3864
Fax: (0131) 650 6526
E Mail: Applied.Lingiustics@ed.ac.uk

MSc Applied Linguistics
Full Time 1 year £2540 (non E.U. £6550)
Contact: Stuart Lawson
Entry requirements: Preference is given to honours graduates but professional achievement and experience are also taken into account. Substantial teaching experience is normally expected.

The course is divided into two parts, a 9 month period of course work consisting of a core course and a set of options between October and June, and a dissertation in the summer. The aim of the core course is to provide a basic foundation in linguistics, socio- and psycho-linguistics, modern linguistic descriptions of English grammar and discourse, and an introduction to the concepts and research techniques. Participants follow eight options from 28 available. Students successfully completing the course work qualify for a Diploma. The dissertation is required for the award of the MSc.

MLitt and PhD in Applied Linguistics
The department welcomes applications from intending research students who wish to study for a higher degree.

University of Essex
Department of Language and Linguistics
Wivenhoe Park
COLCHESTER
CO4 3SQ
Tel: (01206) 872083
Fax: (01206) 872085
E mail: laladms@essex.ac.uk

MA ELT
Full Time 9 and 12 mths £2540 (non E.U. £6310)
Part Time 24, 33, 36 mths
Contact: Phil Scholfield
Entry requirements: A good first degree and three years active professional involvement with ELT. Preference is given to honours graduates, but professional achievement and experience are also taken into account. Substantial teaching experience is normally expected.

This is a practical course designed to increase awareness of contemporary issues and techniques in ELT.

University of Exeter
Department of Applied Linguistics
Queens Building
The Queens Drive
EXETER
EX4 4QH
Tel: (01392) 264302
Fax: (01392) 264361

MA/Dip Lexicography
Please contact Jo Whitmore for further details.

University of Hertfordshire
School of Humanities and Education
Watford Campus, Wall Hall
Aldenham, Watford
HERTFORDSHIRE WD2 8AT
Tel: (01423) 352235
Fax: (01423) 353449

MA Linguistics
Please contact Pat Morton in School of Humanities and Education for further information.

University of Hull
Language Institute
HULL
HU6 7RX
Tel: (01482) 465900
Fax: (01482) 466180
E mail: langc@hull.ac.uk

MA/Dip Applied Language and New Technologies
Full Time 1 year £2540 (non E.U. £6200)
Part Time 2 years £1050 (non E.U. £3100)
Contact: Ms. V. Hunter
Entry requirements: Normally a good honours degree in English, Dutch, German, Italian, Spanish or Swedish. Or graduates in other disciplines who have substantial experience in language teaching.

The course is designed for those who have an interest in language teaching or developing course materials etc.. The MA course does not offer any practical teaching qualifications, but the content is designed to help candidates to become more reflective practitioners.

University of Lancaster
Department of Linguistics and Modern English Language
LANCASTER LA1 4YT
Tel: (01524) 593028
Fax: (01524) 843085
E mail: M.F.Robinson@lancaster.ac.uk

Linguistics for ELT
For further information please contact Majorie Robinson.

The University also encourages applications from intending research students for Mphil or PhD.

University of Leeds
School of Education
LEEDS LS2 9JT
Tel: (0113) 233 4528
Fax: (0113) 233 4541
E Mail: m.bygate@education.leeds.ac.uk

MA Linguistics and ELT
Full Time 1 year £2540 (non E.U. £6350)
Part Time £300 per module (non E.U. £794)
Contact: The Secretary
Entry requirements: Initial qualification and at least 3 years relevant teaching experience.

The aim of the course is to promote an awareness of the uses of technology in ELT, and to develop practical skills in the use of educational technologies in the ELT classroom.

MEd TESOL
Full Time 1 year £2540 (non E.U. £6350)
Part Time £300 per module (non E.U. £794)
Contact: The Secretary
Entry requirements: An initial qualification and at least 3 years relevant teaching experience.

The aim of the course is to promote an awareness of the uses of technology in ELT, and to develop practical skills in the use of educational technologies in the ELT classroom.

University of Leicester
School of Education
21 University Road
LEICESTER
LE1 7RF
Tel: (0116) 252 3669
Fax: (0116) 252 3653
E mail: hw8@le.ac.uk

Advanced Certificate TESOL
MA Applied Linguistics/TESOL
Distance Training maximum 5 years £445 per module (£495 non E.U.)
Contact: Helen Whitfield
Entry requirements: A first degree and teaching experience.

The Advanced certificate in TESOL and the MA Applied linguistics/TESOL by distance learning are designed for practising graduate teachers who require a higher qualification and further study in TESOL. The Advanced Certificate is offered as an independent module. In addition, it counts as one contributory module of the distance learning MA Applied Linguistics/TESOL.

University of Liverpool
Applied English Language Studies Unit
Department of English Language and Literature
PO Box 147
LIVERPOOL L69 3BX
Tel: (0151) 794 2771
Fax: (0151) 794 2739

MA Language Teaching and Learning
For further details of fees etc. please contact the MA Course Director
Entry requirements: First degree and relevant experience.

The course sets out to explore the three areas of language; language learning, language teaching and methodology, with particular emphasis on the relationship between them.

University of Manchester
CELSE
School of Education
Oxford Road
MANCHESTER M13 9PL
Tel: (0161) 275 3467
Fax: (0161) 275 3480
E Mail: celse@man.ac.uk

Diploma in Advanced Study in TESOL
Full Time 1 year £2540 (non E.U. £6350)
Part Time £300 per module (non E.U. £794)
Contact: The Secretary
Entry requirements: Applicants should be graduates with an initial qualification and 1-2 years relevant teaching experience.

The course aims to provide advanced training for experienced teachers through a core course of theoretical and practical studies.

MEd TESOL
Full Time 1 year £2540 (non E.U. £6350)
Part Time £300 per module (non E.U. £794)
Contact: The Secretary
Entry requirements: Applicants should be graduates with an initial qualification and at least 3 years relevant teaching experience.

The aim of the course is; to enhance the professional development of experienced languages teachers through a self-selected course of theoretical and practical studies; to encourage the development of classroom skills, and to assist long-term career development in language teaching, materials, design, teacher training and course evaluation.

MEd in Educational Technology and TESOL
Full Time 1 year £2540 (non E.U. £6350)
Part Time £300 per module (non E.U. £794)
Contact: The Secretary
Entry requirements: Applicants should be graduates with an initial qualification and at least 3 years relevant teaching experience.

The aim of the course is; to promote an awareness of the uses of technology in ELT, and to develop practical skills in the use of educational technologies in the ELT classroom.

MEd ELT
Full Time 1 year £3500
Part Time £480 per module and £620 for dissertation
Contact: The Secretary
Entry requirements: Applicants should be graduates with an initial qualification and at least 3 years relevant teaching experience.

The aim of the course is; to enhance the professional development of experienced languages teachers through a self-selected course of theoretical and practical studies; to encourage the development of classroom skills, and to assist long-term career development in language teaching, materials, design, teacher training and course evaluation.

MEd in Educational Technology and ELT
Full Time 1 year £3500
Part Time £480 per module and £620 for dissertation
Contact: The Secretary
Entry requirements: Applicants should be graduates with an initial qualification and at least 3 years relevant teaching experience.

The aim of the course is; to promote an awareness of the uses of technology in ELT, and to develop practical skills in the use of educational technologies in the ELT classroom.

University of Newcastle Upon Tyne
Language Centre
Old Library Building
NEWCASTLE, NE1 7RU
Tel: (0191) 222 7535
Fax: (0191) 261 1182
E-mail: admissions-enquiries@ncl.ac.uk

MA Linguistics for TESOL
Full Time 1 year £2350 (non E.U. £6060)
Contact: Admissions Officer
Entry requirements: First degree a teaching qualification and 2 years TEFL experience.

The course is designed to provide a thorough introduction to the following: classroom processes and methodology, language acquisition and psycholinguistics, materials and course design and evaluation, research methods for second language learning and teaching, the syntax and phonetics of English and sociolinguistics and discourse.

Also, options are available in: literature in language teaching, translation in language teaching, the communicative use of language laboratories, video in language teaching, computer assisted language learning and theoretical and computational linguistics.

Media Tech for TEFL MA
Full Time 1 year £2350 (non E.U. £6060)
Contact: Admissions Officer
Entry requirements: First degree and a teaching qualification and 2 years TEFL experience.

The course is designed to help teachers of English as a Foreign Language update their knowledge of recent developments in the methodology of TEFL and acquire new skills in the use of technological aids. No previous experience of using computers or video is assumed and appropriate training will be given. The course provides a thorough introduction to Media Technology and TESOL.

University of Nottingham
Department of English Studies
University Park
NOTTINGHAM
NG7 2RD
Tel: (0115) 951 4513
Fax: (0115) 979 1506
E-mail: barbara.sinclair@nottingham.ac.uk

ELT TESOL MA
Full Time 1 year £2610 (non E.U. £6500)
Part Time 2 years £930
Contact: Barbara Sinclair
Entry requirements: First degree, a teaching qualification and 2 years TEFL experience.

The course is designed for teachers of English and other professionals in ELT wishing to take up senior positions in ELT.

University of Portsmouth
School of Language
Park Building
King Henry 1 Street
PORTSMOUTH
PO1 2DZ
Tel: (01705) 846102
Fax: (01705) 846040
E-mail: yvonne.fraser@port.ac.uk

Applied Linguistics and TEFL
Full Time 1 year £2610 (non E.U. £6500)
Part Time 2 years £700 (non E.U. £2,345)
Contact: The Course Secretary
Entry requirements: First degree, a teaching qualification and 2 years TEFL experience.

This course is designed for those who wish to enhance their professional competence and career opportunities.

University of Reading
CALS
Whiteknights
P.O. Box 241
READING, RG6 6WB
Tel: (0118) 318512
Fax: (0118) 756506
E-mail: CALS@reading.ac.uk

Cert/Dip/MA TEFL
Full Time I year £3925 (non E.U. £6280)
Contact: Course Administrator
Entry requirements: A university degree and several years TEFL experience.

The programme sets out to connect theory and practice in English Language teaching. If you take this course, you will be given up-to-date knowledge of principles and issues in areas of importance to this field, and will investigate their practical implications. Candidates will receive a thorough grounding that will help you to develop your career as a teacher, trainer, researcher or manager.

The MA course is structured in three parts. Candidates completing part one will qualify for a Pg Cert., those completing parts one and two qualify for the Pg Dip. and those completing parts one, two and three will qualify for the MA. The third part can take the form of a dissertation or a taught section.

University of Sheffield
Department of English and Linguistics
5 Shearwood Road
SHEFFIELD S10 2TN
Tel: (0114) 222 0210
Fax: (0114) 276 8251

MA PgDip Applied Linguistics
Full Time 1 year £2490 (non E.U. £6300)
Contact: Dr Mike Reynolds
Entry requirements: A university degree and relevant TEFL experience.

The programme is designed for those who have a professional concern with language.

The modules for the Diploma and the Masters are the same except with the Masters where a compulsory research methods module is necessary and also a dissertation.

University of Southampton
Faculty of Educational Studies
SOUTHAMPTON
SO17 1BJ
Tel: (01703) 593473
Fax: (01703) 592687
E Mail: rfm3@soton.ac.uk

MA Applied Linguistics for Language Teaching
Full Time 1 year £2490 (non E.U. £6300)
Contact: Dr Ros Mitchell
Entry requirements: A university degree and several years TEFL experience.

The MA ALLT is designed primarily for those wishing to teach Language and Literature. Most of the participants are teachers of mother tongue or second/foreign languages. There are both lectures and seminars, but students are encouraged to participate actively throughout. Because of the problem solving nature of much of applied linguistics, participants are expected to reflect on and to present language related problems and solutions from their own experience, and to participate in regular student led workshops.

MA (Ed) Language in Education
For further details of this course please contact the Faculty directly.

University of Stirling
CELT
STIRLING
FK9 4LA
Tel: (01786) 467934
Fax: (01786) 466131
E Mail: stl@stir.ac.uk

MSc/Dip in TESOL
Full Time 1 year £2500 (non E.U. £6180)
Contact: Staphanie Tytler
Entry requirements: Degree

The course aims to provide practical and thorough training in TESOL. Those who are already experienced teachers may omit basic modules and concentrate on modules in classroom methodology and language analysis. The PgDip consists of the taught component of the programme. Successful candidates can submit a dissertation for the MSc.

MSc CALL and TESOL
Full Time 1 year £2500 (non E.U. £6180)
Contact: Stephanie Tytler
Entry requirements: Degree

The programme offers different levels depending on the candidates previous experience. The course is designed to introduce teachers to the techniques of Computer Assisted Language Learning and to show how CALL can be used to help teachers in practical teaching situations. The course also provides theory and practice of TESOL.

MEd TESOL
Contact: Stephanie Tytler
Entry requirements: A first degree, preferably in English or Education, and substantial teaching experience.

The programme provides professional updating in the theory and practice of teaching English, complemented by the study of the appropriate topics in the field of education.

University of Surrey
English Language Institute
GUILDFORD
GU2 5XH
Tel: (01483) 259174
Fax: (01483) 259507
E-Mail: eli@surrey.ac.uk

PG Dip/MA Linguistics (TESOL)
Full Time 1 year total fee £5200
Contact: Smiljka Gee
Entry requirements: A degree and two years relevant teaching experience.

The course is available by distance learning. The course is aimed at practising teachers who wish to relate their classroom experience to relevant theories of language, language teaching and teaching.

The course gives a solid theoretical background enabling the student to relate theory to practice, to take responsibility for a wide range of pedagogical decisions based on theoretical principles, to undertake a research study, and to acquire skills in managing teaching.

University of Ulster
Coleraine
Northern Ireland
BT52 1SA
Tel: (01265) 324 383
Fax: (01265) 324 897
E-mail: ce.kane@ulst.ac.uk

PG Dip/MA TEFL
Please contact Dr. Rosaline Pritchard for further details on this course.

University of Wales, Cardiff
English Language Studies
PO Box 94
CARDIFF CF1 3XB
Tel: (01222) 874243
Fax: (01222) 874242

MA/Dip Applied Linguistics
Full Time 1 year £2490 (non E.U. £5880)
Contact: Julia Bullough
Entry requirements: Normally a first degree and TEFL experience.

This course is designed for those pursuing, or intending to pursue, a career in Language Education, including TEFL or TESL. It is also valuable for other language professions including lexicography.

MA English Language Studies and Methods
Full Time 1 year £3510 (non E.U. £6795)
Contact: The Secretary
Entry requirements: Normally a first degree in a related field.

The aim of the course is to provide an academic and a professional orientation to the field of ELT for those who wish study or work within this field.

University of Warwick
CELTE
COVENTRY
CV4 7AL
Tel: (01203) 523200
Fax: (01203) 524318
E Mail: A.D.Beale@warwick.ac.uk

MA ELT
Full Time 1 year £3510 (non E.U. £6795)
Contact: The Secretary
Entry requirements: Normally a first degree and TEFL experience.

The course is a full time post-experience programme of study leading to an MA in English Language Teaching. It consists of a taught course followed by a dissertation. Its aims are to provide an understanding of the theoretical foundations of language teaching and to study the ways in which theory can be applied to different aspects of language teaching in order to bring about improvements in practice.

MA ELT and Admin Dip
Full Time 1 year £3510 (non E.U. £6795)
Contact: The Secretary
Entry requirements: Normally a first degree and TEFL experience.

The aim of the course is to develop awareness of, and expertise in, the practical teaching and administrative skills involved in running English Language programmes in different types of institutions.

MA ELT (Young Learners)
Full Time 1 year £3510 (non E.U. £6795)
Contact: The Secretary
Entry requirements: Normally a first degree and TEFL experience.

The course is a full time post experience programme of study leading to an MA in English Language Teaching. It consists of a taught course followed by a dissertation. Its aim is to provide an understanding of the theoretical foundations of language development and language teaching and to study the ways in which theory can be applied to the teaching of young learners (children between the ages of 5 and 11) in order to bring about improvements in practice.

MA ELT (ESP)
Full Time 1 year £3510 (non E.U. £6795)
Contact: The Secretary
Entry requirements: Normally a first degree and TEFL experience.

The course is a full time post experience programme of study leading to an MA in English Language Teaching for Specific Purposes. It consists of a taught course followed by a dissertation. Its aim is to provide theoretical grounding in language teaching and an introduction to the practice and theory of English for Specific Purposes (ESP), incorporating English for Occupational Purposes. The emphasis is on the practical application of theory to the students' own areas of interest.

Taught Master's Degrees and Doctoral Studies in Languages in Education, including TESOL

INSTITUTE OF EDUCATION
UNIVERSITY OF LONDON
Pursuing Excellence in Education

The Languages in Education Group at the Institute of Education is concerned with the study of all aspects of the Teaching of English to Speakers of Other Languages, and also seeks to assess developments in, and promote fresh and vigorous thinking about, modern language teaching and learning.

Our modular programme leading to the degree of **MA in TESOL** may be undertaken on a full-time or part-time basis in London; there is also a part-time Internet route to the degree. Our **MA in Modern Languages in Education** degree programme is available on either a full-time or part-time basis. We also offer a research degree programme leading to the degrees of **MPhil/PhD**, which will be of interest to specialists in TESOL and Modern Language Teaching.

The Institute of Education, University of London, is a world centre for the study of education

For further information about these degree programmes please contact:

Student Programmes Office
Room 511,
Institute of Education
University of London
20 Bedford Way
London WC1H 0AL

Telephone: 0171 612 6104
Fax: 0171 612 6097
E-mail: home.liaison@ioe.ac.uk

Defining the Field...
Books for the language teacher and student

NEW AND FORTHCOMING TITLES

Communication Strategies:
Psycholinguistic and Sociolinguistic Perspectives
Edited by G. Kasper & E. Kellerman
Paper 0 582 10017 8   £17.99   416pp   Due late 1997
Applied Linguistics and Language Study Series

Teaching and Language Corpora
Edited by A. Wichmann, S. Fligelstone, G. Knowles & A. McEnery
Paper 0 582 27609 8   £18.99   368pp   Due late 1997
Applied Linguistics and Language Study Series

Errors in Language Learning and Use:
Exploring Error Analysis
C. James
Paper 0 582 25763 8   £14.99 (est.)   320pp   Due early 1998
Applied Linguistics and Language Study Series

Strategies in Learning and Using a Second Language
A. Cohen
Paper 0 582 30588 8   £16.99 (est.)   312pp   Due early 1998
Applied Linguistics and Language Study Series

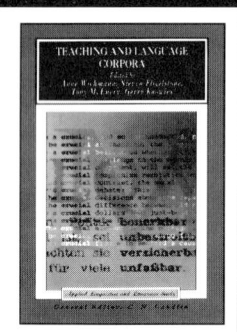

For further information, please contact Simon Collins,
Tel: (01279) 623087   Fax: (01279) 623862   e-mail: simon.collins@awl.co.uk
http://www.awl-he.com

Addison Wesley Longman

SECTION 9
Countries of the world

Top 69 TEFL consumer countries

"Where to go, what to expect when you get there, and what to take with you"

page 100

Argentina

While there are a number of schools that still employ gringos, your best bet is teaching Business English.

Argentina is a diverse country, both socially and geographically. Buenos Aires is a big bustling city with a strong cultural tradition, but cities in the interior can be a bit on the rustic side. The culture is macho and the Argentinians are a proud people. The economy and society are recovering well from the crisis years, but do avoid making political jokes. Although English, French and German are widely spoken, a smattering of Spanish will be appreciated. You will need to be qualified and to have had some experience as competition is quite strong. Private classes will be difficult to find. Night life and food in Buenos Aires are highly recommended, though vegetarians may find life difficult. In all, Aregentina is both a nice place to visit and live in with no worries about CJD.

Entry requirements:
Working on a three month renewable tourist visa is possible. Going the full bureaucratic course is best done before leaving home if you wish to avoid an enormous amount of hassle. It can take 6 to 8 months to get the necessary permits.

Vaccinations:
You will need malaria shots for some areas, but should get Hepatitis A, Typhoid and Polio. Conditions of hygiene in the interior can be somewhat primitive.

Tax and insurance:
If you register with the tax office you will pay around 15%. Get private medical insurance as Argentinian hospitals are expensive.

Wages:
Variable, depending on experience and qualifications. Expect about £750 a month in contracted employment or about £20 an hour or less outside Buenos Aires.

Accommodation:
If you want a flat you usually have to pay a two month deposit with rent at £300 to £350 a month. You will be better off staying in a pensione (digs to you).

Useful contacts:
The British Embassy and the British Council. Note that the British Council does not give English courses.
Language Training Center for Management, Maipu 742, Piso 8°H, Buenos Aires I006.
International Schools have a centre at Arcos 1830, 1428 Capital Federal.
Instituto Cultural Argentino-Britanico, Calle I2, No 1900, La Plata.

Austria

Vienna, gently decaying and gerontocratic, has something of the atmosphere of Bournemouth in mid-winter. Young people tend to emigrate to Germany in search of better prospects. Vienna is fascinating for its museums and architecture. You will need a good knowledge of German. Expect stiff competition from resident foreigners. Now that Austria is a member of the EU, you can apply for jobs in state schools, but you will find work teaching children or business people. Summer camp work is also a possibility. The scenery is marvellous and there are many places worth visiting (Salzburg is a must). Food and drink are very good, but you will find the country expensive. As it is an EU country you will be able to transfer social security credits back to the UK. Use form E303. This applies to all EU Countries.

Entry requirements:
For EU country citizens, no work permit is required, however, as in all EU countries, after three months you must apply for a residency permit/identity card. The situation for non-EU country citizens is more complicated requiring work permits etc.. See your local Austrian Embassy or Consulate.

Vaccinations:
Nothing to worry about here.

Tax and insurance:
Get health insurance. Income tax and social security can take 40% from your salary.

Wages:
£10 to £12 an hour or more at good institutes. Contracted employees can expect £850 a month or more.

Accommodation:
Expect to pay around £350 a month for a one-bedroom flat.

Useful contacts:
The Austro-British Society, Wickensburggasse 19, 1080 Vienna.
Business Language Center, Charles La Fond & Co., KEG, Trattnerhof 2, 1010 Vienna.
English for Children, Kannalstrasse 44, PO Box 160, 1220 Vienna.

Bahrain

Perhaps the most liberal of the Oil States. That said, prepare for a culture shock. Mixed classes and women teachers are acceptable; smoking in public during Ramadan, alcohol at any time except in your own home, eating pork or using your left hand at the table are not. Choose your lifestyle; live as an expat or try to learn a little Arabic and make some local friends. Respect Islam at all times. Electronic goods are cheap. You must have some qualifications to be able to teach. Bahrain is an island with a population of some 2.3m. Apart from oil, there is an aluminium smelting industry and the island has become a centre for banking and commerce: a sort of Islamic Cayman Islands. Take great care over contracts etc. before you leave home.

Entry requirements:
UK nationals born in the UK do not need visas. Other nationals may need a No Objection Certificate before entering. Three and five day visas can be issued on arrival which gives your employer time to make arrangements, including the work permit required for all nationalities. You will also need to take a medical check-up. Check with your local embassy before leaving as to any new bureaucratic wrinkles.

Vaccinations:
Hepatitis A, Polio and Typhoid.

Tax and insurance:
No tax. Rejoice. Get health insurance. It can be obtained locally at reasonable rates, but do get it.

Wages:
Salaries range from £125 to £135 if you have a certificate, and from £135 to £165 if you have a diploma. Hourly rates for part-time work range from £1.50 to £1.90.

Accommodation:
For a flat, you will have to pay three months rent in advance. Rent for a two bedroom flat will be from £45 to £70.

Useful contacts:
The British Council, AMA Centre, (PO Box 452), Manama 356, Tel. 261555.
Bahrain Computer & Management Institute, PO Box 26176, Manama. Tel. 293493.
Gulf School of Languages, PO Box 20236. Manama. Tel 290209.

Bangladesh

There is a great demand for English teachers, but you will need money of your own for funding. There is a teaching centre in Dhaka run by the British Council. They recruit in the UK. Part-time work is possible, but mainly outside the capital. This is a very poor country with low wages but low living costs. Work permits are difficult to get. You will need to have secured a position, confirmed by a letter from your employer and then apply to the Indian Embassy. Don't hold your breath in anticipation. Sanitation is poor in the capital, so take lots of the necessary pills with you. The cool season lasts from September to November. The rest of the year is rain, monsoon and heavy humid heat. Expect sea flooding if it's raining. Or even if it is not. You may end up teacher training.

Entry requirements:
Everybody needs a work permit and an entry permit. It is illegal to work on the three month tourist visa. You will not like it if you are caught.

Vaccinations:
Hepatitis A, Polio, Tetanus, Malaria, Meningitis, and Yellow Fever. Rabies is also a good idea, as is Typhoid. Your doctor may recommend others.

Tax and insurance:
Get health insurance. Lots of it. No information on income tax.

Wages:
Low.

Accommodation:
Quite easy to find due to a surge in the construction industry. On the other hand, it will cost you in the region of £300 a month. The British Council has accommodation for its teachers.

Useful contacts:
Try to get information from the British Council.

Belgium

Good beer, in fact, very good beer. Brussels has sometimes been compared to Swindon for exciting night life. Be aware of the social distinctions between the Walloons and the rest. In spite of the enormous number of language schools and language teaching, there is no shortage of teachers. There are opportunities in private primary teaching. Expect competition from the spouses of expats and EU officials. A useful thing to do is to register as a freelance teacher with the British Council, giving proof of qualifications (degrees, etc.). Failing this, go to a university and pin up a notice somewhere (student's union?). Summer camps are also a possibility. One good thing is that you will be nicely placed for weekend trips to Holland, France, Luxembourg and Germany. Culturally fascinating in itself but also for its proximity to other highly civilized places.

Entry requirements:
For those from outside the EU, apply to your local embassy with a letter confirming employment. EU nationals; as for Austria.

Vaccinations:
Take a hangover remedy with you.

Tax and insurance:
Sticky. Most people register as self-employed. You will have to deal with your own tax and social security payments. Expect to contribute about 30%. Do this in the beginning and avoid hassle. Some do try to work illegally and declare nothing. Belgian tax inspectors are singularly lacking in a sense of humour. Remember form E303 (re. Austria). Get health insurance.

Wages:
Private teaching can earn you £17 an hour. Otherwise expect from £10 to £13 an hour.

Accommodation:
Don't expect help from your employer. Rents run from £200 a month outside Brussels to £300 in the capital.

Useful contacts:
British Council, rue de la Chaité 15, 1210 Brussels. Tel. 2 227 0840.
Berlitz Language Centre at Britslei 15, 2018 Antwerpen and Leuvenselaan 17, 3300 Tienen Linguarama, Avenue des Artes, Kunstlaan 19, 1040 Brussels. Tel. 217 9055.
Brussels Language Studies (BLS), rue du Marteau 8, 1210 Brussels. Tel. 2 217 2373.
* Most schools will want an interview at the school.

Botswana

As English is the official language, demand is low. At the time of writing the political situation renders this country a dangerous place to be. Check with the Foreign Office. Employers prefer locals to foreigners. Be prepared for a culture shock. Female teachers may encounter social problems. Scenery marvellous, wild life exuberant, shame about the politics. There is also a crime problem. Teachers are often recruited through the Teachers for Botswana Recruitment Scheme. Contact the British Council in Manchester. You will need recognised qualifications, the more impressive the better. Recruitment takes place twice a year. Cost of living is cheap.

Entry requirements:
An entry permit can be obtained on production of a return ticket and proof of sufficient money. This is valid for 30 days. After that, you must obtain a renewable work permit from the Department of Labour.

Vaccinations:
Hepatitis A, Malaria, Polio, Tetanus and Typhoid. As in all sub-Saharan Africa, beware of AIDS.

Tax and insurance:
Get health insurance. Although it sounds awful, making out a will is a wise precaution. No information on income tax.

Wages:
For those with a degree, expect £450 a month or so. Postgraduates can get up to £600 a month.

Accommodation:
Most state schools will subsidise accommodation. A fee of 15% is usual. There is a great shortage of housing. A flat (subsidised) could cost from £70 to £110, while a private flat will run from £260 to £430.

Useful contacts:
Contact the British Council in Manchester and the Foreign Office.

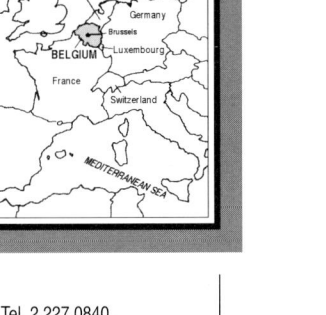

Brazil

With cultural traditions ranging from West African, through Portuguese, French, Italian, German and Arabic, for diversity you need go no further. Food and drink are excellent. The people are friendly and open. Brazil still has many problems due to unequal distribution of land and money. There is a crime problem in Rio de Janeiro and São Paulo, but other cities suffer from it to a lesser degree. São Paulo (Sampa, to the initiated) is an enormous city of 14m inhabitants. Rio is still living on past glories and is, sadly, no longer the paradise it once was. Brasília is full of opportunities for the teacher and is a less stressful place to live than either Rio or São Paulo. Try other, less known cities away from the three mentioned above. Do not miss Carnival, in fact, do a Carnival before you die. You will not regret teaching in this country.

Entry requirements:
This is the downside. It will be up to you to arrange a work permit. This can take from 4 to 6 months. You can find work and pick up your visa in a neighbouring country (Paraguay is the usual choice). Be prepared for enormous amounts of red tape. Try not to leave home without your permits etc..

Vaccinations:
Cholera, Hepatitis A, Polio, Typhoid, Malaria (especially in the Amazons) and Yellow Fever. There is a noticeable incidence of AIDS so take care, especially during Carnival.

Taxes and insurance:
Tax will vary from 12.5% to 25%, and there is also a social security deduction (INPS). Get health insurance. Local policies do not usually cover dental treatment.

Wages:
You can expect approx. £220 a month for full time work. Private classes can be lucrative, but beware of possible tax problems. Salaries are paid 13 times a year.

Accommodation:
This varies enormously from city to city, state to state. Some schools will offer subsidised accommodation. Expect to pay around 30% of your salary for a (generally) unfurnished flat.

Useful contacts:
The various branches of the British Council vary from the astonishingly incompetent to the surprisingly efficient. Take your pick. At the last count there were 45 branches of Cultura Inglesa all over the country. In Brasília, try the Independent British Institute (Instituto Britanico Independente) at SHCGN 703, Area Especial s/n°, Brasília DF 70730-700. Tel. 55 61 322 8373.
The British Council has a leaflet, "Teaching English in Brazil" which will give a list of approved schools (LAURELS etc.).

Brunei

This is a country of a quarter of a million people whose ruler donated a TV to every household. Find it on a map first. Remember this is an Islamic state. There is a great, and officially sanctioned, demand for EFL. You will need a degree and at least two year's experience, but will get loadsamoney. Get an International Driving Licence or a local one. There is almost no public transport, but schools may offer the loan of a car. Be prepared for a weekend of Friday and Sunday. There are no seasons to speak of and temperatures range from 24°C to 30°C. It may get a bit rainy and humid, but generally has a pleasant climate. You are in the middle of S.E. Asia and well placed for further travel. Malay is the official language. You could do a lot worse than teaching in this politically stable and pleasant country. Respect local laws at all times. There are restrictions on alcohol and dress. Forget alcohol.

Entry requirements:
You will need proof of a job offer with which you must apply to the Brunei High Commission. Do all job hunting before leaving home. On arrival, you will get a stamp on your passport for a stay of length at the Immigration Officer's discretion. Private sector teachers will need their employer to apply for a Labour Licence as well as a work permit.

Vaccinations:
Hepatitis A, Polio, Yellow Fever and Typhoid.

Tax and insurance:
Usually no income tax. Get health insurance and check-ups (medical and dental) before you go.

Wages:
A fluctuating exchange rate makes it difficult to give exact figures. Usually between £14,000 and £35,000 p.a. tax free plus air fares and other perks. You will not starve.

Accommodation:
Usually provided or subsidised. A three-month deposit is usually required for a flat. Be sure of details in your contract. Rent may run to £700 a month otherwise.

Useful contacts:
The Ministry of Education (Old Airport, Berakas, Bandar Seri Begawan 1170).
The British Council, English Language Centre, 45 Simpang 100, Jalan Tungku Link, Bandar Seri Begawan 3192.
Contact CfBT Education Services, 1 The Chambers, East St, Reading RG1 4JD.

Bulgaria

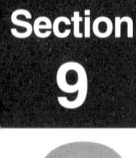

Education is taken very seriously in this country. Be prepared to work very hard. You may expect a rewarding experience, but must be prepared for failures in various sectors (food supply, energy supply, transport, etc.). Bear in mind that everyone is trying hard in Bulgaria, so do your bit. You will not regret it. Never compare a Bulgarian to a Turk, as there are serious cultural differences. Since the fall of communism, the country has gone through many difficulties, but is now forging ahead. You will be in a somewhat disturbed part of the world. The political situation in neighbouring countries is unstable. The scenery and countryside is marvellous. The cuisine is good too, excellent if you like garlic. Winter can be abysmal at times. Visit the Black Sea resorts if you can. Bear in mind that a nod of the head means "no", and a shake means "yes".

Entry requirements:
You will need an entry visa from the Bulgarian Consular Service in your country. Your school will help you with the rest of the paperwork. You will need to send the original certificate of your degree plus two letters of academic reference. See contacts below.

Vaccinations:
Hepatitis A, Polio, Typhoid and Tetanus.

Taxes and insurance:
No information on income tax. Get health insurance. If you have a UK passport and an NHS card you will have access to all medical treatment.

Wages:
Around £100 a month. Remember that your air fares will be paid, furnished accommodation and holidays. You may also get a bonus paid in $US or £GBP. This is above the salary paid to highly qualified nationals.

Accommodation:
Provided in most cases.

Useful contacts:
From September, through the Central Bureau and the British Council; The Bulgarian Ministry of Education, 18 Boulevard Stamboliisky, 1540 Sofia. Tel. 2-8481. The British Council in Sofia can provide a list of schools. 7 Tulova Street, 1504 Sofia.
Business & Accountancy Private High School, 3 Kamen Petkov St., Plovdiv 4000 New School of English, 13 Serdika St., Sofia.
Alliance, Centre for Teaching of Foreign Languages, 3 Slaveikov Square, 1000 Sofia; Institute of Tourism, Park Ezero, 8000 Bourgas.

Cambodia

A huge demand for teachers. The political instability and the general lawlessness makes this a dangerous place to live and work. The people are friendly and the cuisine is excellent. The scenery is almost beyond description. Casual work can be found without great difficulty, but contracts are usually obtained through volunteer aid organisations, such as; VSO, USAID etc.. Business English is also in great demand but expect a bias to US English. You will be well placed for other countries in S.E. Asia. French is widely spoken. The climate is tropical monsoon; heavy and humid. Cambodia is now a totally despoiled paradise, trying desperately to get itself together. It will be a sobering experience. Travel restrictions in force.

Entry requirements:
A visa will be arranged by your employer for full-time contracts obtained before arrival. Working on a business visa is possible. This can be arranged on arrival at the airport. Don't try working on a tourist visa.

Vaccinations:
Yellow Fever, Polio, Hepatitis A, Malaria and Typhoid.

Tax and insurance:
No information on income tax. Get health insurance covering repatriation.

Wages:
Ranging from £4.50 an hour if unqualified to £7.50 to £16 an hour if qualified.

Accommodation:
Can be expensive. Usually £250 a month for a flat or small house. Situation very fluid.

Useful contacts:
Australian Centre for Education (ACE), PO Box 860, Phnom Penh, Cambodia. Tel. (18)810443.
American School for Language Arts, Piey Sianouk Raj Academy, Phnom Penh. There are opportunities in other cities, but the instability of the situation makes recommendations difficult.

Chile

In spite of Pinochet, this is the most politically mature country in South America. The economic growth rate is now around 10% and unemployment is around the 5% level. It also has some of the best wine in the world. Competition is tough, and you must have qualifications and experience. You will have to show a high degree of competency. The recent trade agreements (MERCOSUR) have meant that demand for EFL is high. Foreigners may not teach in the state sector without a qualification from a Chilean university. There are some 30 schools around the country, the best being in Santiago. Other cities may prove more receptive and less competitive. The country is 175km by 4,300km. The mountain ranges boast excellent skiing facilities, and the coast (at least in the north) has some good warm beaches.

Entry requirements:
Apply for permits and visas before arriving. Applying for a work permit after arrival will mean that you must prove that you intend to stay for a minimum of one year. Don't try working on a tourist visa.

Vaccinations:
Hepatitis A, Polio and Typhoid.

Tax and insurance:
Get health insurance. Tax runs at around 10%.

Wages:
Minimum wage is set at around £250 a month for teachers on contract. If qualified you may expect from £5 to £7 an hour.

Accommodation:
Don't expect too much help from schools. Hotels are cheap and will offer long-term rates. If you want a flat, expect to pay around £250 a month, with a month's deposit and a month in advance. Rooms will be about £80 to £160 a month or more.

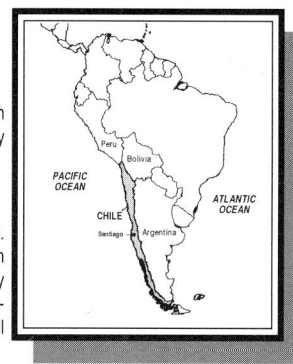

Useful contacts:
Instituto Chileno-Britanico de Cultura, 3 Norte 824, Casilla 929, Vina del Mar. Tel. (32) 971061.
Let's do English, Villa Vicenio 361, Office 109, Santiago. Tel. (2) 632 4984.
Redland School, Camino El Alba 11357, Las Condes, Santiago. Tel 2-214 1265.

China

The bureaucracy will drive you crazy. A fascinating experience awaits you, but you may not wish to extend your contract. 200 million students are learning English. There are no official private language schools. You will either be a Foreign Teacher (under 25 with a degree) or a Foreign Expert (experienced teachers with an MA in a related field). Standard class size is 60 pupils. While facilities may often be lacking, furniture for example, the students' enthusiasm will make up for it. You will need to be inventive and resourceful. There is no doubt the experience you gain will make you a better teacher. Don't expect food as in your local take-away. That is only for the rich. No politics in the classroom, or outside it, for that matter.

Entry requirements:
Theory: teacher sorts out job and employer notifies Bureau of Foreign Experts who then send you a letter of qualification for a work visa. Practice: teacher enters country on visitor's visa and employer sorts out paperwork, hopefully, befor the visa expires. Try and sort out as much as possible before arriving. This will save grey hairs later.

Vaccinations:
Hepatitis A, Malaria, Polio, Tetanus, Typhoid and Yellow Fever.

Tax and insurance:
Get health insurance. No tax.

Wages:
From £76 to £92 a month for a Foreign Teacher. Foreign Experts may expect from £154 to £270. Teachers don't get all the perks. Experts do.

Accommodation:
Make sure that the employer (as is normal) will supply it. Very difficult otherwise.

Useful contacts:
Chinese Education Association for International Exchange (CEAIE), 37, Damucang Hutong, Beijing 100816. Tel. 10-660 20 731. This organisation will help enormously.
You will also need to contact the Chinese Embassy's Education Section in the UK; 5-13 Birch Grove, Acton, London W3 9SW. In the USA; 2300 Connecticut Avenue NW, Washington DC 20008.

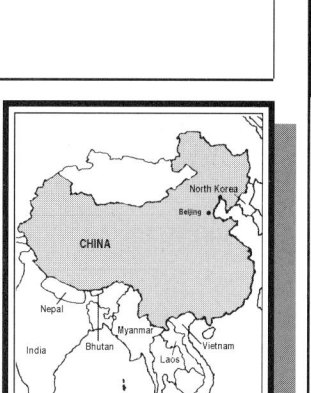

Colombia

Don't be too put off by the stories of drug barons and guerillas. You may get your pocket picked or even be mugged in the big cities, but you are very unlikely to be involved in anything else. Wages are low, but demand is high. American English is most sought after, but British English still has a snob cachet. Outside the big cities the people are warm and welcoming. Travel is best done by plane, as the mountainous terrain makes bus travel a chore. Be careful of acclimatisation in Bogota. At an altitude of 2,650m, walking and smoking are not compatible. Running up stairs is strictly out. Visit Cartagena for its history and see the gold museum in Bogota. Never get involved in politics at any level. Be prepared for a great deal of petty corruption and red tape.

Entry requirements:
You must have a work permit before entering the country. Private schools can intervene with the Ministry of Foreign Affairs, but those employed by officially approved institutions may obtain the visa (relatively) more simply. The application process will be lengthy and expensive. You will be investigated by DAS (read FBI or MI5) before a visa is granted.

Vaccinations:
Hepatitis A, Polio, Malaria, Typhoid and Yellow Fever.

Tax and Insurance:
Hospitals are expensive and so are doctors. Get health insurance. Expect 10% or more for tax.

Wages:
Wages are paid 14 times a year. Inflation makes it difficult to give dependable figures, but as a guide; £1.60 per hour, £530 to £710 a month, sometimes more.

Accommodation:
Expensive; total costs for an apartment can reach £250 per month.

Useful contacts:
Ministerio de Relaciones Exteriores, Calle 10 N° 5-51, Santafé de Bogotá. Tel. 1-281-2099 for visa applications.
Centro Cultural Colo-bo-Americano, Barranquilla, Carrera 43, N° 51-95, Apartado Aereo 2097, Barranquilla. Tel. (5) 340 8084.
First Class English Ltda., Carrera 12, N° 93-78, Piso 4°, Santafé de Bogotá, D.C. Tel. (6) 232374/232375.
Oxford Centre, AA 102420, Bogotá. Tel. (1) 674 5812.

Costa Rica

Safe but quite expensive. Wonderful scenery. Physically beautiful people. Poor facilities and mixed ability classes. The government has recently decided to start teaching English in primary schools. This has greatly increased demand for teachers. Work permits are very difficult to obtain and most people work on a visitors' visa, even for long stays. Work may be found by volunteering assistance and then making contacts. It is such a pleasant country that you may well end up staying for much longer than you had planned. You will be well placed for further travel to the rest of Central America, and also for North and South America.

Entry requirements:
As getting a work permit is not a realistic possibility, a visitors' visa will suffice.

Vaccinations:
No definite information, but Hepatitis A, Malaria, Typhoid and possibly Yellow Fever would all be prudent.

Tax and insurance:
No definite information. Get health insurance.

Wages:
£250 to £300 or more per month.

Accommodation:
£60 to £120 a month for a shared flat. Employers sometimes help out.

Useful contacts:
The Instituto Britanico, PO Box 8184-1000, San Jose. Tel. 256 0256.
World Education Forum, PO Box 383-4005, San Antonio de Belen, Heredia. Tel. 239 2245.

Croatia

The political situation is still a little unstable. Check with your local government for updates. A great demand for English. Full-time contracts are normal. Job finding may be a little problematic if unqualified, but there are opportunities for private lessons. Beautiful scenery and an island dotted coastline. The British Council can provide a list of schools. Good towns to look for work are; Zagreb, Karlovac and Varazdin. Sample Slivovitz (plum brandy) in moderation, as the hangover can be crippling.

Entry requirements:
UK or Irish citizens need no visa, but everyone else does. Jobs arranged in advance will mean your prospective employer sends you a Labour Permit to present to your local embassy. It may be possible to fix something up after arrival.

Vaccinations:
Hepatitis A, Polio and Typhoid.

Tax and insurance:
Tax will be deducted by your employer. Health insurance is a good idea. UK nationals have access to medical and some dental treatment.

Wages:
£320 to £480 per month paid in Deutschmarks. More is possible if better experienced.

Accommodation:
Hard to find and expensive. A bedsit could cost £160 while a flat will cost £200 a month with up to six month's rent in advance. Rents are usually paid in hard currency. Your employer may help with finding a place.

Useful contacts:
British Council, Ilica 12/1, PO Box 55, 10000 Zagreb. Tel. 1 273491.
Services for Open Learning (SOL), North Devon Professional Centre, Vicarage St, Barnstaple, Devon EX32 7BH. Tel. (01271) 327319. This institute is good for contacts in most of Eastern and Central Europe.
Linguar Centar, Miroslava Krleze 4c, 47000 Karlovac. Tel. 47 621900.
Skola Stranih Jezika, Cesarceva10, 42000 Varazdin. Tel. 42 215055.
Vern Lingua, Senoina 28, 10000 Zagreb. Tel. 41 428548.

Cuba

In deep trouble after the fall of the former Soviet Union, but tourism is on the increase and providing some money. Good food if you are a foreigner or rich. Spectacular scenery outside the capital, and crumbling architectural marvels within it. The economy has suffered greatly from the USA's blockade and the lack of the former Soviet Union's support. The country and the people deserve better.

Entry requirements:
See your local Cuban Embassy for details.

Vaccinations:
The usual tropical ones are a good idea.

Tax and insurance:
No tax. Health care is free, but insurance is prudent.

Wages:
Wages are set by the government. Private schools may pay a small salary in US dollars, which you can use on the black market.

Accommodation:
Hard to find.

Useful contacts:
The Project Trust, The Hebridean Centre, Ballyhough, Isle of Coll, Argyll PA78 6TE. Tel. (01979) 230444.
Universidade de Cienfuegos, Departamento de Inglés, Carretera a Rodas, Km 4, Cuatro Cam. Cienfuegos 55100.

Cyprus

Bear in mind that this island is divided between Turkey (no private language schools, few job prospects) and Greece (English is the second language, poor job prospects even so). Government policy protects Cypriot nationals for employment and you will not be able to find work in the state sector unless you speak Greek, and even then you will find it difficult. There are private schools in the Greek part, and these are a possibility. There will be much competition from English speaking ex-pats who have settled on the island. 77% of the population is Greek speaking Orthodox Christian and 18% are Turkish speaking Muslim. The remaining 5% are Armenian, Maronite, Latin and other minorities. Climate is typical Mediterranean. The mean January temperature is 10°C on the central plain and 4°C in the mountains. In July and August the mean temperatures are 22°C in the mountains and much higher on the plain. Snow is frequent in the mountains in winter.

Entry requirements:
It is illegal to work on a tourist visa. To qualify for a work permit, you must have a degree in English Literature or English Language. Locals will always be considered before you. See Useful Contacts below.

Vaccinations:
Nothing special here. Check with your doctor.

Tax and insurance:
Variable. Good health services available.

Wages:
Around £5 to £6 an hour.

Accommodation:
You may have to pay a month's rent in advance for a flat. Rent will be around £190 to £250 a month. Rooms are difficult to find.

Useful contacts:
For Cyprus and many other places try this Internet site: http://www.isp.acad.umn.edu/istc/Work/TEFL/Europe.html. To advertise your services in Greek Cyprus: Cyprus Mail (PO Box 1144, Nicosia) or Cyprus Weekly, (PO Box 4977, Nicosia 1306). International Language Institute (ILI), 12 Richard & Verengaria Street, Limmassol. Tel. 371017.
Massouras Private Institute Ltd, 1 Liperti St, Flat 103, Paphos. Tel. (61) 246118/244288.
The British Council, 3 Museum Street, (PO Box 5654), 1387 Nicosia. Tel. 2 442152.

Czech Republic

Warm friendly people and excellent beer. The chief problem here is the competition. It is such a good place to live and work and demand is so high that to succeed, the more qualifications, the better. The government recruits through its Embassies for primary and secondary schools outside the capital. You could advertise in a paper (see Useful Contacts below). The cost of living is low and public transport in the capital is good and cheap. Prague is rich in history; don't miss the Old Town Hall clock - a 15th century astronomical marvel. Traffic is a problem, but the underground system is good. You will get much better treatment in the state sector than in the private one. Private lessons are a good source of supplementary income.

Entry requirements:
A work permit is essential. It will take your employer about 2.5 months to obtain the visa. You could apply for work and residency permits after checking out the job situation, but it will take the same amount of time, during which you will be unemployed.

Vaccinations:
Nothing special here. Check with your doctor.

Tax and insurance:
UK nationals have access to hospital and other treatment. Get health insurance anyway. Taxes are 25 to 30%.

Wages:
£120 to £140 after tax in the state sector. A private school may get you £190 to £300 a month. Private classes run to £3.50 an hour.

Accommodation:
Difficult. One month's rent deposit and £70 a month rent. Some employers may help.

Useful contacts:
The Prague Post (Na Porící 12, 115 30 Prague 1). Fax. 2-24 87 50 00. An information service for tourists and teachers is: Infotel s.r.o. (PO Box 67, 110 01 Prague 1). Tel. 2-69 24 237. Accent Language School, Radmila Prochazkova, Bitovska 3, 140 00 Prague 4. Tel. 420 420 595. This school offers free R.S.A. courses if you make a commitment for three years. Bell School, Nedvezska 29, 100 00 Prague 1. Tel. 2 781 5342. International House Brno, Sokolska 1, 602 00 Brno. Tel. 5 41 24 0493. International House Prague, Lupacova 1, 130 00 Prague 3. Tel. 2 27 5789. The British Council, Narodni 10, 12501 Prague 1. Tel. 2 249 91 21 79. International Training Solutions Ltd, Colleen Kelly, Thamova 24, 186 00 Prague 8. Good information source for Hungary, Latvia, Lithuania, Poland, Russia Slovakia, Slovenia and the Ukraine as well as the Czech Republic.

Denmark

Since indulging in a lot of raping, pillage and other healthy outdoor pursuits in the early part of the millennium, the Danes have calmed down a lot and are now very civilized indeed. You should like pickled fish, butter and pork. Probably the best beer in the world. Danes can drink anyone else (except perhaps a Finn) under the table at any time, and they do. Frequently. Having said this, the Danes are probably the most law-abiding and sober (behaviour-wise) people in Europe. They are a friendly people. Much unemployment makes it difficult to find a job. Teaching in the public sector requires good Danish. The private sector is small, but Business English is a possibility. Copenhagen is a delightful capital, rich in history and culture, but very expensive.

Entry requirements:
If you are not an EU national, forget about work permits.

Vaccinations:
Nothing special here. Check with your doctor.

Tax and insurance:
Tax is an eye-watering 50%. Non-EU nationals should get health insurance, although excellent free treatment is available.

Wages:
Fixed by law. £20 an hour. Danish teachers are amongst the highest paid in the world as they are expected to teach any subject to any pupil.

Accommodation:
High standards. £900 to £1,100 a month. Outside Copenhagen, rent is less.

Useful contacts:
Cambridge Institute Foundation, Vimmelskaftet 48, 1161 Copenhagen. Tel. 33 13 33 02. This institute has 40 branches around the country.
Center for Undervisning, arhous amt, Ulla sørensen, Vesterkovvej 4, 8660 Skanderborg. Tel. 86 511511. Offers many services.
European Education Centre Aps (Inlingua), Lyngbyvej 72, 2100 Copenhagen.
Berlitz International, Vimmelskaftet 42a, 1161 Copenhagen.
Babel Sprogtræning, Vordingborggrade 18, 2100 Copenhagen.

Ecuador

If you are planning to work your way around South America, start here. Easy to find work. The currency is worth little outside Ecuador, so just spend and enjoy; the cost of living is low. Classes start early, around 07:00hrs, to avoid the mid-day heat. 49% of the population live on the coastal plain between the Andean Sierra and the Pacific. The country has the highest active volcano in the world (Cotopaxi, 5,896m). The climate on the coast is hot and humid, but Quito (high in the mountains) has spring-like days and chilly nights, with heavy rain in the afternoon. Politically stable. Friendly people. Spectacular scenery. Quechua is spoken, but Spanish is the main language.

Entry requirements:
Although it is illegal to work on a tourist visa, many people do. UK nationals can stay 6 months on a tourist visa; USA nationals, 9 days. You must produce a return air ticket to work legally. No swapping of visas so if you get a job you will have to nip over the border to sort out the paperwork.

Vaccinations:
Hepatitis A, Polio, Typhoid, Malaria and Yellow Fever.

Tax and insurance:
Tax is 7% for all teachers, legal or not. Don't leave home without health insurance.

Wages:
Unqualified teachers will get from £150 to £250 a month. The British Council only employs qualified teachers and is fussy, but pays £600 a month.

Accommodation:
No great problem. Rooms, flats and houses are available. £40 a month for a room in a shared flat or £100 for your own flat. Two month's rent deposit.

Useful contacts:
Centro de Estudos Interamericanos/CEDEI, Casilla 597, Cuenca. Tel. 7-839003. E-mail: ptamariz@ecua.net.ec.
International Benedict School of Languages, PO Box 09-01-8916, Guayaquil. Tel. 4-444418.
Experimento de Convivencia International del Ecuador, Les Embleton, Hernando de la Cruz 218 y Mariana de Jesus, Quito. Tel. 593 2 551937/550179. This is the most prestigious private school in the country.

Egypt

In spite of recent negative publicity due to Islamic extremists, most Egyptians will be pleased to see you and employ you. Respect Islam at all times. Demand for Business English is high, but jobs are also available teaching young learners. Beware of different attitudes to learning. This is not a western-type culture. Exercise caution in accepting job offers; look before you leap. Apart from the narrow strip of land flanking the Nile, most of the country is desert. Cairo (El Qahira) is an enormous city of almost 10,000,000 inhabitants. Disorganization is incredible, but it all seems to work somehow. Simply putting up bilingual posters can get you a job. Women will find less difficulties here than in other Islamic countries. Cost of living is low.

Entry requirements:
Work permit applications are only processed in Egypt. Most job-seekers enter the country on a one month tourist visa, get a job and then apply for a permit to the Ministry of the Interior. It takes about two weeks to process.

Vaccinations:
Hepatitis A, Polio, Typhoid, Malaria and Yellow Fever.

Tax and insurance:
Between 5 and 7%. Get health insurance.

Wages:
£5 to £9 an hour in a school or for private lessons £13 to £20.

Accomodation:
Don't expect western standards. Cheap and easy to find, but basic. A room may cost up to £100 a month.

Useful contacts:
Job advert placing: Cairo Today, 24 Syria Street, Mohandasin, Cairo. Tel. 2-349-0986 or
Maadi Messenger, Port Said Road and Road 17, Maadi, Cairo. Tel. 2-351-2755.
Community Services Administration, CSA Road 21, Maadi, Cairo. There are notice boards here. Put up a bilingual poster.
International Language Learning Institute, 34 Talaat Harb Street, 5th Floor, Cairo. Tel. 748355/392 7244.
International Language Institute (ILI), 2 Muhammed Bayoumi Street, Heliopolis, Cairo. Tel. 202 2291 9295 (affiliated with International House).

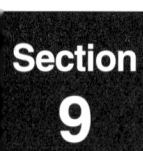

Estonia

Try to get there before winter starts in November. Now progressing rapidly after independence. Of the other Baltic states (Latvia and Lithuania) this is the most progressive. There are 1,512 lakes, and forest covers 36% of the country. Population is just over 1.5m. The capital is Tallinn (population approximately 500,000). The language is related to Finnish. Good luck if you try to learn it. Estonians are heartily glad to be independent from the former Soviet Union, and have a strong sense of national identity. An interesting country to visit. See the 13th century citadel, the former Governor's Palace (1767 -73) and the Toomkirik Cathedral (13th to 15th centuries).

Entry requirements:
Quite easy to get a work permit after getting a job.

Vaccinations:
Nothing special here.

Tax and insurance:
No information on income tax. Health insurance is a good idea.

Wages:
Low. You will need to take private classes to make ends meet.

Accommodation:
Expect to pay around £125 a month for a flat.

Useful contacts:
The British Council will provide a list of schools.

Finland

Second only to Belgium for exciting night life. Alcohol is very expensive, but the Finns are legendary drinkers. The binge type. More than 90% of Finnish children learn English in school. Relatively easy to find work, and contracts may include travel and accommodation. Look for work in the spring. The second language is Swedish with English being the third. You could try to learn Finnish... on the other hand, Chinese might be easier. This is the third most sparsely inhabited country in Europe (after Iceland and Norway). There are 60,000 lakes and forest covers 65% of the country. Interestingly enough, Finland is still emerging from the sea and its land area increases by 7km^2 each year. The cost of living is high. The Finnish sense of humour would be interesting if found.

Entry requirements:
EU nationals have no problems. Non-EU nationals must apply for a permit (once a job is found) and it could take up to three months. There is a US placement service (see Useful contacts, below).

Vaccinations:
Nothing special here, unless there is one against cold weather.

Tax and insurance:
Excellent health care available. The tax rate is 25%, you may be responsible for arranging payment.

Wages:
45 minute lessons pay from £10 to £17 each. Salaries range from £870 to £1,200.

Accomodation
Easy to find and schools frequently help. One/two month's rent deposit and £135 rent which will include heating (for which you will be very grateful).

Useful contacts:
US placement service: InterExchange, 161 Sixth Avenue, Suite 902, New York, NY 10013 will help graduates with experience find jobs.
Federation of Finnish-British Societies, Puistokatu 1 b A, 00140 Helsinki. Tel. 0-639 625.
The British Council will provide a list of schools.
Richard Lewis Communications, Itatuulenkuja 10 B, 02100 Espo, Helsinki. Tel. 455 4811.
International House, Mariankatu 15 B 7, 00170, Helsinki. Tel. 0 90 177 266.
Liguarama Suomi, David Eade, Annankatu 26, 00100 Helsinki. Tel. 9/680 3230.

France

Parisians can be somewhat less than polite, but, outside the capital, people are friendly if you try to speak French. Expensive. Commercial experience is a great advantage in finding a good job as recent legislation has forced companies to put by 1% for training. A widely varying country where people can be very different from region to region. The culture continues to be about as insular as Britain's, but entry into the EU has changed attitudes. Paris is as fascinating as ever, with museums, art galleries, historic sites etc.. An unmissable country for any roving EFL teacher, in spite of rude Parisian waiters. Treatment of employees may leave something to be desired.

Entry requirements:
EU nationals will have to apply for a carte de sejour within three months of arrival. If applying before this time, you must show you have enough money to live on. It may take several months to come through. Find a job first. Non-EU nationals will find it difficult. There are heavy fines and deportation for those (non-EU nationals) found working on a tourist visa.

Vaccinations:
Nothing special here. Garlic is very healthy.

Tax and insurance:
Variable, depending on status. Around 20% would seem to be a guide. Hospitals and doctors may prove expensive so health insurance is a good idea.

Wages:
From £10 to £14 an hour, £700 to £1,000 a month. Universities may pay up to £26 an hour.

Accommodation:
Outside Paris, cheap (£210 a month), but in Paris expect to pay around £410 for a one bedroom flat. Everything is cheaper outside Paris.

Useful contacts:
The British Council, 9/11 rue de Constatine, 75007 Paris. Tel. 49 55 73 00. They have a very useful publication; Teaching English as a Foreign Language in France. International House, Centre d'Anglais d'Angers, 16 rue de Deux Haies, 49000 Angers. Tel. 41 87 01 06.
Linguarama, 6 rue Roland Garros, 38320 Eybens. Tel. 76 62 00 18.
Executive Language Services, 20 rue Sainte Croix de la Bretonnerie, 75004 Paris. Tel. 44 54 58 88.

Georgia

Enormous demand for native speakers. It may be possible to pick up jobs merely by visiting the country. Georgians are not to be confused with Russians; they are good-time, happy, hospitable people. The country is known for its fruit and wines. It also has the largest manganese mines in the world. It is still a poor country, but rapidly getting richer. Some areas may not be safe yet; check with your local External Affairs service. Some nice places to visit on the Black Sea coast. If you don't make much money, you'll enjoy your stay.

Entry requirements:
No big problems. Schools just ask for visa extensions for their teachers. Flexibility is the keyword.

Vaccinations:
Hepatitis A, Polio and Typhoid.

Tax and insurance:
Taxation is at source. The rates are low. Health insurance is essential.

Wages:
£2 to £2.50 an hour in private schools. Private lessons can get up to £6.25 an hour. You will need to give private lessons to make ends meet.

Accommodation:
£95 to £125 a month for a flat.

Useful contacts:
The British Council Resource Centre in Tblisi.

Germany

Now that it has been discovered that frowning uses more energy than smiling the Germans find it admissible to have a sense of humour. The high level of teaching in schools means that the commercial sector is the best bet. You should have some commercial experience, especially with financial matters. If you can speak German, so much the better. You may expect high earnings if working as a freelancer, but will not have good benefits or health cover. Official status means an awful lot of bureaucracy. Contracts are usually for a year. Germany is an expensive place to live, but this is the richest country in the EU and the level of technology and access to information is awesome.

Entry requirements:
EU nationals have no problems. Non-EU nationals should apply for work permits before travelling. The process is easier than in other EU countries. Everybody has to go through a process of registering with local authorities.

Vaccinations:
Nothing special here.

Tax and insurance:
30% on earnings over £4,800 p.a. British nationals can work for two years tax-free. Freelancers must pay 13% for social security. Freelancers should get health insurance.

Wages:
For a 45 minute lesson, you may expect around £10. If freelance, £20 to £50.

Accommodation:
Schools may give assistance, but expect to pay around £400 a month with three months rent as a deposit. Some landlords will take double rent until the deposit is paid.

Useful contacts:
For US citizens; the USIA Fulbright Program, 809 UN Plaza, New York NY10017-3580 and German Academic Exchange Service (DAAD), 950 Third Avenue, 19th Floor, New York NY 10022.
English Language Teaching Associations: Dresden - 351 2210 172; Frankfurt - 6131 479 915; Hamburg - 40 796 7996 Munich - 89 692 4670; Ravensburg - 752 222 109; Rhine - 220 313 266; Stuttgart - 70 238 084. These places will give advice and lists of schools in the area.
British Council, Hardenburgstr. 20, 10623 Berlin. Tel. 3110990.
International House, Poststrasse 51, 20345 Hamburg. Tel. 40 459 520.

Greece

One quarter of all candidates for Cambridge First Certificate and Proficiency exams worldwide are from Greece. The demand is there. That said, competition is fierce and you must be a graduate. The state school system is weak and children go to private language schools. Standards in private schools have risen, and the cowboys are disappearing. Even so, exercise caution. Possibly the most beautiful country in the world to live in, although pollution in Athens is a big problem. Food is excellent and the cost of living is quite low. Students have to work very hard in the state schools and in their (essential) private lessons, so may not always be present in both body and spirit. It can get cold in north-eastern Greece in winter. Facilities of all types may be basic, but it should be fun.

Entry requirements:
EU nationals must get a teacher's licence first. You will need to have your degree certificate translated into Greek and, once in Greece, get a chest X-ray. Non-EU nationals must obtain a letter of hire sent to an address outside Greece and then apply to the nearest Greek consulate for a work visa. It takes about two months to process a visa, once obtained you should then follow the rest of the procedure above.

Vaccinations:
Nothing special here.

Tax and insurance:
Around 20% (if you declare everything). Health insurance a good idea.

Wages:
Expect around £4 an hour, but this could go up to over £6. If freelance, double.

Accommodation:
Expect to pay around a third of your salary. Schools usually help. Don't expect a phone (the waiting list for installation is ten years). Heating bills will surprise you in winter.

Useful contacts:
British Council, Ethnikis Amynis 9, P0 Box 50007, 54013 Thessalonika. Tel. 30 31 235 236.
Featham School of English, Mrs. A. Featham, P0 Box 12, 50 Ep. Marouli St., Rethymon 74100. Tel. 30 (0) 831 23482.
Kakkos School of English, Constantine Kakkos, A Par. Papastratou 5, Arginio 30100. Tel. 30 641 23449.
Enossi Foreign Languages (The Language Centre), Stadiou 7, Syntagma, 10562 Athens. Tel. 3230 356/3250081.

Hungary

Great demand; it is necessary to have passed an exam in English to enter university. Pay is poor and competition in the capital is strong. Try the provinces. If you can speak Hungarian it will greatly increase your employment chances. The language ranks with Finnish as an intellectual challenge. Food excellent, if on the heavy side. Excellent wines. The capital, Budapest, is in reality, two towns; Buda (the old town with hills and woods) and Pest (modern shopping and business centre). It has the best and cheapest public transport system in Europe. There are some thirty spa baths to relax in between lessons.

Entry requirements:
UK and Irish citizens do not need a visa. Everybody else does. Regulations are very strict and your employer must produce a letter saying that no Hungarian is available to do the job. Arrange permits before travelling. A health certificate will also be necessary.

Vaccinations:
Tetanus.

Tax and insurance:
Find out if your salary is gross or net. 25% can go in taxes. Health insurance is advisable and should include repatriation.

Wages:
State sector; £90 to £115 after tax. Private lessons approximately £175 a month after tax. Which works out at £2.50 to £4 an hour.

Accommodation:
Hard to find, even when schools help. Rents from £115 to £330 for a small flat. £400 a month for a large flat. One month's rent deposit.

Useful contacts:
Central European Teaching Program (CEPT), Beloit College, Box 242, 700 College Street, Beloit, Wisconsin 53511-5595, USA. Tel. 1 608 363 2619.
International Business School Budapest, 1115 Etele u. 68, Budapest. Tel. 203 0050.
International House Budapest, Language School and Teacher Training Institute, PO Box 95, 1364 Budapest. Tel. 1 212 4010.
Living Language Seminar, Fejer Gyorgy u 8-10, 1053 Budapest. Tel. 1 326 3251.

India

India is rapidly encroaching on China to be the most populated country on Earth, (estimates suggest the population will be larger than China by 2002). Among the educated classes, English is virtually a first language but opportunities for foreign teachers to work in any comfort are few and far between. The majority of the small number of foreign teachers in India teach in private language schools, which in themselves are few and far between. Teaching in the state sector is possible but facilities are often terrible with a lack of resources, space and, some would say more importantly, pay. You may also find that your local colleagues lack ability, enthusiasm and finance. As a result you are quite likely to be little depressed about it all. There are a number of agencies that place volunteer teachers, some of which require candidates to be self funding.

Entry requirements:
Work permits are generally not easy to obtain, however, you should try and get an offer from an employer and submit this to the Indian Embassy. It has been known for teachers to volunteer to teach in state schools by walking through the front door and offering their services.

Vaccinations:
Hepatitis A, Polio, Tetanus, Malaria, Meningitis, Yellow Fever and Typhoid. Any others your doctor may recommend. Rabies is a good idea too if you are likely to be in an isolated area. Also, it is worth being aware of the risk of AIDS. However, I personally know a lot of people who have gone there and returned!

Tax and insurance:
Get health insurance, as much as you can. Income tax exists but little is known.

Wages:
Low could be an understatement, very few teachers find it possible to survive on a local salary alone.

Accommodation:
Some schools will provide accommodation, but you can expect to pay up £100 per month for somewhere that you might want to live.

Useful contacts:
English Joint Assistance Centre 6-17, Gurgaon District, Haryana 122002 India. This organisation can arrange placement for self funding volunteers.
Jaffe International Education Service, Kunnuparambil Buildings, Kurichy, Kottayam 686549, India. Tel/Fax: (481) 430470. This organisation arranges placement for volunteers in various parts of India.
Teaching Abroad, 46 Beech View, Angmering, Sussex BN16 4DE. This organisation also arranges short term placement for volunteers.

Indonesia

In terms of population, Indonesia ranks fifth in the world. Oil revenues keep the economy going and the demand for English is high, particularly in the commercial sector. Having a certificate will make finding a job easier, but just asking around may result, such is the demand. Don't expect sophisticated resources and plush classrooms. Food is superb. Cost of living is low. The language is easy to learn. Indonesians are warm and welcoming. The country is actually the world's largest island group comprising of 5 main islands and 30 smaller archipelagos. Total 13,677 islands. The island of Jawa has 115 volcanic peaks, of which 15 are currently active. Climate is equatorial, with an average temperature of 27°C. Hot and humid. The chief religion is Islam.

Entry requirements:
Tourists visas are valid for two months, but don't work on them. If caught you will be deported and refused further entry into the country. If arriving as a tourist, show an onward ticket to avoid hassle. You must have a letter confirming employment with which you apply for the work permit from outside the country. As a tourist, you could do this from Singapore.

Vaccinations:
Hepatitis A, Polio, Typhoid, Malaria and Yellow Fever.

Tax and insurance:
Tax is around 10%. Health insurance a good idea.

Wages:
Around £600 a month for full-time work. More is possible.

Accommodation:
You may need to pay a full year's rent in advance, but schools often help out with an interest-free loan or may even offer you somewhere (sometimes with a phone).

Useful contacts:
The British Institute (TBI), Ken Trolland, Plaza Setiabudi 2, Jalan HR Rasuna Said, Jakarta 12920. Tel. 62 21 525 6750.
UCLES approved ELS International, Jalan Tanjung Karang 7 c d, Jakarta Pusat. Tel. 323211.
Indonesia-Australia Language Foundation (IALF), Wisma Budi, Suite 503, Jalan HR Rasuna Said Kav c-6, Kuningan, Jakarta Selatan 12940. Tel. 521 3350.
Oxford Course Indonesia (OCI), Jalan Cempaka Putih Tengah 33C-2, Jakarta Pusat 10510. Tel. 21 424 3224.

Israel

The very high number of English speakers in Israel means that native-speaker teachers are not in great demand. The political situation does not make this a safe or attractive country in which to work. The British Council operates some schools, but recruits locally. Voluntary work may be available, but in the most dangerous areas.

Entry requirements:
You can enter the country on a tourist visa, but must be sponsored by a school to apply for a work permit.

Vaccinations:
Hepatitis A, Polio and Typhoid.

Tax and insurance:
Tax up to 40%. If you are not Jewish, you must have your own health insurance.

Wages:
£12.50 to £17.50 an hour.

Accommodation:
Cheaper outside Tel Aviv, but still quite expensive.

Useful contacts:
The British Council at; 140 Hayarkon Street, (PO Box 3302), Tel Aviv 61032. Tel. 3 522 2194 14-706 Al-Nasra Street, (PO Box 355), Al-Rimal. Gaza City. Ein Sarah Street, (PO Box 277), Hebron.
British Council Teaching Centre, Al-Nuzha Building, 2 Abu Obeida Street, (PO Box 19136), East Jerusalem.

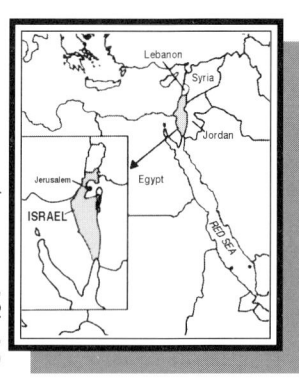

Italy

Great demand, but great supply. Exercise caution in accepting positions. Some schools claim to provide more than they actually can. Food and drink excellent. A marvellously varied and attractive country where things seem to happen in spite of attempts at organisation. That said, the centre-north can be a model of social organisation. The south, less so. As far as historical interest goes, where else could you find such riches? Warm-hearted, friendly people. Some schools had to close during the recession of the mid 90s, and demand slackened a little. However, the state school teaching of English is inadequate which creates a demand. The north can be cold in winter.

Entry requirements:
UK and Irish citizens will have no problems. Employers will provide assistance. All other nationalities should apply before leaving home. It won't be easy.

Vaccinations:
Nothing special here.

Tax and insurance:
20% tax plus 10% for social security. Non-EU nationals should get health insurance.

Wages:
After tax; £600 to £800 a month.

Accommodation:
Easy to find but expensive. A small flat may cost £400 a month in a big city. Two or three month's rent for a deposit. Schools may help with the search.

Useful contacts:
The British Council, Palazzo del Drago, Via Quattro Fontane 20, 00184 Rome. Tel. 6 478141.
The British School of Bari, Via Celentano 27, 70121 Bari. Tel. 080 524 7335.
The English Language Studio, Via Antonio Bondi 27, 40138 Bologna. Tel. 51347394.
Regency School, Via dell' Arcivescovado 7, 16121 Turin. Tel. 11 562 7456.
The English Centre, Via P Paoli 34, 07100 Sassari, Sardinia. Tel. 79 232154.

Jamaica

The official language is English, but there are jobs teaching new residents, business clients and remedial English. This is an enjoyable place to teach and live, but certain areas are not very safe due to a regrettable attitude towards foreigners (particularly white foreigners). However, this is not an attitude shared by the majority. Jamaica continues to be a pleasant place to live and work. The island itself is beautiful. There is a train which goes across the island allowing stunning views of the mountainous interior. Bus trips are an adventure; Jamaican bus drivers appear to have learnt driving with Finnish rally drivers.

Entry requirements:
No entry visa. A work permit is required, but this should be applied for in Jamaica.

Vaccinations:
Hepatitis A, Polio, Yellow Fever and Typhoid.

Tax and insurance:
Income tax is 25% and there is a consumption tax of 15%. Health insurance is a good idea.

Wages:
Around £10 an hour, say £7,400 a year. For private lessons you can earn £15 to £37 an hour.

Accommodation:
Hard to find. One or two month's rent as a deposit. As a guide; £500 to £1,500 for a flat.

Useful contacts:
Teach in Jamaica programme organised by BUNAC, 16, Bowling Green Lane, London EC1R 0BD. Tel. 0171 251 3472. Fee of £245 for programme.
Language Training Centre Ltd., 24, Parkington Plaza, Kingston 10. Tel. (809) 926 3756.
Target English Associates, 9a Duquesnam Avenue, Kingston 10. Tel. (809) 929 2473.

Japan

No shortage of schools, but a lot of competition. The more qualifications, the better. A very expensive place to live. Japanese students are the hardest working in the world. Night schools serve as a back-up to the excellent state system, but almost all students attend at least one because competition for university entrance is so stiff. This is no place for the semi-professional - a high standard is needed and expected. You must have a degree to get a work visa. Beware of culture shock and prepare yourself well for a very strong and ancient culture that has little in common with the west, even now. There are many wonderful things to see in Japan; Kyoto is not to be missed, Hokkaido has some beautiful sights and Sapporo is almost un-Japanese. Visit Akihabara market in Tokyo if you are into consumer electronics.

Entry requirements:
Australian, New Zealand and Canadian citizens can work on a working holiday visa obtainable in the respective countries. Everybody else needs a work visa. You need a degree and must be sponsored by a school or person in Japan. This person/entity applies to the Ministry of Justice in Tokyo so as to obtain a Certificate of Eligibility. With this, your passport, a photo and an application form you apply to your local embassy. It should take around a week. You could look for a job on a tourist visa, go to Korea until the paperwork is done and then go back.

Vaccinations:
Nothing special here.

Tax and insurance:
Around 10% income tax. Health insurance may be provided by your school, but is a good idea anyway.

Wages:
Usually about £2,000 a month. Lessons go from £20 to £40 an hour.

Accommodation:
You may find landlords are reluctant to rent to foreigners. Rent can vary from £500 to £800 a month. There may be a deposit of up to £3,000. Schools often help out and it may even be included in your contract.

Useful contacts:
Council on International Educational Exchange, 52 Poland Street, London W1V 4J4. Tel. 0171 478 2010. They administer the JET (Japanese Exchange and Teaching) scheme in the UK. In the USA, contact the Japanese Embassy in Washington, 2520 Massachusetts Avenue NW, DC 20008. Tel. 800-INFOJET/202 939 6772/3.
ICA Kokusai Kaiwa Gakuin (International Conversation Academy), 1 Mikasa 2 Building, 1-6-10 Nishi.
CIC English School, Kawamoto Building, Imaddegawaagaru Nishigawa Kaeasumadori, Kamigyo-ku, Kyoto.
Kobe Language Centre, 3-18 Wakinoharnacho, 1-chome, Chuo-ku, Kobe 651. Tel. 78 2614316.
Sumikin-Intercom Inc., Andrew Vaughan, 7-28 Kitahama 4-Chome, Chou-ku, Osaka 541. Tel. 06 220 5500.
Cosmopolitan Language Institute, Yashima B Building 4f, 1-8-9 Yesu Chuo-ku, Tokyo 104.

Jordan

Lots of demand since a certain amount of liberalisation was introduced. The state system cannot cope very well. Do all job hunting and visa work before leaving home. Situated next to Israel with a small coast to the Red Sea, most of the country is desert. The chief export is phosphate rock, though oil shipping helps the economy. Before going, check on the political situation. The climate is hot and sunny, though in winter there may be snow in the mountains.

Entry requirements:
If you get your contract before travelling, your employer will sort out the paperwork. Otherwise, you will pay a certain amount each year for a work permit (£300).

Vaccinations:
Hepatitis A, Polio, Typhoid and Yellow Fever.

Tax and insurance:
No information on tax. Get health insurance.

Wages:
Full-time; £900 a month. Lessons go for around £10 an hour. Private language schools (except the British Council) pay less.

Accommodation:
The refugee situation makes it difficult to find. One year's rent is often asked for in advance. Rents at £300 a month. Negotiate with the landlord.

Useful contacts:
The British Council, First Circle, Jebel Amman, PO Box 634, Amman 11118.
American Language Centre, Amman. Tel. 659859.
The Ahliyyeh School for Girls, Amman. Tel. 624872.
Yarmouk Cultural Centre, PO Box 960312, Amman. Tel. 6 671447.

Kuwait

Still recovering from the Iraqi invasion. The market for English teachers is not yet at the pre-invasion level, but getting there. Qualifications are very necessary. 90% of the population (approximately 1.4m) live within 10km of the Arabian Gulf. The terrain is stony with sparse vegetation. The climate is hot and humid, but frosts can occur at night on high ground. There is little rainfall. Petroleum continues to be the mainstay of the economy. Until the discovery of oil in 1938, Kuwait was a country of nomads and fishermen. At one point, due to oil, Kuwait had the third largest GNP in the world. Practically no public transport. Get a driving licence.

Entry requirements:
You will need to take an HIV and a TB test first off. After that, you must have a work permit and an entry visa. The best way to get around all this is to advertise in a Kuwaiti newspaper to get a job offer and do the rest before travelling. (Arab Times, Kuwaiti Times).

Vaccinations:
Hepatitis A, Polio and Typhoid.

Tax and insurance:
No income tax. Get health insurance.

Wages:
Expect around £15,000 a year for full-time work.

Accommodation:
Most schools help out. Rent is from £400 to £550 with a month's rent in advance.

Useful contacts:
British Council, 2 Al Arabi Street, Block 2, PO Box 345, 13004 Safat, Mansourrija.
ELU The Kuwait Institute of Banking Studies, PO Box 1080, Safat 13011.
Institute for Private Education, PO Box 6320, 32038 Hawalli. Tel. 573 7811.
Fahaheel English School, PO Box 7209, Fahaheel 64003. Tel. 3711070.

Lithuania

Few opportunities for unqualified teachers, but a few for the qualified. Foreign currency problems make material expensive and difficult to find. There are organisations which can help with placement (see Useful Contacts below). Lithuania has had a patchy history; from 1385 to 1795 it was united with Poland, then it went to Russia. It was occupied by Germany from 1915 to 1918 when the Republic was proclaimed, then it was annexed by the Soviet Union in 1940. It has been independent since the breakup of the Soviet Union and is now trying hard to make a go of things. A flat country, with a cold climate. The language is related to the Indo-European group, but was declared a 'critical' language in 1985 by the US Department of Education in the sense that the learning of it would significantly help the spread of knowledge.

Entry requirements:
UK citizens do not need a visa. The situation for other nationalities varies, but it will not be a problem once you have a job.

Vaccinations:
Nothing special here.

Tax and insurance:
No information on taxes. Health insurance advisable.

Wages:
Can start as low as £50 a month.

Accommodation:
No information.

Useful contacts:
Teaching Abroad, 46 Beech View, Angmering, Sussex BN16 4DE. Tel. (01903) 859911. This organisation recruits teaching assistants for Lithuania, Ukraine, Russia, India and Ghana. A fee will be charged.
The Lithuanian Ministry of Education and Science runs a placement scheme run by Mrs. Ausra Svilpiene, Ministry of Science and Education, Teacher Training Department, 2691 Volano Gatve 2/7, Vilnius. Tel. 2-622483.
Klaipeda International School of Languages, Mark Uribe, Zveju g.25800 Klaipeda. Tel. (3706) 3111190.
Siauliai Pedagogical Institute, P. Visinkio 25, 5419 Siauliai. Tel. 370 143 2592.

Malaysia

Strong demand for English. Openings for qualified and unqualified teachers. The country is the bit hanging off the end of Thailand, right next to Indonesia and includes a bit of the island of Borneo. Right on the end of the peninsula is Singapore. Essentially, a ridge of mountains separating the West and East coastal plains. Sarawak (the bit on Borneo) is a narrow swampy coastal belt. High humidity and a climate influenced by monsoons. Sarawak has the largest and most varied bird population in the world. Abundant natural resources have enabled Malaysia to achieve one of the highest living standards in SE Asia. Kuala Lumpur has the highest building in the world, the Petronas Twin Towers - 88 floors and 451.9m high.

Entry requirements:
Get a visa before travelling. It is possible to work on a tourist visa while waiting for the work permit. Permits are only granted to teachers with at least an MA.

Vaccinations:
Hepatitis A, Polio, Tetanus, Malaria and Yellow Fever.

Tax and insurance:
30% tax, but if you can qualify for resident status, 15%. Health insurance is a good idea, but some schools offer it.

Wages:
Salaries from £475 to £950. Private classes from £9.50 to £12 an hour.

Accommodation:
Easy to find. Rents around £200 a month. Two months rent up front and a month's rent deposit.

Useful contacts:
CfBT Education Services, 1 The Chambers, East Street, Reading RG1 4JD. Tel. (0118) 952 3900. Will recruit teachers for many countries including Malaysia.
Bangsar English Language Centre, 60-1 Jalan Ma'arof Bangsar Baru, 59100 Kuala Lumpur. Tel. 3 282 3166/68.
The English Language Centre, 1st Floor, Lot 2067, Block 10, K.C.L.D., Jalan Keretapi, PO Box 253, 93150 Kuching, Sarawak.
Centre for Promoting Language and Knowledge, University Malaysia Sabah, Temporary Campus Likas Bay, Locked bag 2073, 88999 Kota Kinabalu, Sabah.

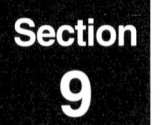

Mexico

Since Mexico joined NAFTA, demand has increased greatly. Business English, in particular, is a rapidly-growing field. Permits are almost impossible to get, but there are lots of ways around this. A certain amount of political instability is apparent in certain areas as the struggle for land reform (a long term problem in Mexico) comes once more to the fore. In general, the further away from the US border, the nicer the people. The 'mordida' (little bite - a bribe) will still solve many problems. Most officials are flexible in this respect. Do not forget that this is the home of 'machismo'. Mexicans (particularly men) are very proud people, but are also warm-hearted and hospitable. There are many worse places to be.

Entry requirements:
Marginally easier for US and Canadian citizens. The official position is implacable: practically no way. However, people do work on other's tax forms, and employers can sometimes arrange this. Beware of immigration inspectors posing as teachers so as to catch the teacher working on a tourist visa. They also pose as students to catch teachers giving private classes. To apply for a visa you will need a CV translated into Spanish, an authenticated TEFL and University qualification validated by a Mexican consulate. The process is costly.

Vaccinations:
Hepatitis A, Polio, Typhoid, Malaria and Yellow Fever.

Tax and insurance:
Get health insurance, as health care is expensive. 15% income tax.

Wages:
Around £250 a month. Private classes around £6 an hour.

Accommodation:
Look outside city centres for reasonably priced places. Expect to pay around £100 a month. You will spend between 25 and 30% of your salary on accommodation. Usually unfurnished.

Useful contacts:
Anglo-Mexican Cultural Institute, Rio Nazas 116, Colonia Cuauhtémoc, 06500 Mexico, D.F. Tel. 5 208 5547.
Colégio Internacional de Cuernavaca, Apartado Postal 1334, Cuernavaca, Morelos. Tel. 73 132905.
Universidad Autonoma de Yucatan, Fac. de Educacion, Calle 61 N° 525 (entre 66 y 68), 97000 Merida, Yuc.

Morocco

While traditionally a French and Arabic speaking country, English is in great demand. It is needed for University entrance. The number of foreign teachers in any institution cannot exceed 50% of all teaching staff. Knowledge of French would be a distinct advantage. The northern part of Morocco can be quite lush, but the rest is more and more desert-like as one goes south. The Atlas mountains and Marrakesh are sights not to be missed. Rabat and Casablanca are just big cities. Don't miss the Roman ruins at Volubilis. Although it may appear very westernised, this is still a very traditional country in the interior. Respect Islam. An interesting country to visit, if only for its history. The shrine-town of Moulay Idris is a wonderful place. Non-Muslims can only enter during daylight.

Entry requirements:
You must be offered a contract. The school then applies for a residence permit. It is better to do this before arriving. You will need your birth certificate (original), your degree diploma and teaching certificate.

Vaccinations:
Hepatitis A, Polio and Typhoid

Tax and insurance:
25% taxes etc. on a rising scale. Get health insurance.

Wages:
£4 to £8 an hour.

Accommodation:
Varies greatly. In big towns, £175 to £280 a month as a guide.

Useful contacts:
British Centre, 3 rue Nolly, Casablanca. Tel. 27 31 90.
British Council, 36 rue de Tanger, B.P. 427, Rabat. Tel. 7 76 0836.
Business and Professional English Centre, 74 rue Jean Jaures, Casablanca.
American Language Centre, 4 Zankat Tanja, Rabat 10000. Tel. 7 76 1269.

Mozambique

Slowly recovering from a disastrous civil war. Portuguese is the dominant language, but efforts are being made to make English a much more important language. VSO can help with volunteer work. The future will be promising if the country can get itself together. There are immense natural resources - coal, diamonds, tin and other metals and oil. A potentially unstable area, given the fragile stability of neighbouring countries. The people can be exceptionally welcoming and hospitable, but there is a rising crime rate.

Entry requirements:
You can get a visa through your local embassy. Work permits are obtained by the employer's application.

Vaccinations:
Hepatitis A, Polio, Meningitis, Malaria and Yellow Fever. Take all precautions against AIDS.

Tax and insurance:
Around 13%. Get health insurance.

Wages:
Around £1,100 a month.

Accommodation:
One month's rent deposit, then from £200 to £350 a month.

Useful contacts:
Skillshare Africa, 3 Belvoir Street, Leicester LE1 6SL. Tel. (0116) 254 0517.

Myanmar

Formerly Burma, this country poses a bit of a puzzle. Private enterprise and private teaching are illegal, but there is a demand for English. Teaching and teachers are tolerated (possibly because English is deemed essential) and work is possible. This is done by arranging a one-month tourist visa from home, and then extending it in Myanmar. The school will have to apply for a work permit. The country is surrounded on the North, East and West by mountain ranges of over 5,000m in height. The South is coastline. The climate is tropical monsoon. In 1987 the country was given least developed status by the UN. It had been the richest nation in South East Asia. The country's name was changed to Myanmar in 1989. The political situation is complex and unstable.

Entry requirements:
As outlined above.

Vaccinations:
Hepatitis A, Malaria, Polio, Typhoid, Tetanus and Yellow Fever.

Tax and insurance:
10% tax. Get health insurance.

Wages:
£4,000 to £12,000 a year depending on qualifications.

Accommodation:
Easily found, but limited choice. Schools may help to find it. Rents are around £200 to £350 a month. Deposits of £650 to £1350 are refundable.

Useful contacts:
Press adverts in Singapore are a good source. The local newspaper 'New Light of Myanmar' may also prove useful.

Nepal

Unless you can get a job with the British Council or the American Language Center, you will need some savings to survive. Even if you lose on the deal, the experience will be enriching and will prove an interesting addition to your CV. On the other hand, jobs are easy to find and it is a better place to work than India. Interesting voluntary work is available also. This is the only official Hindu kingdom in the world. Bringing in Indian currency is prohibited. The terrain rises from a swampy region near the Ganges to mountains of over 8,000m in height, including Everest at 8,848m. In Katmandu, the temperature varies from 40°C in May to 1.6°C in December.

Entry requirements:
Three-month tourist visas are available on arrival. Residency and work permits will be arranged by your employer. It is illegal to work on a tourist visa, but it is done. You will need to renew the visa twice a year and can only stay for 3 months out of any 12.

Vaccinations:
Hepatitis A, Polio, Tetanus, Encephalitis, Typhoid, Meningitis and Yellow Fever.

Tax and insurance:
No information on tax. Wages are so low it would hardly matter. Get health insurance.

Wages:
Local schools offer as low as £12 a month. The British Council and the American Language Center pay more realistic rates.

Accommodation:
A flat can be found by agents for a small fee. Expect £60 to £90 a month. A deposit may be required if your employer finds the flat - anything from £200. Accommodation will be found for volunteers.

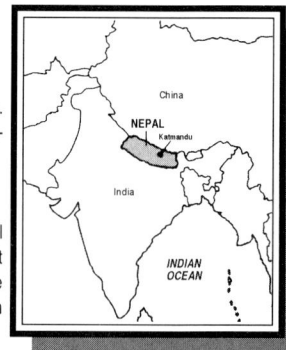

Useful contacts:
Children's Model School, PO Box 4747, Katmandu.
Three Star English School, Dhungin, Faika, Kapan, Katmandu.
America Language Centre, PO Box 58, Katmandu. Tel 1 419933.
Fill the Gap, World Challenge Expeditions Ltd., Black Arrow House, 2 Chandos Road, London NW10 6NF. Tel. 0181 961 1122.
British Council, Kantipath, (PO Box 640), Katmandu. Tel. (1) 221305.

Netherlands

Depressingly, most young Dutch people are able to speak better English than the average inhabitant of Birmingham or Bristol. Most of the opportunities are in Business English. Contracts are not usual, however, long term freelancers are acceptable. Don't expect a stable income. Possibly the best way to arrange work is through the Dutch version of 'Yellow Pages' (category; talen institut). This is possibly the most civilised country in the world, and one of the most liberal. Apart from the various attractions of Amsterdam, there is the sober and serious city of s'Gravenhage (The Hague) and the enormous port city of Rotterdam. Behave in a responsible manner, and you may well end up staying in this country. The Dutch are very tolerant.

Entry requirements:
UK and Irish citizens need no visa, but must obtain a tax number from the police when the they arrive. Any other nationalities will encounter many rules and regulations. It can take up to three months to get a work permit.

Vaccinations:
Nothing special here.

Tax and insurance:
Around 30% tax. If you pay tax, the excellent Dutch health schemes will take care of you.

Wages:
£11 to £20 per lesson, if qualified.

Accommodation:
Expensive. Expect to pay £180 a month for a flat. One month's deposit is required.

Useful contacts:
Avoc Teleninstiuut, Heugemerweg 2d, 6229 As Maastricht.
Berlitz Language Centre, Rokin 87-89, 1012 K1 Amsterdam. Tel. (20) 622 1375.
Educational Holidays, Beuksraat 149, 2565 Xz Den Haag.
Language Partners - Rotterdam, Wtc Beursplein 37, 3011 A, Rotterdam.
British Council, Keizersgracht 343, 1016 EH Amsterdam. Tel. (20) 622 36 44.

Oman

Do not expect lavish levels of pay; good, yes; extravagant, no. A popular place to teach for Westerners, as alcohol is permitted and women are employed. This is the second largest country in Arabia. It has a frontier with the Rub al Khäli (Empty Quarter) of Saudi Arabia (re: T.E. Lawrence). Expect temperatures of up to 47°C. Oil was discovered in 1964. More than 90% of the government's revenues are from oil. The country is situated on the other side of the Strait of Hormuz from Iran.

Entry requirements:
Your employer must sponsor you. Don't hold your breath waiting for a response. It may take some time.

Vaccinations:
No information. Check with local health authorities.

Tax and insurance:
No income tax. Allah akh'bah. Health insurance advisable.

Wages:
£360 to £460 per month. Check for sterling equivalent.

Accommodation:
Around £160 per month when not provided.

Useful contacts:
British Council, Road One, Medinat Qaboos West, (PO Box 73), Postal Code 115, Muscat. Tel. 600548.
Polyglot Institute, PO Box 221, Ruwi, Oman. Tel. 701261.

Papua New Guinea

There are over 800 language groups in this country. English is (more or less) the second language. Low wages and high taxes. On the other hand, a country so diversified, partially unexplored and beautiful would be hard to find. Pidgin English is a better description of the dominant language. A mountainous country (highest peak; Mount Wilhelm - 4,508m), but also has the most extensive swamps in the world. It rains a lot and the average temperature is high (33°C). Good mineral resources provide 66% of the country's income. Some areas are controlled by bandits.

Entry requirements:
Your employer will have to lodge an application with the authorities and with the immigration department of any Papua New Guinea High Commission.

Vaccinations:
Check with your local health authority.

Tax and insurance:
No information. Health insurance a good idea.

Wages:
No information.

Accommodation:
No information. If a voluntary worker, it will be provided.

Useful contacts:
VSO (Voluntary Service Overseas), 317 Putney Bridge Road, London SW15 2PN. Tel. (Enquiries Unit) 0181 780 1331.

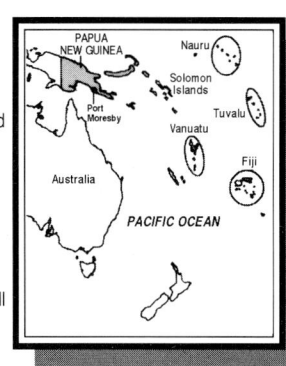

Peru

The Sendero Luminoso and other guerrilla groups make life difficult in the interior and the political situation is not entirely stable. However, most Peruvians are rather phlegmatic about politics and are hospitable pleasant people. Business English is a growth area. That said, Lima is a stressful place to live. Unemployment is high and wages are low. Demand is very high, however. The official languages are Spanish and Quechua. Ayamara is also spoken around Lake Titicaca. There are three geographical regions; the central mountains, the tropical eastern lowlands and the western coastal plains. Simon Bólivar and Jose San Martin led the country to independence in 1821 (ratified in 1842) and are national heroes of great renown. Obvious tourist sights are Machu Picchu and Cuzco. Revel in the history and sympathise with the state of the country today.

Entry requirements:
Try to get a contract before leaving home. Working on a tourist visa is out, also swapping a tourist visa for a work permit is out while in the country. Work visas are very difficult to get.

Vaccinations:
Hepatitis A, Polio, Yellow Fever, Typhoid and Malaria.

Tax and insurance:
16% tax. Get health insurance.

Wages:
£3,000 to £5,000 in private schools. The British Council pays more.

Accommodation:
£150 to £200 a month. Two month's rent deposit. Schools sometimes help out.

Useful contacts:
The British Council, Calle Alberto Lynch 110, San Isidro, Lima 27. Tel. (1) 2217552.
William Shakespeare Instituto de Inglese, Avenida dos Mayo 1105, San Isidro, Lima. Tel. (14) 221313.
Markham College, Apartado 18-1048, Miraflores, Lima. Tel. (14) 241 7677.
Asociacion Cultural Peruano Britanica, Av. Arequipa 3495, San Isidro, Lima. Tel. (1) 421 6004.

Poland

Enormous demand as Poland forges ahead in its continuing economic development in spite of having a language that (apparently) dispenses with vowels. Do beware of a certain degree of culture clash - the Poles' vision of you and your vision of the Poles may not meet. However, their enthusiasm will bridge most divides. Apart from the private and state sectors, Business English and young learners are also growth areas. The climate is one of severe winters and hot summers. The terrain in mostly flat, except to the south where there is a range of mountains. The capital, Warsaw, is rich in history. Since the break up of the former Soviet Union, the Polish have embraced capitalism with great fervour.

Entry requirements:
Apply for a work permit before travelling. You must present your degree diploma (notarised), your TEFL certificate (also notarised) and a job confirmation from your employer to your local Polish consulate. No working on a tourist visa.

Vaccinations:
Nothing special here.

Tax and insurance:
20% tax. If you have a UK NHS medical card, you will have access to medical care and some dental treatment. Otherwise, insurance is a good idea.

Wages:
State sector - £80 to £190. Private sector - £300. Overtime is offered in some schools at £7 to £9 an hour. Accommodation and airfares may be included in the contract.

Accommodation:
If not provided, difficult to find and wildly variable in price. Exchanging English lessons for a room is an option.

Useful contacts:
The British Council, Al Jerozolimskie 59, 00-697 Warsaw. Tel. (2) 628 74 01/3.
The Eagle English Centre, Al Stanow Zjednoczonych 26 m 25, 03-965 Warszawa.
International House - Krakow, ul. Pilsudskiego 6, lp, 31-110, Krakow. Tel. 12 219440.
Warsaw School of Commerce, Kursy Handlowe, al Chlodna 9, Warszawa.

Portugal

This country was stuck in a 1930s time warp until 1974 and the surprisingly peaceful revolution. There are still areas stuck in the past, but the country as a whole is forging ahead with a strong economy very well managed. Portuguese bureaucracy can be a cause of high blood pressure. Food and drink excellent. There are many opportunities outside Lisbon, but the capital is still the place to go for variety. The north is the richest part with the most 'old money'. Everything south of the Tagus is rather poor (but fascinating for tourism) until the Algarve (south coast) is reached. Take the train down the Valley of the Douro for the most interesting train ride of your life. There are more cinemas per head of population in Lisbon than in New York.

Entry requirements:
After three months, EU nationals must get a residency permit. A letter of confirmation from your employer will make this process infinitely easier. Non-EU nationals should remember the comment on bureaucracy above and get a contract before travelling.

Vaccinations:
Nothing special here.

Tax and insurance:
After nine months you must start to pay tax; around 20%. EU nationals can get health care, but it is a good idea to have insurance.

Wages:
£6 to £8 an hour, £480 to £675 a month. Salaries are paid 14 times a year normally, but you will get a bonus after 12 months if this does not apply.

Accommodation:
Ridiculously expensive in Oporto and Lisbon due to a housing shortage and outdated rent laws. Flats there can cost up to £350 a month. Try sharing. Two month's rent is required as a deposit.

Useful contacts:
British Council, Rue de São Marçal 174, 1294 Lisboa codex. Tel. 347 6141.
IF - Inglês Funcional, Ap 303, 2430 Marinha Grande. Tel. 44 568351.
British Council, Rua do Breyner 155, 4050 Oporto. Tel. 200 5577.
Lisbon Language Learners, Rua Conde Redondo 33-r/c Esq., 1100 Lisboa.
Cambridge School, Avenida de Liberdade 173-4, 1200 Lisboa. Tel. 352 74 74.
Centro de Estudos IPFEL, Rua Edith Cavell 8, 1900 Lisboa.

Romania

Still recovering from the Ceaucescu dictatorship. Don't expect to save money. Look for private lessons with the rich. Take savings. The language is Latin based with some Slavic influences - not difficult to learn. The country is host to the World Dracula Congress every year. Take lots of material with you; photocopiers and videos are rare items. Nice resorts along the Black Sea coast. The country will be in a sad state for some time to come, but the experience will be useful. Take lots of warm clothes for winter.

Entry requirements:
A tourist visa on arriving will suffice. After getting a job your employer will apply to the local authorities with you for a work permit.

Vaccinations:
Hepatitis A, Polio and Typhoid.

Tax and insurance:
No information on tax. UK nationals have access to medical and some dental care. All other nationalities should get insurance.

Wages:
Private classes £3 to £8 an hour. Schools will pay local rates of about £50 a month, perhaps with a supplement.

Accommodation:
If on a volunteer scheme, it will be provided. Otherwise, the inferior housing on offer may take up all your salary.

Useful contacts:
International House, B1. Republicii 9, 1900 Timisoara. Tel. 56 190593.
Open Doors School of English, Michelle Penta, str. L. Blaga nr. 4, Timisoara. Tel. 40 56 194252.
PROSPER-ASE Language Centre, Suite 4210, et. 2, Calea Grivetiei 2-2A, Bucharest. Tel. (1) 211 7800.
British Council, Calea Dorobantilor 14, Bucharest. Tel. (1) 210 5374.

Russia

Still a great demand. Good places to look for work are in the Siberian oilfields and other industrial districts. Moscow and St. Petersburg continue to be good options. Salaries are low, but private classes can be lucrative. 20m people tune in to the BBC English lessons every day. Street conditions and the crime rate make, at least, Moscow a place in which to take some care. The housing situation is out of control. Try for digs. If all else fails, you can at least take the legendary Siberian Express all the way to Yokohama and teach in Japan.

Entry requirements:
It is easy to get a tourist visa. However, if you have a Russian contact or employer, get a business visa. This will get you discounts on purchases. Alternatively, you could try for a multiple entry visa from home with an invitation from a Russian company. The invitation need only be for 'consultation'. Fee; £100.

Vaccinations:
Nothing special here.

Tax and insurance:
If paid in hard currency - 40%. Get health insurance. UK nationals have access to state hospitals.

Wages:
£300 to £375 a month, £8 to £12 an hour - £19 an hour is possible in big cities for private lessons.

Accommodation:
Agencies will charge a fee of around £125 to find a flat. The rent will be around £300 a month. A bedsit may run to £180. Deposits are usually one month's rent.

Useful contacts:
Benedict School, Novosibirsk 630099. Tel. 3832 23 24 33.
System-3 Language and Communication, Arnold Rubinstein, Kantemirovskaya Street 16 #531, Moscow 115522. Tel. 9210141.
Moscow International School, 2nd Ulitsa Marynoy Rosschi 2a, Moscow.
Sunny School, P0 Box 23, 125057 Moscow. Tel. 95 151 2500.

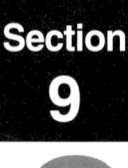

Saudi Arabia

A classic case of band-wagon jumping has created some problems - too many schools on a 'get rich quick' kick. There are many opportunities in Business English. Do not forget that there is no alcohol, men and women intermingling is out and so are women drivers. For a single man (no left-handers) it might be interesting, but if you are in a family see about funding for your children's education. Women must wear head to foot clothing in public and men must adhere to a formal dress code. Beware of unprofessional treatment by both recruiters and schools. Make sure all contracts are very firm and specific. The Arabic word 'malesh' is frequently used - it means (literally) tomorrow but actually means 'sometime in the future'. Bear this in mind when dealing with bureaucracy.

Entry requirements:
No working on a tourist visa. You must be sponsored by a company in Saudi Arabia which will do the rest for you.

Vaccinations:
Hepatitis A, Polio, Typhoid, Malaria, Meningitis and Yellow Fever.

Tax and insurance:
No tax. Get health insurance if it is not in your contract.

Wages:
Expect between £16,000 and £35,000 a year.

Accommodation:
Usually part of the contract. If not, the employer will help out.

Useful contacts:
The British Council, Al Moajil Building, 5th Floor, Dhahran Street, Mohamed Street, PO Box 8387, Daman. Tel. 834 3484.
Girl's College of Arts - General Presidency for Female Institute for Languages and Translation, c/o King Saud University, PO Box 2465, Riyadh 11451.
Riyadh Military Hospital - Training Division, PO Box 7897, Riyadh 11159.
King Fahd University of Petroleum and Minerals, English Language Centre, Dhahran 31261. Tel. 3 860 2393.

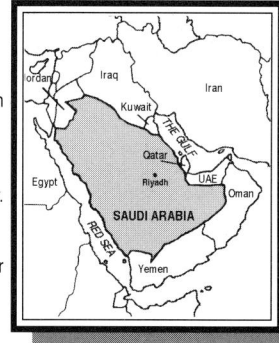

Singapore

Often called a 'fine country' - because you can and will get fined for the slightest thing. Qualifications and a conventional appearance are 'musts'. The country has also been described as a large shopping mall. On the positive side, it is clean, safe and well ordered. Contracts are a minimum of one year. You will be well placed for the rest of Asia, and also for Malaysia (over the border) and Thailand. The country is really just an island on the southern tip of Malaysia. The population is just over 2.5m. It is about the size of the Isle of Wight. High humidity. Daily temperatures range from 21° to 34°C.

Entry requirements:
You will need copies of your education certificates, medical certificates and sponsorship from an employer. You will not be able to get a visa without a letter from the employer.

Vaccinations:
Hepatitis A, Polio, Typhoid and Yellow Fever.

Tax and insurance:
Tax is 15.2%. Get health insurance.

Wages:
£900 to £2,300 a month. Hourly rates start at £9.

Accommodation:
Easy to find. Many people share. Rents around £250 a month. Three months deposit is usually required.

Useful contacts:
Inlingua School of Languages, 68 Orchard Road, 07-04 Plaza Singapura, Singapore 238839. Tel. 737 6666.
Coleman Commercial and Language Centre, Peninsula Plaza, Singapore. Tel. 336 3462.
Seamo Regional Language Centre, 30 Orange Grove Road, Singapore. Tel. 737 9044.
Morris Allen Study Centre, 1 Newton Road 02-47/49, Goldhill Plaza, Singapore. Tel. 253 5737.

Slovakia

When the former Czechoslovakia split into the Czech Republic and the Slovak Republic, a lot of the prosperity seems to have stayed with the Czechs. However, Slovakia has been coming on slowly and demand is strong. Cultural organisations will help with placements (see Useful Contacts below). There is very little crime and good opportunities for tourism (particularly if you like skiing). Wages are low, but so is the cost of living. There are many attractive features to this rather neglected country.

Entry requirements:
See Czech Republic. You will also need to undergo a medical examination.

Vaccinations:
Hepatitis A, Polio, Typhoid and Tetanus.

Tax and insurance:
No information on income tax. Get health insurance. UK nationals can get hospital treatment and other medical care.

Wages:
£160 to £190 a month.

Accommodation:
Usually provided.

Useful contacts:
SAIA, Na vrsku 8, (PO Box 108), 81000 Bratislava 1. Tel. 7-53 33 010/53 33 762.
This agency will help place teachers in the state system. Also contact the local Slovak Embassy.
Akademia Vzdelavania, Gorkého 10, 815 17 Bratislava. Tel. (7) 367 580.
American Language Institute (ALI), Drienova 34, PO Box 78, 820 09 Bratislava. Tel. 7-293 114.
Foundation for a Civil Society, V Záihradfách 29A, 811 02 Bratislava. Tel. (7) 580 2491.
VSMU, Katedra Jazykov, Ventúrska 3, 813 01 Bratislava. Tel. (7) 533 2306.

Slovenia

Although it was part of the mess that was once Yugoslavia, it managed to stay out of the regrettable lapse into barbarism that the rest of the country indulged in. The economy is strong, and a well-established ELT industry is thriving. Slovenia is situated in the northern part of the former Yugoslavia and has borders with Hungary, Austria and Italy to the North, and Croatia to the South. The cost of living is low and your salary will be paid in Deutschmarks.

Entry requirements:
You will need a work visa before travelling. Some daring souls work on a tourist visa (unofficially).

Vaccinations:
Nothing special here.

Tax and insurance:
Tax depends on status and experience. Health insurance is a good idea; if you are a UK national you will have access to some medical and dental care.

Wages:
£6 to £8 an hour.

Accommodation:
Usually provided. If not - £60 a month plus a month's deposit. Six month's deposit may sometimes be asked.

Useful contacts:
Jeizikovni Center International, Gornji Trg 4, 1101 Ljubljana. Tel. (61) 125 5317.
Krona Plus D.0.0., Trzaska Cesta 2, 1111 Ljubljana. Tel. (61) 126 1266.
Yurena, Marjana Kozine 49A 8000 Novo Mesto. Tel. (68) 341434.

South Korea

Despite recent financial setbacks, the demand is still strong in this fascinating country. Known as the 'Land of the Morning Calm', you may not be so calm when starting your classes at around 7:00 in the morning. Everybody works and studies hard. Parents have been known to spend up to US$10,000 on their children's English classes. English is studied by those wishing to enter an American university (i.e. most students). Food is excellent - get used to 'kimchi' - rather like sauerkraut, but made with garlic and peppers as well as cabbage. It is almost a staple food. Life here moves at a frantic pace (at least in Seoul) but there are still some poor people.

Entry requirements:
No longer the easy casual option of the past. If caught working on a tourist visa, you will be deported and your employer may be put out of business. Try to do it in advance - your employer will need to send you a contract, documents of sponsorship and a copy of their Business Registration Certificate. Send these, along with your CV, an authenticated copy of your degree diploma (notarised by a consular official), two photographs and the required fee to your local Korean embassy.

Vaccinations:
Hepatitis A, Polio, Typhoid and Tetanus.

Tax and insurance:
Perhaps tax-free (depending on field and school), if not, between 4 and 11%. Get health insurance. Your employer may pay for this.

Wages:
Expect around £950 a month. Private lessons may net you around £30 an hour, but this is viewed as illegal working.

Accommodation:
It is usual to give a year's rent as a deposit. Expect around £500 a month for an unfurnished flat. Most schools will help out with this.

Useful contacts:
Dong-A Educational Foundation, 50-10 Jayang-Dong, Dong-ku, Taejon 300-100. Fax 42 624 7294.
YBM/ELSI Si-Sa-Yong-0-Sa Language Institutes, Yeoksam Heights Building, 2nd Floor, 642-19 Yeoksam-dong, Kangnam-gu, Seoul 135-081. Tel. 2 538 4380.
Keimyung Junior College, 2139 Dae-Myung Dong, Nam-ku, Taegu 705-037. Tel. 53 620 2648.
Korea Foreign Language Institute, 16-1 Kwancheol-Dong, Chongro-ku, Seoul. Tel. 2 739 8000.

Spain

Now one of the stronger economies of Europe, it still retains a great deal of charm. Be aware of the internal differences - the North-East is still poor and backward; Madrid and surrounding areas are sophisticated; the South-East (Catalunia) is almost another country with sober and hard-working people. Take a walk down 'Las Ramblas' in Barcelona on a Sunday morning and see how liberal they are too. There is a lot of cut-throat competition among schools, and some unprofessional treatment. Take care with contracts. The economic growth has led to many imbalances and allowed a lot of petty corruption. Even so, it is a delightful country. The language is among the easiest to learn of all.

Entry requirements:
EU nationals can get a residency permit with a copy of their contract. Non-EU nationals may need up to two years to get a permit.

Vaccinations:
Nothing special here.

Tax and insurance:
Variable tax rates. Get health insurance. Residents pay 15% tax plus 6% social security. Tax is only paid after nine months in the country.

Wages:
From £475 to £570 or even £650 upwards in some cases. Around £10 an hour in Madrid.

Accommodation:
Expect to pay around 25% of your salary. Two month's deposit and from £300 to £500 a month. Sharing is a good idea.

Useful contacts:
The British Council, Miguel Angel, 1 dpdo, Alfonso X, 4, 28010 Madrid. Tel. (1) 337 3592.
Calle Amigo 83, 08021 Barcelona. Tel. (3) 209 6090.
Aljarafe Language Academy, Crta Castilleja-Toamres 83, Toamres, Sevilla.
Britannia School, Leopoldo Lugones 3-1B, 33420 Lugones, Asturias. Tel. 85 26 2800.
International House, Calle Zurbano 8, 28010 Madrid. Tel. 34 1 310 13 14.
York House, English Language Centre, Muntaner 479, 08021 Barcelona. Tel. 32 113200.

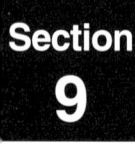

Sri Lanka

While this may be Arthur C. Clarke's paradise, for the rest of the population there is a civil war going on (though mainly in the north and east). Check the political situation before you go. The demand is there, encouraged by the government to help bridge the gap between the Sinhalese and the Tamils. Wages will be very low, so you should take some savings. All this said, the island is incredibly beautiful. The beaches are idyllic, the mountains are majestic - all in all an entirely inappropriate place for a civil war and terrorist activity.

Entry requirements:
You will have to get a visa. Your employer will arrange the work permit. Consult your local embassy.

Vaccinations:
Hepatitis A, Polio, Typhoid, Malaria and Yellow Fever.

Tax and insurance:
No tax in the first year. Health insurance a good idea.

Wages:
About £2,000 p.a. British Council employees can get £11,000 to £13,000.

Accommodation:
A year's rent up front and about £250 a month.

Useful contacts:
The British Council, 49, Alfred House Gardens, (PO Box 753), Colombo 3. Tel. (1) 581171/2.

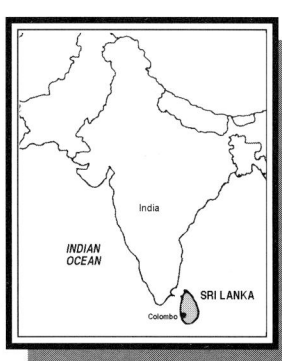

Sudan

What was once the country with the best education system in Africa, is now in trouble after its civil war. Education budgets have been cut and an Arabicisation has led to a decline in education and an official halt in foreign teacher recruitment. Jobs are there, but not in abundance and not well paid. This is the largest country in Africa. 75% of the population are employed in agriculture. The usual restrictions in Islamic countries apply.

Entry requirements:
An entry visa takes about three weeks to process. Arab country nationals do not need a permit, but everyone else does. Get all the paperwork done before leaving home.

Vaccinations:
Yellow Fever, Hepatitis A, Typhoid, Tetanus, Meningitis and Polio.

Tax and insurance:
Tax is 20%. A very good idea is some sort of long-term travel insurance, as well as health insurance.

Wages:
£5 to £10 an hour for private work. Otherwise negotiate (haggle).

Accommodation:
Rent around £40 a month with six month's deposit. Easy to find and schools often help out.

Useful contacts:
Sudanese Embassy, 3 Cleveland Row, St. James, London SW1A 1DD. Tel. (0171) 839 8080.

Swaziland

English is the official language of this, the smallest country in Southern Africa. Although 70% of the population is employed in agriculture, there are reserves of asbestos, iron ore and coal. Most opportunities are in the state sector, though there are some private schools. The borders to the north are with Mozambique and the south with South Africa. This is a fairly quiet rural country. The culture is definitely male-dominated.

Entry requirements:
No visa for Commonwealth citizens. Everyone must get a work permit. This is obtained by the employer showing a certificate that no Swazi citizen or resident can do the job.

Vaccinations:
Hepatitis A, Polio, Tetanus, Typhoid and Yellow Fever.

Tax and insurance:
If you get more than £220 a month you will pay tax. Maximum rate is 33%. Health insurance a good idea.

Wages:
£200 to £250 a month in the state sector. Private schools should pay more.

Accommodation:
Cheap places are difficult to find. A good place will cost you around £200 a month. One month's rent deposit. State schools will usually provide accommodation.

Useful contacts:
Skillshare Africa, 3 Belvoir Street, Leicester LE1 6SL. Tel. (0116) 254 0517. A placement organisation for Lesotho, Botswana and Mozambique as well as Swaziland.

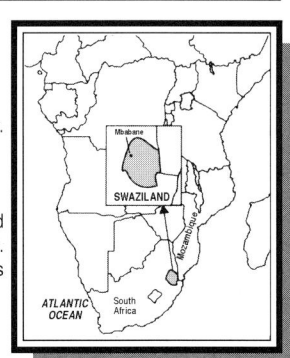

Sweden

While most Swedes already speak very good English (the state school system is very good), there are opportunities with the Swedish equivalent of the Open University - the Folk University. There is a demand for Business English, but you will need a good network of contacts. Swedes sometimes smile in spite of themselves - they are a serious and somewhat dour people, but also take enormous pains to be fair and just. A highly civilized country and a safe (if expensive) place to live and work.

Entry requirements:
EU nationals need no visa. Non-EU members will need to already be resident or married to a resident or Swedish citizen. The Folk University only recruits UK nationals.

Vaccinations:
Nothing special here.

Tax and insurance:
Between 25 and 33%. Health insurance is a good idea.

Wages:
The Folk University offers £1,000 a month minimum. This is a living wage in Sweden.

Accommodation:
You will spend between 25 and 35% of your salary on a place to live. £230 to £320 a month including (mercifully) hot water and heating. No deposit.

Useful contacts:
Folkuniversitetet, Nina Saevig, Box 26152, 100 41 Stockholm. Tel. 46 8 679 2950.
The British Institute, Stochholm, Michael Eyre, Hagatan 3, 511348 Stockholm. Tel. 46 8 341200.

Switzerland

Six hundred years of peace and civilization, having culminated in the invention of the Cuckoo Clock (Orson Welles), should be discounted. The country runs like, well... clockwork. Sober and serious people (you can get fined for singing in the street), the Swiss can be divided into three types; German Swiss (very correct), French Swiss (a little less correct, but still Swiss) and the Italian Swiss (looked down on by the rest, but still Swiss). There is a demand for Business English, but you must be qualified and the entry requirements are stringent (see below). The country is an expensive place to live, but has many cultural attractions - the museums in the big cities and the architecture are magnificent. And there is always the skiing.

Entry requirements:
As the EU has still not reached acceptable Swiss standards, everybody has to go through the same procedures. There are two types - Premis A, for seasonal employment, and Premis B, for contracted employment of a year's duration. Your employer must prove that no Swiss can do the job and must guarantee a minimum number of hours. This can be difficult to obtain and has often been refused.

Vaccinations:
Nothing special here.

Tax and insurance:
Tax is around 15%. Get health insurance.

Wages:
As a guide - £20 an hour.

Accommodation:
Expensive. Schools may help out. One month's rent as a deposit. If living in an apartment, there are strict rules about not making noise after 22:00. Even taking a shower is out after this time.

Useful contacts:
Basilingua Sprachschule, Birigstrasse 2, 4054 Basel. Tel. 61 281 3954.
Markus Frei Sprachschulen, Neugasse 6, 6300 Zug. Tel. 41 710 4240.
Village Camps, 1296 Coppet. Tel. (22) 776 20 59 (summer address; Chalet Seneca, 1854 Leysin). Tel. (25) 34 23 38. A language summer camp.
Bell Language School, 12 Chemin des Colombettes, 1202 Geneva. Tel. 00 41 22 740 20.

Syria

A country with a rich and distinguished history is, today, far too involved in Middle East politics. However, it is still much safer than some of its neighbours (Lebanon, Israel, Iraq). Demand is there, both in private tuition and through schools. This is a poor country. The usual restrictions for Islamic countries apply. 60% of the country is desert but the coast has a Mediterranean climate. The khamsin wind at the beginning and end of summer can raise temperatures to 49°C. The temperatures in Damascus range from 7°C in January to 27°C in July. Credit cards, cheque books and traveler's cheques are not used.

Entry requirements:
Get an entrance visa from your local Syrian Embassy. A residence card may be acquired by registering on an Arabic course.

Vaccinations:
No information; check with embassy.

Tax and insurance:
No information on tax. Get health insurance.

Wages:
£3.75 to £6.25 an hour. Expect about £280 a month. There is an annual bonus of £2,000 to £6,000.

Accommodation:
Around £200 a month in Damascus. Renting a room may cost around £60 a month. It is illegal to cohabit with a person of the opposite sex if not legally married.

Useful contacts:
Al Razi English Language Centre, PO Box 2533, Damascus. Tel. 457301.
American Language Center, PO Box 29, Rawda Circle, Damascus. Tel. 963 11 3327236.
Al Kindi English Language Centre, 29 May Street, Damascus.

Taiwan

There is a demand for English, but positions are not advertised outside the country. Try to arrive in the summer as schools close, just in time for the summer school jobs. There are many jobs for teaching young learners. Being able to speak Chinese is not an advantage. American English (and accents) are preferred. The economy continues to flourish as local industries become more sophisticated. The political regime is firmly right-wing and maintains close ties with the USA. The country is an island just off the south coast of the People's Republic. Previous plaintive claims to be preparing to invade the PR have now hushed. The opposite may happen one day. Cost of living is high.

Entry requirements:
Very complicated. You must have a degree and be sponsored, have a contract of employment and documents of approval from the Ministry of Education. Working on a tourist visa is out, and if you find work you will have to leave the country to get the paperwork finalised. Try to do it all before leaving home.

Vaccinations:
Hepatitis A, Polio, Typhoid and Yellow Fever.

Tax and insurance:
Schools will help with health insurance, and you may join a government scheme from £5 a month. Tax is 20% for the first 183 days. After that it's around 6-10%. A tax rebate is available for the first period after all the paperwork is sorted out.

Wages:
About £9 an hour. In-company classes may double this. Freelance teaching is not considered legal, but it can net you £13 to £22 an hour.

Accommodation:
A room in a shared flat can cost over £150 a month in Taipei. Landlords want two month's rent in advance. A bed in a dormitory outside town is an option. £3.50 to £4.50 a night.

Useful contacts:
Gram English Institute, 7th Floor, 216 Tun Hwa South Road, Sec 1, Taipei. Tel. 2 741 0970.
Kang Ning English School, PO Box 95, Chutung 310. Tel. 3 594 3322.
Shane English School, David Roberts, 5F, 41 Roosevelt Road, Section 2, Taipei. Tel. 886 (02) 351 7755.
Word of Mouth English, 4F-2, 163 Nan King East Road, Sec. 5, Taipei. Tel. 2 762 7114.

Thailand

Great demand due to tourism. Posts are rarely advertised outside the country. This also means that many schools are not entirely serious. There are too many teacher-travellers with scanty qualifications. A wonderful country to visit - the scenery and the people are wonderful. An unfortunately high incidence of AIDS and commercial sex may be off-putting, but that is just the seedy side of Bangkok. There is more to the country than that. Food is excellent. The cost of living is low, and lower still outside Bangkok. You will be well-placed for the rest of Asia.

Entry requirements:
Only New Zealanders don't need visas. To get a work permit (all nationalities) you must have a degree, a certificate and be employed in a recognised institution. Although it is illegal to work on a tourist visa, many do. A non-immigrant visa (90 days) may be obtained with a letter of invitation from your employer or a Thai national.

Vaccinations:
Hepatitis A, Polio, Tetanus, Typhoid, Malaria and Yellow Fever.

Tax and insurance:
With a work permit - around 2% tax. Get health insurance.

Wages:
If qualified - £330 to £475 a month or £6 to £11 an hour.

Accommodation:
Difficult - get a Thai speaker to help. £64 to £83 a month if you find a flat, plus three month's rent deposit. Otherwise try to find a budget hostel.

Useful contacts:
ECC, Paul McCleave, 430/17-24 Chula Soi 64, Siam Square, Bangkok 10330. Tel. 255 1856-9.
Inligua School of Languages, Central Chidlom Tower, 22 Plenchit Road, Pathumwan, Bangkok 10330. Tel. 2 254 7029.
ELS International, 419/3 Rajavithee Road, Phyathai, Bangkok 10400. Tel. 2 247 8088.

Tunisia

Although a French-speaking country, English is fast becoming the language of business. A knowledge of Arabic and/or French would be a distinct advantage. Geographically, rather an odd country. Tunis, the capital, is on the Mediterranean coast in the north. The coastline extends south to the border with Libya. In the midwest, the Atlas mountains intrude, and the far south is well into the Sahara. Tunisia is the world's fourth largest producer of olive oil. Agriculture employs some 50% of the population. Oil and phosphate rock are also produced. A popular place for a holiday and, as yet, relatively unaffected by fundamentalism. The usual restrictions with Islamic countries apply.

Entry requirements:
It can take more than three months to arrange. Your employer should arrange a temporary work permit or letter of confirmation from your employer. Originals of your birth certificate and degree diploma will be needed.

Vaccinations:
Hepatitis A, Polio, Typhoid and Yellow Fever.

Tax and insurance:
Tax is around 20%. Get health insurance.

Wages:
£5.50 to £7.50 an hour. Maximum £7,100 a year.

Accommodation:
Easy to find. Usually unfurnished. £160 to £220 a month with one month's deposit.

Useful contacts:
AMIDEAST, 10 rue 8003, Cite Montplaisir, Tunis. Tel. 790559.
English Language Training Centre, British Council, 47 Avenue Habib Bourgiba, Tunis.
Institute Bourgiba des Languages Vivantes (IBLV), 47 Avenue de la Liberté, Tunis. Tel. 2161 932418.

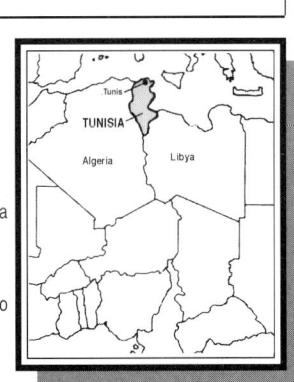

Turkey

Trying desperately to be accepted into the EU, but its record on human rights and bad treatment to the Kurdish minority keep hindering it. Slowly moving into the modern world in the interior and firmly in it in Istanbul. There is still poverty in some places, but there is also great individual wealth. The quest for EU membership has meant an increasing demand for English. Some schools are guilty of poor treatment of teachers. Take care with contracts. That said, the Turkish people are warm-hearted and hospitable. Ankara, Istanbul and Izmir are all good places for jobs. This is still an Islamic country and western attitudes are not to be expected.

Entry requirements:
Only UK nationals need an entry visa. Everyone needs a work permit. You must have a degree and a teaching qualification. Try to do all the paperwork from home, as it can take up to six months in Turkey.

Vaccinations:
Hepatitis A, Polio, Typhoid and Malaria.

Tax and insurance:
Tax is 25%, but salaries are usually quoted net. Get health insurance. State care is available, but of poor quality.

Wages:
£375 to £1,000 a month. Private classes can net you £10 an hour. High inflation, check for mid-term index-linked corrections or some payment in foreign currency.

Accommodation:
Usually provided by the school (shared). If not, rent is around £100 a month with one month's deposit.

Useful contacts:
Interlang, Russell Baulk, Zuhtu Pasa Mah, Recep Peker Cd, Sefikbey Sok No 17, Kiziltoprak, Istanbul. Tel. 216 418 3910.
Cambridge English, Kazim Ozalp Sok. No 15, Kat. 4, Saskinbakkal, Istanbul. Tel. 216 385 8431.

United Arab Emirates

Good prospects here; excellent if you have qualifications. Pay is good and the contract may include travel and accommodation. The country is a federation of Abu Dhabi, Dubai and Sharjah principally. There are 7 member states. In 1984, oil reserves were estimated at 32 billion barrels. Natural gas reserves are about 3% of world total. The restrictions on women teachers are not so severe here, though it should be remembered that this is an Islamic country. Climate is mainly hot and dry. There is some agricultural production and a certain amount of industry.

Entry requirements:
To live and work here, you need a sponsor employer. Rules change often. Check with your local UAE embassy.

Vaccinations:
Hepatitis A, Polio, Typhoid and Malaria.

Tax and insurance:
No tax. You can get a health card for about £130.

Wages:
£720 to £1,440 a month. About £14 to £28 an hour.

Accommodation:
If not provided, expect to pay from £3,000 to £5,000 a year for a single flat.

Useful contacts:
Arabic Language Centre, (Dubai World Trade Centre), PO Box 9292, Dubai. Tel. 3086036.
International Training Solutions, Lynne Haboubi, PO Box 4234, Dubai. Tel. 97 16 363249.
ELS International, PO Box 2380, Dubai. Tel. 827616.
International Language Institute, PO Box 3253, Sharjah. Tel. 06 377257.

Uruguay

Once known as the Switzerland of South America, such was the efficiency of the welfare state, it embarked on a military inspired bid to become an industrial country. The resulting economic crisis and repressive measures imposed by the military led to the military not appearing in uniform on the street - people would spit on them. Things have calmed down a lot now, and there are many opportunities. The Uruguayans are a civilised and educated people. Montevideo has many attractions and the country is a pleasant place to live. Food and drink excellent.

Entry requirements:
Rather complicated. Enter on a tourist visa and nip across the border to finalise the paperwork. Argentina is within easy reach by ferry from Montevideo.

Vaccinations:
Hepatitis A, Polio and Typhoid.

Tax and insurance:
19% tax. Get health insurance.

Wages:
Around £450 a month. Private classes net more.

Accommodation:
Expensive. £125 to £250 a month with two month's rent deposit.

Useful contacts:
London Institute School of Languages, Caramura 5609, Montevideo. Tel. 61 33 83.
English Lighthouse Institute, Sarandi 881, Maldonado. Tel. 42 34538.
Instituto Cultural Anglo-Uruguayo Casilla de Correo 5087 Sec. 1, San Jose 1426, Montevideo.

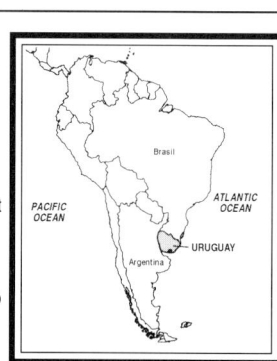

Venezuela

An economic crisis has hit this country, and although the effects are fading, inflation is still high. There are opportunities, but American English (and accents) are preferred. Caracas is a crowded and busy city, but wonderfully situated behind a range of mountains from the sea and the airport. Try the cableway to the mountains on a cloudless day (you will be above the cloudbase) for a stunning view of Caracas. Each street corner has a special name and people give directions using the names. Unfortunately the names are not on any maps. Maracaibo is worth a visit also. Food and drink excellent. Somewhat conservative, but hospitable people.

Entry requirements:
Much paperwork to face. Try to enter on a tourist visa, get a job and then go over the border (to Colombia to the West, or British Guyana to the East) to finalise the permit.

Vaccinations:
Hepatitis A, Polio and Typhoid.

Tax and insurance:
No information on taxes. Get health insurance.

Wages:
Around £3 an hour.

Accommodation:
Expensive. Haggle for it to be included in your contract.

Useful contacts:
Loscher Ebbinhaus; La Trinidad, Calle San Jose, Quinta Katheriñe, Sorocaima. Tel. 932459.
La Campina, Centro Commercial Avenida Libertador, Crn. Calle Negrin (2nd Floor), Caracas. Tel. 2-762 5501/761. Also in Valencia, Tel. 41 236052.
This place will have you take a psychometric test and requires teachers to wear jackets at all times in class.
English Lab S.R.L., Apartado Postal 4004, Carmelitas, Caracas 1101. Tel. (2) 574 2511/573 6120.
The British Council, Torre La Noria, Piso 6, Paseo Enrique Eraso, Urb. Altamira, Caracas. Tel. 263 11 06/262 17 64.

Yemen

A very poor country. However, this is what Arabian countries were like before the discovery of oil. Intelligent, courteous people. Do not forget that illiteracy is over 80% and the usual restrictions with Islamic countries apply; women must wear long dresses, no alcohol and don't use your left hand. Don't go to the north as there are bandits about who kidnap people. The Red Sea coast is hot and humid with mean temperatures of 29°C. The highlands (the capital San'a is here) have a maximum of 29°C. Cold winters with frosts are not uncommon.

Entry requirements:
While people work on tourist visas, it is illegal. Get an invitation from a Yemeni school and present it to your local Yemeni embassy or consulate.

Vaccinations:
Hepatitis A, Polio, Typhoid and Yellow Fever.

Tax and insurance:
No tax. Get health insurance.

Wages:
£625 to £940 a month. More at the British Council. Payment must be in hard currency.

Accommodation:
Easy to find. Rent is around £80 a month with two or three month's deposit.

Useful contacts:
The British Council, As-Sabain Street No 7, (PO Box 2157), Sana'a. Tel. (1) 244121/2.
The Modern Yemen School, PO Box 13335, Sana'a. Tel. 206 548.
Al Farouq Institute, PO Box 16927. Tel. 209 721.
Sana'a International School, PO Box 2002, Sana'a. Tel. 234 437.

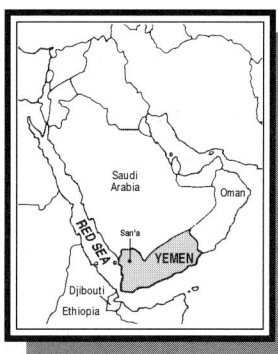

Zimbabwe

Zimbabwe still retains at least one hangover from British rule, English remains the principle medium for teaching and learning. Unfortunately, until independence in 1980, there was a strong bias toward educating the white population, to the detriment of others. In the following years, the new Government has tried hard to redress the balance. This led to a great demand for able and qualified teachers which still exists today. Although introducing new teacher training programmes to try and foster local teachers, Zimbabwe still relies on a considerable number of foreign teachers. These are recruited through the Zimbabwean Government directly, or through a number of volunteer organisations (VSO, Christians Abroad etc.). Most Government contracts are 3 years in duration. Teachers are needed for all areas of education, not just English. Teachers may find themselves teaching mixed ability classes, this is emphasised as state schools do not operate a system of streaming for exams. Adaptability is very important, but the enthusiasm of your students may well make up for any other short comings.

Entry requirements:
It is possible to apply for work while on a tourist visa, and if you are UK or a US citizen you do not need to a tourist visa. However to work you must obtain a residence permit and a work permit. This can take a long time and be painfully slow, if possible employment and permits etc. should be arranged before travel. People applying direct to the Ministry of Education will need to provide identification, proof of qualifications (degree at the minimum) and experience and also a medical certificate and a chest X-ray.

Vaccinations:
Hepatitis A, Polio, Malaria, Tetanus, Typhoid and Yellow Fever. Any others your doctor may recommend. Also it is worth being aware of the risk of AIDS.

Tax and insurance:
Get health insurance.

Wages:
Although wages are not high (up to Z$3000 per month) most people are able to live comfortably, primarily because there is very little on which to spend money.

Accommodation:
Schools will generally provide accommodation, taking the strain off living expenses.

Useful contacts:
The first stop should be your local Zimbabwean High Commission. 429 Strand, London WC2R 0SA who will forward your applications to the Zimbabwe Ministry of Education in Harare.
VSO, 317 Putney Bridge Road, London SW15 2PN. Tel (0181) 780 7500.
Christians Abroad, 1 Stockwell Green, London SW9 HP Tel: (0171) 7377811

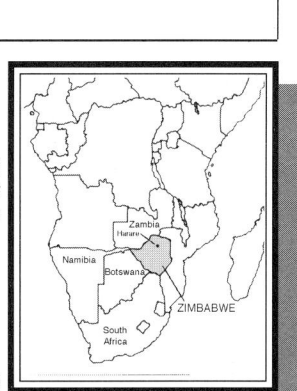

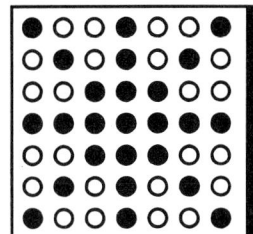

BRITISH COUNCIL INTERNATIONAL SEMINARS

"A CULTURAL AND EDUCATIONAL OPPORTUNITY THAT WILL REMAIN A LIFETIME MEMORY"
(NEW ZEALAND)

"More than fulfilled all expectation"
(SOUTH AFRICA)

"The most stimulating and rewarding professional experience of my career"
(CANADA)

Our 50 years of experience in events management, combined with The British Council's unequalled global network, guarantees top quality events of international acclaim spanning every area of the ELT field.

Why participate in our ELT International Events?

- Access to a global network within the ELT field
- Opportunity for delegate contribution and exchange
- Direction by leading experts
- Professional Seminar Manager in daily attendance
- Lasting personal contacts
- Opportunity to enjoy the richness and variety of British Culture
- Contributors from leading-edge institutions
- Excellent value for money
- Exposure to latest developments in ELT

http://www.britcoun.org/seminars/

The British Council, registered in England as a charity no. 209131, is
The United Kingdom's international network for education, culture and development services.

FOR FULL DETAILS OF THE FORTHCOMING PROGRAMME OF ELT INTERNATIONAL EVENTS PLEASE COMPLETE AND RETURN THIS SLIP TO THE ADDRESS BELOW. (TR)

Name: ....

Address: ....

....

....

International Seminars, The British Council, 1 Beaumont Place, Oxford OX1 2PJ.
Tel: +44(0) 1865 316636.   Fax +44(0) 1865 557368/516590.

Other Stuff

Useful contacts

Addresses, contact details and internet sites.

page 126

British council centres

The main office for each country is listed first.

Argentina
Director: Mr Mike P Potter
Marcelo T de Alvear 590
(4th floor), 1058 Buenos Aires
Tel: (+00 54 1) 3119814
Fax: (+00 54 1) 3117747

Australia
Director: Mr James Potts
Edgecliff Centre
401/203 New South Head Road
PO Box 88 Edgecliff
Sydney NSW 2027
Tel: (+00 61 2) 3262022
Fax: (+00 61 2) 3274868
E-mail: bc.sydney@bc-sydney.sprit.com

Austria
Director: Mr Mark Evans
Schenkenstrasse 4
A-1010 Vienna
Tel: (+00431) 5332616
Fax: (+00431) 533216685
E-mail: bc.vienna@british-council.sprint.com

Bahrain
Director: Mr John Shorter
AMA Centre
146 Shaikh Salman Highway
PO Box 452, Manama 356
Bahrain
Tel: (+00 973) 261555
Fax: (+00 973) 241272
E-mail: britcon@baTel:co.com.bh

Baltic States
(Latvia, Lithuania & Estonia)
Director Baltic States
Mr Ian Stewart
Lazaretes iela 3, Riga LV-1010
Latvia
Tel: (+00 371) 7320468
Fax: (+00 371) 7830031
E-mail: bc.riga@british-council.sprint.com

Resource Centre Manager:
Ms Virginija Ziukiene
Vilniaus 39/6, 2600 Vilnius
Lithuania
Tel: (+00 370 2) 616607
Fax: (+00 370 2) 221602
E-mail: bc.lithuania@british-council.sprint.com

Resource Centre Manager:
Ms Imbi-Reet Kaasik
Vana Posti 7, Tallinn EE0001
Estonia
Tel: (+00 372 6) 314010
Fax: (+00 372 6) 313111
E-mail: tallinn@british-council.sprint.com

Bangladesh
Director: Mr Tom Cowin
5 Fuller Road, PO Box 161
Dhaka 1000, Bangladesh
Tel: (+00 880 2) 868905
Fax: (+00 880 2) 863375
E-mail: ubarlow@
bcdhaka.pradeshta.net

Manager Chittagong:
 Mrs Sutapa Barua
British Council, Laldighi South
PO Box 327, Chittagong
Tel: (+00 880 31) 223632

Belgium and Luxembourg
Director: Dr Ken Churchill OBE
Leifdaigheidstraat/
Rue de la Charité 15
1210 Brussels
Tel: (+00 32 2) 2270840
Fax: (+00 32 2) 2270849
E-mail: bc.brussels@bc-brussels.sprint.com

Director:
Ms Fiona Clouder- Richards
United Kingdom Research and Higher
Education European Office
Rue de la Loi 83
BP10, 1040 Brussels
Tel: (+00 32 2) 2305275
Fax: (+00 32 2) 2304803
E-mail: ukeo@bbsrc.ac.uk

Botswana
Director: Ms Anne Hewling
British High Commission Building
Queen's Road, The Mall
PO Box 439, Gaborone Botswana
Tel: (+00 267) 353602
Fax: (+00 267)356643
E-mail: bc.gaborone@british-council.sprint.com

Brazil
Director:
Mr Howard Thompson OBE
Edificio Morro Vermilbo
Quandra 1, Blococ 21
SCS 70399-900
Brasilia, DF, Brasil
Tel: (+00 55 61) 323 6080
Fax: (+00 55 61) 323 7440
E-mail: brasilia@britcoun.org.br

Director Recife:
Mr Edward Edmundson
Av. Domingos Ferreira 4150
Boa Viagem
Caixa Postal 4079
51021-040 Recife PE
Tel: (+00 55 81) 4657744
Fax: (+00 55 81) 4657271
E-mail: bcrecife@it.com.br

Director Rio de Janeiro:
Mr Tom Walsh
Rua Elmano Cardim 10
Urca, Caixa Postal 2237
22291 Rio de Janerio RJ
Tel: (+00 55 21) 2957782
Fax: (+00 55 21) 5413693
E-mail: bcconrj@ibm.net

Director São Paulo:
Mr John Coope OBE
Avenida Brigadiero Faria Lima
2000 (10o Andar)
Torre Norte 01452-002
São Paulo SP, Brasil
Tel: (+00 55 011) 30390500
Fax: (+00 55 011)30390503
E-mail: bcsaopaulo@mcimail.com

Brueni
Director Malaysia supervises work in Brunei
Manager: Ms Susan Mathews
Room 505, 5th Floor
Hong Kong Bank Chambers
Jalan Pemancha 2085
Bandar Seri Begawan
Postal address: PO Box 3049
Bandar Seri Begawan 1930
Brunei
Tel: (+00 673 2) 227480
Fax: (+00 673 2) 241769
E-mail: bcbrunei@pso.brunet.bn

Bulgaria
Director
7 Tulovo Street
1504 Sofia
Tel: (+00 359 2) 9460098
Fax: (+00 359 2) 9460102
E-mail: bc.sofi@
bc-sofia.sprint.com

Canada
Director and Cultural Counsellor:
Mr Sean Lewis
British High Commission
80 Elgin Street, Ottawa
Ontario K1P 5K7
Tel: (+00 1 613) 2371530
Fax: (+00 1 613) 5691478
E-mail: af572@freenet.carleton.ca

Director Montréal : Ms Sarah Dawbarn
1000 ouest rue de la Gauchetière
Bureau 4200
Montréal, Quebec H3B 4W5
Tel: (+00 1 514) 8665863
Fax: (+00 1 514) 8665322
E-mail: britcnl@alcor.concordia.ca

Caribbean
Director: Mr David Tarr
PCMB Building
64 Knutsford Boulevard
PO Box 575, Kingston 5
Jamaica
Tel: (+00 1 809) 9296915
Fax: (+00 1 809) 9297090
E-mail: bc.kingston@mail.toj.com

Liason Officer: Ms Marcia Pillai
British High Commission
19 St Clair Avenue
St Clair, PO Box 778
Port of Spain, Trinidad & Tobago
Tel: (+00 1 809) 6281234
Fax: (+00 1 809) 6224555
E-mail: bc.trini@wow.net

Chile
Director: Mr David Stokes
Eliodoro Yáñez 832
Casilla 115 Correo 55, Santiago
Tel: (+00 56 2) 2357375
E-mail: bcchile@mailnet.rdc.cl

China
Counsellor (Cultural): Mr Martin Davidson
British Embassy, Cultural and Education
Section, 4th Floor, Landmark Building
8 North Dongsnahuan Road
Chaoyang District
Beijing 100006
Tel: (+00 86 10) 65011903
Fax: (+00 86 10) 65011977
E-mail: bc.beijing@bc-beijing.sprint.com

Consul (Cultural) Shanghai:
Ms Barbara Wickham
244 Yong Fu Lu
Shanghai 200031
Tel: (+00 86 21) 64714849
Fax: (+00 86 21) 64333115
E-mail: britcoun@public.sta.net.cn

First Secretary (Cultural) South China:
Mr Jonathan Greenwood
5/F, 3 Supreme Court Road
Admiralty, Hong Kong
Tel: (+00 852) 29135201
Fax: (+00 852) 29135205
E-mail: bc.southchina@
britcoun.org.hk

Colombia
Director: Mrs Kate Board
Calle 87 No 12-79
Apartado Aéreo 089231
Santafé de Bogotá

Tel: (+00 571) 6180107
Fax: (+00 571) 2187754
E-mail: brit.council@sprintcol.sprint.com

Croatia
Director: Mr Ian Stewart
Ilica 12/1, PO Box 55
10001 Zagreb
Tel: (+00 385 1) 273491
Fax: (+00 385 1) 421725
E-mail: bc.zagreb@bc.Tel:.hf

Cyprus
The Director
Shakespear Reading Room
3 Museum Street
1097 Nicosia
PO Box 5654, 1387 Nicosia
Tel: (+00 357 2) 442152
Fax: (+00 357 2) 477257
E-mail: bc.nicosia@britcoun.org.cy

Czech Republic
Director: Mrs Mary O'Neil
Narodni 10, 12501 Prague 1
Tel: (+00 420 2) 24912179
Fax: (+00 420 2) 24913839
E-mail: bcprague@britcoun.anet.cz

Denmark
Director Nordic Countries: Mr Len Tyler
Gammel Mont 12.3
1117 Copenhagen K, Denmark
Tel: (+00 45) 33112044
Fax: (+00 45) 33321501
E-mail: british.council@britcoun.dk

East Jerusalem
(West Bank and Gaza)
Director: Mr Peter Skelton
Al-Nuzha Building
2 Abu Obeida Street
PO Box 19136, Jerusalem
Tel: (+00 972 2) 6282545
Fax: (+00 972 2) 6283021

Manager Gaza: Ms Susannah Pickering
14-706 Al Nasra Street
Al-Rimal, PO Box 355, Gaza City
Tel: (+00 972 7) 822290
Fax: (+00 972 7) 820512

Manager Nablus: Mohammed Kobari
Harwash Building
Radidia Main Street
PO Box 497 Nablus
Tel: (+00 972 9) 385951
Fax: (+00 972 9) 375953

Officer-in-charge: Ma'im Daour
Ein Sarah Street
PO Box 277, Hebron

Ecuador
Director: Mr Antony Deyes
Avda Amazonas
1646 y Orellana

Casilla 17-07-8829, Quito
Tel: (+00 593 2) 540225
Fax: (+00 593 2) 508283
E-mail: eyre@britcoun.org.ec

Manager Guayaquil: Mr John Crowther
Costanera 504, entre Ebanos y Las
Monjas-Urdesa, Casilla 09-01-06547
Guayaquil
Tel: (+00 593 4) 885100
Fax: (+00 593 4) 884932

Egypt
Director: Mr David Marier OBE
192 Sharia el Nil
Agouza, Cairo
Tel: (+00 20 2) 3031514
Fax: (+00 20 2) 3443076
E-mail: bc.cairo@bc-cairo.sprint.com

Director Alexandria: Amanda Burrell
9 Batalsa Street, Bab Shark, Alexandria
Tel: (+00 20 3) 4820199
Fax: (+00 20 3) 4826630
E-mail: bc.alexandria@bc-
alexandria.sprint.com

Estonia
see Baltic States

Finland
see Nordic Countries

France
Director and Cultural Counsellor:
Dr Christine Gamble
9/11 rue de Constantine
75007 Paris
Tel: (+00 33 1) 49557300
Fax: (+00 33 1) 47057702
E-mail: bc.paris@bc-paris.sprint.com

Georgia
Director Russia is reponsible for work in Georgia
Centre Manager: Ms Maya Kiasishivili
Tskhvedadze 36
Tbilisi, Geogia
(Mail sent via BC in Moscow)
Tel: (+00 78 832) 952361
Fax: (+00 78 832) 220253
E-mail: bc.moscow@bc-moscow.sprint.com

Germany
Director: Mr Keith Dobson OBE
Hahnenstrasse 6, 50667
Cologne
Tel: (+00 49 221) 206440
Fax: (+00 49 221) 2064455
E-mail: bc.cologne@
british-council.sprint.com

Director Eastern Länder: Dr Simon Cole
Hardenbergstrasse 20
10623 Berlin
Tel: (+00 49 30) 31109930
Fax: (+00 49 30) 31109920

Officer-in-charge Hamburg: Frau Heidrun
Schachtebeck-Janik
Rothenbaumchaussee 34
20148 Hamburg
Tel: (+00 49 40) 446057
Fax: (+00 49 40) 447114

Director Leipzig: Ms Katherine Stewart
Lumumbastasse 11-13
04105 Leipzig
Tel: (+00 49 341) 5647153
Fax: (+00 49 341) 5647152
E-mail: bc.leipzig@bc-leipzig.transnet

Director Munich: Mr Stephen Ashworth
Training Manager: Ms Valerie Howarth
Rumfordsrasse 7, 80469 Munich
Tel: (+00 49 89) 2900860
Fax: (+00 49 89) 29008688
E-mail: bc-muc@bc-munich.transnet

Greece
Director (designate): Mr Peter Chenery
17 Plateia Philikis Etarias, PO Box 3488,
Kolonaki Square 102 10, Athens
Tel: (+00 30 1) 3633211
Fax: (+00 30 1) 3634769
E-mail: bc.athens@bc-athens.sprint.com

Director Thessaloniki: Mr Andrew Hadly
Ethnikis Amynis 9, PO Box 50007
540 13 Thessaloniki
Tel: (+00 30 31) 235236
Fax: (+00 30 31) 282498
E-mail: bc.thessaloniki@british-
council.sprint.com

Hungary
Director: Dr Paul Dick
Budapest VI, Benczur Utca 26
H-1068 Budapest VI
Tel: (+00 36 1) 3228246
Fax: (+00 36 1) 3425728
E-mail: hungary@britcoun.hu

India
Minister (Cultural Affairs):
Mr Colin Perchard OBE
British High Commission
British Council Division
17 Kasturba Gandhi Marg
New Delhi
Tel: (+00 91 11) 3711401
Fax: (+00 91 11) 3710717

Director West India
British Deputy High Commission
British Council Division
Mittal Tower, C Wing
Nariman Point, Bombay 400021
Tel: (+00 91 22) 2823560
Fax: (+00 91 22) 2852024

Director East India: Mr Adrian Thomas
British Deputy High Commission
British Council Division
5 Shakespeare Sarani
Calcutta 700 071
Tel: (+00 91 33) 2429144
Fax: (+00 91 33) 2424804

Director South India: Mr Jasper Utley
British Deputy High Commission
British Council Division
737 Anna Salai, Madras 600 002
Tel: (+00 91 44) 8525002
Fax: (+00 91 44) 8523234

Indonesia
Director: Dr Neil Kemp
S. Widjojo Centre
Jalan Jenderal
Sudirman 71, Jakarta 12190
Tel: (+00 62 21) 2524115
Fax: (+00 62 21) 2524129
E-mail: bc.jakarta@bc-jakarta.sprint.com

Ireland
Director: Mr Harold Fish OBE
Newmount House
22/24 Lower Mount Street, Dublin 2
Tel: (+00 3531) 6764088
Fax: (+00 3531) 6766945
E-mail: forename.surname@britcoun.org

Israel
Director: Mr Harley Brookes
140 Hayarkon Street
PO Box 3302, Tel: Aviv 61032
Tel: (+00 972 3) 5222194
Fax: (+00 972 3) 5221229
E-mail: bc.Tel:aviv@british-
council.sprint.com

Office Manager: Ms Caron Sethill
3 Shimshon Street
PO Box 10304, Jersalem
Tel: (+00 972 2) 6736733
Fax: (+00 972 2) 6736737

Senior Teacher: Mr Jeremy Budlow
1002/27 Anis Kardosh Street
PO Box 2651, Nazareth 16000
Tel:/Fax: (+00 972 6) 550436

Italy
Director: Mr Richard Alford OBE
Via Quattro Fontane 20, 00184 Rome
Tel: (+00 39 6) 478141
Fax: (+00 39 6) 4814296
E-mail: bc.rome@british-council.sprint.com

Director Bologna: Ms Carmelita Caruana
Corte Isolani 8, Strada Maggiore 19
40125 Bologna
Tel: (+00 39 51) 225142
Fax: (+00 39 51) 224238
E-mail: 101354.2004@compuserve.com

Director Milan: Ms Gill Caldicott
Via Manzoni 38, 20121 Milan
Tel: (+00 39 2) 782016
Fax: (+00 39 2) 781119
E-mail: 101354.2005@compuserve.com

Director Naples:
Mr Ian Arrowsmith
92/98 Via Crispi, Naples
(mail routed through Rome)
E-mail: 101354.2007@compuserve.com

Jamaica
see Caribbean

Japan
Director: Mr Michael Barrett OBE
2 Kagurazaka 1-chome
Shinjuku-ku, Tokyo 162
Tel: (+00 81 3) 32358031
Fax: (+00 81 3) 32358040
E-mail: bc.tokyo@
bc-tokyo.sprint.com

Director Western Japan:
Mr Mark Baurnfield
DTOM: Jeff Streeter
77 Kitashirakawa, Nishimachi
Sakyo-ku, Kyoto 606
Tel: (+00 81 75) 7917151
Fax: (+00 81 75) 7917154
E-mail: bc.kyoto@
bc-kyoto.sprint.com

Liaison Officer:
Mr Gavin Anderson
Sapporo International Communication
Plazza
MN Building, 3F North 1
West 3, Chuo-ku
Sapporo 060
Tel: (+00 81 11) 2113672
Fax: (+00 81 11) 2191317
E-mail: bc.sapporo@
bc-tokyo.sprint.com

Liaison Officer: Mr Paul Taylor
Nagoya Daiya Building
2-gokan 5F
15-1 Meieki 3-chome
Nakamura-ku, Nagoya 450
Tel: (+00 81 52) 5812016
Fax: (+00 81 52) 5812017
E-mail: bc.nagoya@
bc-tokyo.sprint.com

Jordan
Director: Dr David Burton
DTOM: Mr Hector Low
Rainbow Street (off First Circle)
PO Box 634, Amman 11118
Tel: (+00 962 6) 636147
Fax: (+00 962 6) 656413
E-mail: david.burton@
bc-amman.sprint.com

Korea
Director: Mr Terry Toney
DTOM: Mr Andy Millburn
1st floor, Anglican Church Foundation
Building
3-7 Chung-dong
Choong-ku, 100-120 Seoul

Tel: (+00 82 2) 7377157
Fax: (+00 82 2) 7379911
E-mail: bc.seoul@bc-seoul.sprint.com

Manager: Mr Justin Spence
6th Floor, Kyobo Building
536-6 Boojeon-dong
Pusanjin-ku, Pusan 614-030
Tel: (+00 82 51) 8074612
Fax: (+00 82 51) 8074611
E-mail: 100050.3053@compuserve.com

Kuwait
Director: Mr Carl Reuter
2 Al Arabi Street, Block 2
PO Box 345, 13004 Safat
Mansouriya
Tel: (+00 965) 233204
Fax: (+00 965) 2520069
E-mail: dirkuwu@kuwait.net

Lithuania
see Baltic States

Malaysia
Director: Mr Ted Edmundson
Deputy Director: Mr Michael Wilson
Jalan Bukit Aman, PO Box 10539
50916 Kuala Lumpur
50480 Kuala Lumpur
Tel: (+00 60 3) 2987555
Fax: (+00 60 3) 2937214
E-mail: brcokl@britkl.po.my

Director East Malaysia: Mr Justin Gilbert
Banguan WSK (Public Finance Building)
PO Box 615, 93712 Kuching
Jalan Abell, 93100 Kuching, Sarawak
Tel: (+00 60 82) 256271
Fax: (+00 60 82) 425199
E-mail: brcosar@britsar.po.my

Director East Malaysia: Mr Justin Gilbert
Wing On Life Building, 1st Floor,
1 Lorong Sagunting, PO Box 10746
88808 Kota Kinabalu
88000 Kota Kinabalu, Sabah
Tel: (+00 60 88) 248055
Fax: (+00 60 88) 238059

Area Manager Penang:
Mrs Irene Teoh Ming See
43 Green Hall, PO Box 595
10770 Penang, 10200 Penang
Tel: (+00 60 4) 2630330
Fax: (+00 60 4) 2633589
E-mail: brcopg@britpg.po.my

Mexico
Director: Mr Alan Curry
Maestro Antonio Caso 127
Col. San Rafael, Apartado Postal 30-588
Mexico City 06470 DF
Tel: (+00 52 5) 5666144
Fax: (+00 52 5) 5355984
E-mail:
bc.mexicocity@bc.mexico.sprint.com

Morocco
Director: Mr Tony O'Brien
DTOM: Mr William Bickerdike
36 Rue de Tanger, BP 427, Rabat
Tel: (+00 212 7) 760836
Fax: (+00 212 7) 760850

Mozambique
Director: Mr Paul Woods
Rua John Issa 226
PO Box 4178, Maputo
Tel: (+00 258 1) 421571
Fax: (+00 258 1) 421577
E-mail: root@bcmaputo.uem.mz

Myanmar
Cultural Attaché: Mr Claus Henning
British Embassy, 80 Strand Road
PO Box 638, Rangoon
Tel: (+00 95 1) 281700

Napal
Director: Ms Sarah Ewans
Kantipath, PO Box 640, Kathmandu
Tel: (+00 977 1) 221305
Fax: (+00 977 1) 224076
E-mail: bcnepal@britcoun.mos.com.np

The Netherlands
Dirtector: Mr Tim Butchard
Keizergracht 343
1016 EH Amsterdam
Tel: (+00 31 20) 6223644
Fax: (+00 31 20) 6207389
E-mail:
bc.amsterdam@british.council.sprint.com

New Zealand
Director: Mr Paul Smith
c/o British High Commission
44 Hill Street, PO Box 1812, Wellington
Tel: (+00 64 4) 4726049
Fax: (+00 64 4) 4736261
E-mail: barbara.procter@bc-wellington.sprint.com

Nordic Countries
(Denmark, Norway, Finland, Sweden)
Director Nordic Countries: Mr Len Tyler
Gammel Mont 12.3
1117 Copenhagen K
Tel: (+00 45) 33112044
Fax: (+00 45) 33321501
E-Mail: british.council@britcoun.dk

Manager Finland: Ms Tuija Talvitie
Hakaniemenkatu 2, 00530 Helsinki
Tel: (+00 358) 07018731
Fax: (+00 358) 07018725
E-mail: tuija.talvitie@cimo.fi

Manager Norway: Mrs Rosalind Olsen
Fridtjof Nansens Plass 5
0160 Oslo 1, Norway
Tel: (+00 47 22) 426848
Fax: (+00 47 22) 424039
E-mail: british.council@britcoun.no

Director Sweden: Dr Patrick Spaven
Strandvägen 57A, 4tr S-115 23 Stockholm
Tel: (+00 46 8) 6719190
Fax: (+00 46 8) 6637172

Norway
see Nordic Countries

Oman
Director: Mr Clive Bruton
Road One, Medinat Qaboos West
PO Box 73, Postal Code 115, Muscat
Tel: (+00 968) 600548
Fax: (+00 968) 699163
E-mail: bc.muscat@bc-muscat.sprint.com

Manager Salalah: Mr John Davie
Al Fahya Street, PO Box 18249, Salalah
Tel: (+00 968) 212240
Fax: (+00 968) 212508

Director Administration Sohar:
Mr Nigel Bacon
Al Hadiquah Street, PO Box 854
Postal Code 311, Sohar
Tel: (+00 968) 8433396
Fax: (+00 968) 843398

Peru
Director: Chris Brown
OAS English Language Officer:
Dr Dorothy Bond
Calle Alberto Lynch 110, San Isidro
Lima 27, Apartado 14-0114
Santa Beatriz, Lima 14
Tel: (+00 51 1) 2217552
Fax: (+00 51 1) 4215215
E-mail: bc.lima@bc-lima.sprint.com

Poland
Director: Dr Jerry Eyres
Al Jerozolimskie 59, 00-697 Warsaw
Tel: (+00 4822) 6287401
Fax: (+00 4822) 6219955
E-mail: david.skinner@britcoun.org.pl

Portugal
Director: Mr Bill Jefferson OBE
Rua de São Marçal 174, 1294 Lisbon Codex
Tel: (+00 351 1) 3476141
Fax: (+00 351 1) 3476152
E-mail: allen.swales@bc-lisborn.sprint.com

Director Cascias: Ms Ingrid Rhead Calhau
The British Council, Edificio S. Jose
Av. dos Combatentes da Grande Guerrra
1 piso sala 102, 2750 Cascais
Tel: (+00 351 1) 4573414
Fax: (+00 351 1) 4579918

Director Coimbra:
Ms Carolyn Cemlyn-Jones MBE
Rua de Tomar 4, 3000 Coimbra
Tel: (+00 351 39) 23549
Fax: (+00 351 39) 36705
E-mail: bc.coimbra@british-council.sprint.com

Director Oporto: Bob Carrington
Rua de Breyner 155, 4050 Oporto
Tel: (+00 351 2) 2005577
Fax: (+00 351 2) 2084762
E-mail: bc.oporto@bc-porto.sprint.com

Director Parede: Ms Ingrid Rhead Calhau
Rua De Camilo Dionisio Alvares
Lote 6, 2775 Parede
TEl: (+00 351 1) 4573414
Fax: (+00 351 1) 4579918
E-mail: bc.parede@british-council.sprint.com

Romania
Director: Ms Helen Meixner
Calea Dorobantilor 14, Bucharest
Tel: (+00 40 1) 215347
Fax: (+00 40 1) 2100310
E-mail: bc.romania@bc-bucharest.sprint.com

Russia
Director Russia is responsible for work in Armenia, Belarus, Georgia, Moldova and Turkmenistan
Director: Mr Tony Andrews VGBIL
Ulitsa Nikoloyamskaya, 1
109189 Moscow
Tel: (+00 7 095) 2340201
Fax: (+00 7 095) 9752561
E-mail: bc.moscow@bc-moscow.sprint.com

Nizhnigorodski Institut Razvita
Obrazovaniya, Ulitsa Vanyeva 203
Nizhny Novgorod 603122
Tel: (+00 7 8312) 677654
E-mail: bc.nizhny@british-council.sprint.com

Director St Petersburg: Mr Michael Bird
Biblioteka im Mayakovskovo
Fontanka 46, 191025 St Petersburg
Tel: (+00 7 812) 3256074
Fax: (+00 7 812) 3256073
E-mail: bc.stpetersburg@britco.spb.su

Saudi Arabia
Director: Mr Anthony Lewis
Tower B, 3rd Floor
Al Mousa Centre, Olaya Street
PO Box 58012, Riyadh 11594 Riyadh
Tel: (+00 966 1) 4621818
Fax: (+00 966 1) 4620663

Director West Saudia Arabia:
Mr Colin Hepburn
4th Floor, Middle East Centre
Falasteen Street, PO Box 3424
Jeddah 21471, Jeddah
Tel: (+00 966 2) 6723336
Fax: (+00 966 2) 6726341

Director East Saudi Arabia:
Mr David Baldwin
Al-Moajil Building, 5th Floor
Mohamed Street, PO Box 8387
Dahran 31482
Tel: (+00 966 3) 8343484
Fax: (+00 966 3) 8346895
E-mail: firstname.surname@bc-dahran.sprint.com

Manager Jubail: Mr Michael Roberts
Al-Huwaylat Shopping Centre
1st Floor, Al-Huwaylat, PO Box 11363
Jubail Industrial City 31961
Jubail Industrial City
Tel: (+00 966 3) 3419122
Fax: (+00 966 3) 3419124

Singapore
Director: Mr John Davies
30 Napier Road, Singapore 1025
Tel: (+00 65) 4731111
Fax: (+00 65 4721010
E-mail: bc.singapore@british-council.sprint.com

Slovakia
Director: Mrs Susan Wallace-Shaddad
Panská 17, PO Box 68, 814 99 Bratislava
Tel: (+00 42) 75331793
Fax: (+00 42) 75334705
E-mail: hilary.jenkins@bc.bratislaval.sprint.com

Slovenia
Director: Mr Francis King
Stefanova 1/111
61000 Ljubljana
Tel: (+00 386 61) 1259032
Fax: (+00 386 61) 1259139
E-mail: british.council@guest.arnes.si

Spain
Director: Mr Peter Taylor OBE
Paseo del General Martinez Campos, 31,
28010 Madrid
Tel: (+00 34 1) 3373500
Fax: (+00 34 1) 3373573
E-mail: general.enquires@bc-madrid.sprint.com

Director Barcelona: Mr Andy Mackay
Calle Amigó 83
08021 Barcelona
Tel: (+00 34 3) 2091364
Fax: (+00 34 3) 2023168
E-mail: bc.barcelona@bc-barcelona.sprint.com

Director Bilbao: Mr Jeff Carvell
Avenida Leherndakari Aguirre 29
48014 Deutso Bilbao
Tel: (+00 34 4) 4763650
Fax: (+00 34 4) 4762016
E-mail: 100536.3060@compuserve.com

Manager Las Palmas de Gran Canaria:
Mr David Illsley
Bravo Murillo 25
35003 Las Palmas de Gran Canaria
Tel: (+00 34 28) 368300
Fax: (+00 34 28) 382378

Director Palma de Mallorca:
Mr Iwan Roberts
Edifici Sa Riera
Calle Miguel dels Sants Oliver 2
07012 Palma de Mallorca
Tel: (+00 34 71) 172550
Fax: (+00 34 71) 172552

Co-ordinator Segovia: Ms Teresa Gallagher
Centro de Enseñanza de Inglás
Colegio Universitario, 40001, Segovia
Tel: (+00 34 21) 434813
Fax: (+00 34 21) 443283

Director Valencia: Mr David Rowlands
General San Martin 7, 46004 Valencia
Tel: (+00 34 6) 3518818
Fax: (+00 34 6) 3528688
E-mail: chris.dennison@bc-valencia.sprint.com

Headmaster Madrid: Mr Raymond Halliday
The British Council School
Calle Solana s/n Prado de Somosaguas,
28223-Pozuelo de Alarcón, Madrid
Tel: (+00 34 1) 3373612
Fax: (+00 34 1) 3373634
E-mail: 100536.3105@compuserve.com

Sri Lanka
Director Sri Lanka is responsible for work in Maldive Islands
Director: Mr Peter Ellwood
49 Alfred House Gardens
PO Box 753, Colombo 3
Tel: (+00 94 1) 581171
Fax: (+00 94 1) 587079
E-mail: enquiry@britcoun.lanka.net

Librarian: Ms Lalitha Wirasingha
178 DS Senanayake Veediya, Kandy
Tel: (+00 94 8) 34284
Fax: (+00 94 8) 22410

Sudan
Director: Mr Don Sloan
14 Abu Sin Street
PO Box 1253, Khatoum
Tel: (+00 249 11) 770760
Fax: (+00 249 11) 774935

Swaziland
Director: Ms Felicity Townsend-Mahlundla
Ground Floor
British High Commission Building
Alister Miller Street, Private Bag, Mbabane
Tel: (+00 268)43101
Fax: (+00 268) 42641
E-mail: britishcouncil@britcoun.org.sz

Sweden
see Nordic countries

Switzerland
British Council Manager:
Ms Caroline Morrissey
Sennweg 2, PO Box 532

CH 3000 Berne 9
Tel: (+00 41 31) 3014101
Fax: (+00 41 31) 3011459

Syria
Director: Dr Peter Clark OBE
Abd Malek Bin Marwan Street
Tasheen Tabba' Building
Al Malki, PO Box 33105 Damascus
Tel: (+00 963 11) 3333109
Fax: (+00 963 11) 3310630

Taiwan
Director Hong Kong is responsible for Taiwan
Director ATEC: Mr Patrick Hart
7th Floor, Fu Key Building
99 Jen Al Road, Section 2
Taipei 10625
Tel: (+00 886 2) 3962238
Fax: (+00 886 2) 3415749
E-mail: atecmark@aol.com

Thailand
Director: Dr John Richards
254 Chulalongkorn, Siam Square Soi 2
Pathumwan, Bangkok 10330
Tel: (+00 66 2) 2526136
Fax: (+00 66 2) 2535312
E-mail: bc.bangkok@bc-bangkok.sprint.com

Manager Chiang Mai: Ms Amanda Davies
198 Bumrungraj Road, Chiang Mai 50000
Tel: (+00 66 53) 242103
Fax: (+00 66 53) 244781

Tunisia
Director: Mr John MacKenzie
c/o British Embassy, BP 229
5 Place de la Victoire, Tunis 1015 RP
Tel: (+00 216 1) 259053
Fax: (+00 216 1) 353411
E-mail: geral.enquires@bc-tunis.sprint.com

Turkey
Director Turkey is responsible for work in Azerbaijan & Uzbekistan
Director: Mr Clive Gobby
British Embassy, Kirlangiç Sokak No. 9
Gazi Osman Pasa,06700 Ankara
Tel: (+00 90 312) 4686192
Fax: (+00 90 312) 4276182
E-mail: bc.ankara@bc-ankara.sprint.com

Director Istanbul: Mr Martin Fryer
Office of the Consul for British Council and Cultural Affairs, Örs Turistik Îs Merkezi
Îstiklal Caddesi 251/253
(Kat 2/6) Beyoglu, 80060 Istanbul
Tel: (+00 90 212) 2527474
Fax: (+00 90 212) 2528682
E-mail: bc.istanbul@bc-istanbul.sprint.com

Teacher's Centre Director: Mr Steve Darn
Îsmet Kaptan Mahallesi, 1374 Sokak
Selvili Îs, Merkezi No. 18
Kat 3 Daire 301 / 306

Çankaya 35210, Izmir
Tel: (+00 90 232) 4460130
Fax: (+00 90 232) 4460130

United Arab Emirates
Director Gulf States: Mr Robert Sykes
Villa no. 7, Al Nasr Street Khalidiya
Abu Dhabi
Tel: (+00 971 2) 659300
Fax: (+00 971 2) 664340
E-mail: bc.abudhabi@bc-abudhabi.sprint.com

Director Dubai: Mr Graham McCullock
Tariq bin Zaid Street, near Rashid Hospital
PO Box 1636, Dubai
Tel: (+00 971 4) 370109
Fax: (+00 971 4) 370703
E-mail: bc.dubai@bc-dubai.sprint.com

Manager: Kevin Nolan
Centre for English Studies
PO Box 1870, Al Ain
Tel: (+00 971 3) 643838
Fax: (+00 971 3) 515258

United States of America
Cultural Attaché: Mr David Evans
The Cultural Department
British Embassy
3100 Massachusetts Avenue NW
Washington DC 20008
Tel: (+00 1 202) 5887846
Fax: (+00 1 202) 5887918
E-mail: bc.washington@bc-washingtondc.sprint.com

Venezuela
Director: Mr Paul de Quincey
Torre La Noria, Piso 6, Paseo Enrique
Eraso, Las Mercedes/Sector San Román,
Apartado 65131, Caracas 1065
Tel: (+00 58 2) 915222
Fax: (+00 58 2) 915943
E-mail: bc.caracas@bc-caracas.sprint.com

Yemen
Director: Brendan McSharry OBE
As-Sabin Street No. 7
PO Box 2157, Sana'a
Tel: (+00 967 1) 244121
Fax: (+00 967 1) 244120

Zimbabwe
Director: Mr Jerry Eyres
23 Jason Moyo Avenue
PO Box 664, Harare
Tel: (+00 263 4) 790627
Fax: (+00 263 4) 737877
E-mail: britcoun@harare.iafrica.com

Librarian Bulawayo: Maureen Stewart
75 George Silundika Street
PO Box 557, Bulawayo
Tel: (+00 263 9) 75815
Fax: (+00 263 9) 75815

London
embassies & consulates

American Embassy
24 Grosvenor Square, London W1A
Tel: (0171) 499 9000

Argentine Embassy
65 Brook Street, London W1Y
Tel: (0171) 318 1300

Austrian Embassy
2nd Floor, 23 Lower Belgrave St
London SW1W
Tel: (0171) 235 3731

Australian High Commission
Australia House, Strand, London WC2B
Tel: (0171) 379 4334

Bahrain, State Embassy of
98 Gloucester Road, London SW7
Tel: (0171) 370 5132

Bangladesh High Commision
28 Queens Gate, London SW7
Tel: (0171) 584 0081

Belgian Embassy
103 Eaton Square, London SW1W
Tel: (0171) 470 3700

Botswana High Commission
6 Stratford Place, London W1N
Tel: (0171) 499 0031

Brazillian Consulate General
6 St Albans Street, London SW1Y
Tel: (0171) 930 9055

Brunei Darussalam High Commission
19 Belgrave Square, London SW1X
Tel: (0171) 581 0521

Bulgaria, Embassy of Peoples Republic
186-188 Queens Gate, London SW7
Tel: (0171) 584 9400

Canadian High Commission
MacDonald House, 1 Grosvenor Square
London W1X
Tel: (0171) 258 6600

Chilean Embassy
12 Devonshire Street, London W1N
Tel: (0171) 580 6392

Chinese Embassy
49-51 Portland Place, London W1N
Tel: (0171) 636 5726

Colombian Embassy
3 Hans Crescent, London SW1X
Tel: (0171) 589 9177

Costa Rican Embassy
Flat 1, 14 Lancaster Gate, London W2
Tel: (0171) 706 8844

Croatia, Embassy of the Republic of
21 Conway Street, London W1P
Tel: (0171) 387 1144

Cuban Embassy
167 High Holborn, London WC1
Tel: (0171) 420 3100

Czech Embassy
26 Kensington Palace Gardens
London W8
Tel: (0171) 243 1115

Danish (Royal) Embassy
55 Sloane Street, London SW1X
Tel: (0171) 333 0200

Ecuador, Embassy of
Flat 3b, 3 Hans Crescent, London SW1X
Tel: (0171) 584 1367

Egypt, Embassy of the Arab Republic of
2 Lowndes Street, London SW1X
Tel: (0171) 235 9719

Estonian Embassy
16 Hyde Park Gate, London W11
Tel: (0171) 589 3428

Finnish Embassy
38 Chesham Place, London SW1X
Tel: (0171) 838 6200

French Embassy
58 Knightsbridge, London SW1X
Tel: (0171) 201 1000

Georgian Embassy
3 Hornton Place, Kensington
London W8
Tel: (0171) 937 8233

Germany, Embassy of the Federal Republic of
23 Belgrave Square, London SW1X
Tel: (0171) 824 1300

Greece, Consulate General of
1a Holland Park, London W11
Tel: (0171) 221 6467

Hungary, Embassy of the Republic of
46 Eaton Place, London SW1X
Tel: (0171) 235 8767

India, High Commission of
India House, Aldwych
London WC2B
Tel: (0171) 836 8484

Indonesian Embassy
38 Grovenor Square, London W1X
Tel: (0171) 499 7661

Irish Embassy
17 Grosvenor Place, London W1X
Tel: (0171) 235 2171

Israel, Embassy of
2 Palace Green, London W8
Tel: (0171) 957 9500

Italian Embassy
14 Three Kings Yard, London W1Y
Tel: (0171) 312 2200

Jamaican High Commision
1 Prince Consort Road, London SW7
Tel: (0171) 823 9911

Japanese Embassy
101-104 Piccadilly, London W1V
Tel: (0171) 465 6500

Jordan, Embassy of the Hasamite Kingdom of
6 Upper Phillimore Gardens, London W8
Tel: (0171) 937 3685

Korea, Embassy of the Republic of
60 Buckingham Gate, London W1Y
Tel: (0171) 227 5500

Kuwait, State Embassy of
2 Alberts Gate, London SW1X
Tel: (0171) 590 3400

Lithuania, Embassy of the Republic of
84 Gloucester Place, London W1H
Tel: (0171) 486 6401

Malaysian High Commission
45-46 Belgrave Square, London SW1X
Tel: (0171) 235 8033

Mexican Consulate
8 Halkin Street, London SW1X
Tel: (0171) 235 6393

Moroccan Embassy
49 Queens Gate Gardens, London SW7
Tel: (0171) 581 5001

Mozambique, Embassy of the Peoples Republic of
21 Fitzroy Square, London W1P
Tel: (0171) 383 3800

Myanmar, Embassy of the Union of
19a Charles Street, London W1X
Tel: (0171) 499 8841

Nepalese Embassy, The Royal
12a Kensington Palace Garden
London W8
Tel: (0171) 229 1594

Netherlands Embassy (Royal)
38 Hyde Park Gate
London SW7
Tel: (0171) 590 3200

New Zealand High Commission
New Zealand House, Haymarket
London SW1Y
Tel: (0171) 930 8422

Oman, Embassy of the Sultanate of
167 Queens Gate, London SW7
Tel: (0171) 225 0001

Papua New Guinea High Commission
14 Waterloo Place, London SW1Y
Tel: (0171) 930 0922

Peruvian Consulate General
52 Sloane Street, London SW1X
Tel: (0171) 235 6867

Polish Embassy
47 Portland Place, London W1N
Tel: (0171) 580 4324

Portuguese Consulate General
62 Brompton Road, London SW3
Tel: (0171) 581 8722

Romania, Embassy of
4 Palace Green, London W8
Tel: (0171) 937 9666

Russian Federation, Consulate of the
5 Kensington Palace Gardens, London W8
Tel: (0171) 229 8027

Saudi Arabia, Royal Embassy of
119 Harley Street, London W1N
Tel: (0171) 935 9931

Singapore, High Commisioner for the Republic of
9 Wilton Crescent, London SW1X
Tel: (0171) 235 8315

Slovac Republic Embassy
25 Kensington Palace Gardens, London W8
Tel: (0171) 243 0803

Slovenia, Embassy of the Republic of
Suite 1, Cavendish Court
11-15 Wigmore Street, London W1H
Tel: (0171) 495 7775

Spanish Embassy
39 Chesham Place, London SW1X
Tel: (0171) 235 5555

Sri Lanka High Commissioner
13 Hyde Park Gardens, London W2
Tel: (0171) 262 1841

Sudan, Embassy of
3 Cleveland Row, St James'
London SW1A
Tel: (0171) 839 8080

Sweden, Embassy of
11 Montagu Place, London W1H
Tel: (0171) 917 6400

Swaziland High Commission, Kingdom of
20 Buckingham Gate, London SW1E
Tel: (0171) 630 6611

Switzerland, Embassy of
16-18 Montagu Place, London W1H
Tel: (0171) 616 6000

Syrian Embassy
8 Belgrade Square, London SW1
Tel: (0171) 245 9012

Taipei Representative Office in the UK
50 Grosvenor Gardens, London SW1W
Tel: (0171) 396 9152

Thai (Royal) Embassy
29-30 Queens Gate, London SW7
Tel: (0171) 589 2944

Tunisian Embassy
29 Princes Gate, London SW7
Tel: (0171) 584 8117

Turkish Embassy
43 Belgrave Square, London SW1X
Tel: (0171) 393 0202

United Arab Emirates, Embassy of
30 Princes Gate, London SW7
Tel: (0171) 581 1281

Uruguayan Consulate
140 Brompton Road, London SW3
Tel: (0171) 589 8735

Venezuelan Embassy
1 Cromwell Road, London SW7
Tel: (0171) 584 4206

Yemen, Embassy of Republic
57 Cromwell Road, London SW7
Tel: (0171) 584 6607

Zimbabwe High Commission
429 Strand, London WC2
Tel: (0171) 836 7755

More addresses

ABLS
217-8 Tottenham Court Road
London W1P 9AF
Tel: (0171) 631 0627
Fax: (0171) 637 7291

Addison Wesley Longman
Edinburgh Gate
Burnt Mill, Harlow
Essex CM20 2JE
Tel: (01279) 623 623
Fax: (01279) 623 947

Anglo-Pacific Consultancy
Suite 32, Nevilles Court, Dollis Hill Lane
London NW2 6HG
Tel: (0181) 452 7836

ARELS
2 Pontypool Place, Valentine Place
London SE1
Tel: (0171) 242 3136
Fax: (0171) 928 9378

Authentically English
85 Gloucester Road, London SW7 4SS
Tel: (0171) 244 7301
Fax: (0171) 835 0761

BALEAP
English Lang Unit, Huw Owen Building,
OCW, Penglais, Aberyswyth, Dyfed, Wales

BASELT
Cheltenham and Gloucester College of
Higher Education, Francis Close Hall
Swindon Road, Cheltenham, Gloucester
Tel: (01242) 227099
Fax: (01242) 227055

BATQI
University of Leeds, Leeds LS2 9AJ
Tel: (0113) 233 4528
Fax: (0113) 233 4541

BBC World Service
Bush House, London WC2B 4PH
Tel: (0171) 257 8305
Fax: (0171) 257 8311

Berlitz Publishing
Berlitz House, Peterley Road
Oxford OX4 2TX
Tel: (01865) 747033

Bournemouth English Book Centre
Albion Close, Parkstone, Poole
Dorset BH12 3LL
Tel: (01202) 715555
Fax: (01202) 739609

British Council
10 Spring Gardens, London SW1A 2BN
Tel: (0171) 389 4383

BUNAC
16 Bowling Green Lane
London EC1R 0BD
Tel: (0171) 251 2372

Cambridge International Book Centre
42 Hills Road, Cambridge CB2 1LA
Tel: (01223) 365400

Cambridge University Press
The Edinburgh Building
Shaftesbury Road
Cambridge CB2 2RU
Tel: (01223) 325997
Fax: (01223) 325984

Central Bureau for Educational Visits & Exchanges
10 Spring Gardens, London SW1A 2BN
Tel: (0171) 389 4004
Fax: (0171) 389 4426

CfBT Education Services
1 The Chambers, East Street
Reading RG1 4JD
Tel: (0118) 952 3900
Fax: (0118) 952 3924

Christians Abroad
1 Stockwell Green, London SW9 9HP
Tel: (0171) 737 7811
Fax: (0171) 737 3237

CIEE
52 Poland Street, London W1V 4JQ

CILTS
UCLES, 1 Hills Road, Cambridge CB1 2EU
Tel: (01223) 553789
Fax: (01223) 553086

City & Guilds
1 Giltspur Street, London EC1B 1RW
Tel: (0171) 294 2798
Fax: (0171) 294 2418

Clarity Language Consultants
PO Box 163, Sai Kung, Hong Kong
Tel: (00852) 2791 1787
Fax: (00852) 2791 6484

CMDT
10 Spring Gardens, London SW1A 2BN
Tel: (0171) 389 4931
Fax: (0171) 389 4140

Collins Cobuild *(Harper Collins)*
77/85 Fulham Palace Road, London W8 8JB
Tel: (0181) 741 7070

Contributions Agency
International Services, Room A2119
Longbenton
Newcastle upon Tyne NE98 1YX
Tel: 0645 154811
Fax: 0645 157800

Delta Systems
1400 Miller Parkway
McHenry, IL 60050, USA

DFEE
Santuary Buildings, Great Smith Street
London SW1P 3BT
Tel: (0171) 925 5555
Fax: (0171) 925 6000

Authentically ENGLISH

The magazine for professional teachers of English...worldwide

"Could I have better directions to the resource centre"

Make sure you're prepared for teaching abroad!

Reviews, advice, topical articles, phtocopiable classroom resources, and much more.

For an annual subscripion to the magazine (4 issues), send a cheque or postal order for £17.50 payable to:
Authentically English, 85 Gloucester Road, London SW7 4SS
Tel: 0171 244 7301 Fax: 0171 835 0761

DSS Benefits Agency
Pensions and Overseas Benefits,
Directorate (MED)
Tyneview Park, Whitley Road
Newcastle-upon-Tyne NE98 1BA

Eagle Star International Life Services
4-6 Abbey Street, Reading
Berkshire RG1 3BA

EEP
Carlton House, 27A Carlton Drive
London SW15 2BS
Tel: (0171) 780 2841
Fax: (0171) 780 9592

ECIS
21b Lavant Street, Petersfield
Hampshire GU32 3EL

English Language Bookshop
31 George Street, Brighton BN2 1RH

EL Gazette
1 Malet Street, London WC1E 7JA
Tel: (0171) 255 1969
Fax: (0171) 255 1972

ELS
5761 Buckingham Parkway
Culver, CA 90230-6583, USA
Tel: (001310) 642 0988
Fax: (001310) 649 5231

ELT News & Views
Uruguay 782-3
1015 Capital Federal - Buenos Aires
Argentina
Fax: (00541) 375 3944

English Speaking Board
26a Princes Street
Southport PR8 1EQ
Tel: (01704) 501730
Fax: (01704) 539637

English Worldwide
The Italian Building, Dockhead
London SE1 2BS
Tel: (0171) 252 1402
Fax: (0171) 251 8002

GAP Activity Projects
44 Queen's Road, Reading
Berkshire RG1 4BB
Tel: (0118) 959 4914
Fax: (0118) 957 6634

Georgian Press
56 Sandy Lane, Leyland
Preston, Lancashire PR5 1ED
Tel: (01772) 431 790
Fax: (01772) 431 378

Graduate Teaching Training Registry
Fulton House, Jessop Avenue
Cheltenham GL50 3SL

Heinemann ELT
Halley Court, Jordan Hill, Oxford OX2 8EJ
Tel: (01865) 311 366
Fax: (01865) 314 193

IATEFL
3 Kingsdown Park, Tankerton
Whitstable, Kent CT5 2DJ
Tel: (01227) 276528

ICELS
Oxford Brookes University
Headington, Oxford OX3 6BP
Tel: (01865) 483874
Fax: (01865) 483791

ILC
White Rock, Hastings TN34 1JY
Tel: (01424) 720 109
Fax: (01424) 720 323

Inland Revenue *(General Enquiries)*
Room G1, West Wing, Somerset House
Strand, London WC2R 1LB
Tel: (0171) 438 6420

inlingua Teacher Training & Recruitment
Rodney Lodge, Rodney Roa
Cheltenham GL50 1XY
Tel: (01242) 253 181

INSO Corporation
12 Compton Road, London SW19 7QD
Tel: (0181) 947 1122
Fax: (0181) 947 1810

Institute of Education
University of London TESOL Dept.
20 Bedford Way, London WC1 0AL
Tel: (0171) 612 6104
Fax: (0171) 612 6097

International House
106 Piccadilly, London W1V 9FL
Tel: (0171) 491 2958
Fax: (0171) 491 0959

JALT
Central Office, Urban Edge Building
5th Floor 1-37-9 Taito
Taito-ku, Tokyo 110, Japan
Tel: 0081 3 3837 1630
Fax: 0081 3 3837 1631

JET Programme
CIEE, 52 Poland Street, London W1V 4JQ
Tel: (0171) 478 2000

KELTIC Bookshop
25 Chepstow Corner
Chepstow Place
London W2 4XE
Tel: (0171) 229 8560

Language Project
78-80 Colston Street, Bristol BS1 5BB
Tel: (0117) 927 3993

Language Teaching Publications
35 Church Road, Hove BN3 2BE
Tel: (01273) 736 344
Fax: (01273) 720 898

LCCI Exam Board
Marlow House, Station Road, Sidcup DA15
Tel: (0181) 302 0261

Linguarama
Oceanic House, 89 High Street
Alton, Hampshire GU34 1LG
Tel: (01420) 80899

Link Africa
Orwell House, Orwell Road
Cambridge CB4 4WY
Tel: (01223) 426665
Fax: (01223) 426960

MASTA
Keppel Street, London WC1E 7HT
Tel: (0171) 631 4408

Mini Flashcards
PO Box 1526, London W7 1ND
Tel: (0181) 567 1076

MS Language Systems A/S
Borups Alle 177, PO Box 80
DK-2000 Frederiksberg
Copenhagen, Denmark
Tel: +45 38311 83449

Nord-Anglia International
Overseas Recruitment Dept
10 Eden Place, Cheadle
Stockport, Cheshire SK8 1AT
Tel: (0161) 491 4191

OAS
Medlock Street, Manchester M15 4PR
Tel: (0161) 957 7000

ODA
94 Victoria Street, London SW1E 5JL
Tel: (0171) 917 7000

Oxford University Press
Great Clarendon Street
Oxford OX2 6DP
Tel: (01865) 556767

Peace Corps
Room 8500, 1900 K Street NW
(PO Box 941), Washington
DC 20526, USA
Tel: 001800 424 8580

Penguin ELT
27 Wrights Lane, London W8 5TZ
Tel: (0171) 416 3000
Fax: (0171) 416 3060

Peter Collin Publishing
8 The Causeway, Teddington TW11 0HE
Tel: (0181) 943 3386

Pitman Qualifications
1 Giltspur Street, London EC1A 9DD
Tel: (0171) 331 4021
Fax: (0171) 331 4022

Prentice Hall ELT
Campus 400, Maylands Avenue
Hemel Hempstead HP2 7EZ

Richmond English
19 Berghem Mews, London W14 0HM
Tel: (0171) 371 3976
Fax: (0171) 371 3824

Routledge
11 New Fetter Lane, London EC4P 4EE
Tel: (0171) 842 2098
Fax: (0171) 842 2306

Saxoncourt Recruitment
59 South Molton Street, London W1Y IHH
Tel: (0171) 836 1567
Fax: (0171) 836 1789

Schools Partnership Worldwide
17 Dean's Yard, London SW1P 3PB
Tel: (0171) 222 0138
Fax: (0171) 233 0008

Skillshare Africa
3 Belvoir Road, Leicester LE1 6SL
Tel: (0116) 254 0517

Stern Studios
85 Gloucester Road, London SW7 4SS
Tel: (0171) 244 7301
Fax: (0171) 835 0761

Teaching Abroad
46 Beech View, Angmering, BN16 4DE
Tel: (01903) 859911

TESOL
1600 Cameron Street, Suite 300
Alexandria VA22314, Virginia, USA
Tel: 001703 836 0774
Fax: 001703 836 7864

TOEIC
129 Wendell Road, London W12 9SD
Tel: (0181) 740 6282
Fax: (0181) 740 5207

Transitions Abroad
18 Hulst Road, Amherst
MA 01004-1300, USA

Trinity College London
16 Park Crescent, London W1N 4AH
Tel: (0171) 323 2328
Fax: (0171) 323 5201

UCLES
1 Hills Road, Cambridge CB1 2EU
Tel: (01223) 553311

ULEAC
Stewart House, 32 Russell Square
London WC1B 5DN
Tel: (0171) 331 4021
Fax: (0171) 331 4022

Universities Council for the Education of Teachers
58 Gordon Street, London WC1H 0NT

UNV
Postfach 260 111, D-53153 Bonn, Germany

UODLE
Ewart House, Ewart Place, Summertown
Oxford OX2 7BZ
Tel: (01865) 554291
Fax: (01865) 510085

Verulam Publishing
152a Park Street Lane, Park Street
St Albans, Herts AL2 2AU
Tel: (01272) 872 770
Fax: (01272) 873 866

VSO
317 Putney Bridge Road, London SW15
Tel: (0181) 780 1331

Wida Software
2 Nicholas Gardens, London W5 5HY
Tel: (0181) 567 6941

Worldteach
Harvard Institute for International
Development, 1 Eliot Street, Cambridge
MA 02138, USA
Tel: 001 617 495 5527

Worldwide Education Service
272 Field End Road, Eastcote
Middlesex HA4 9NA
Tel: (0181) 866 4400
Fax: (0181) 429 4838

Women in TEFL
42 Northolme Road, London N5 2UX

TEFL internet sites

Addison Wesley Longman
http://www.aw.com/

Agora Language Marketplace Employment Page
http://www.agoralang.com:2410/agora/employment.html
Employment listings.

Amazon
http://www.amazon.com

Asian CareerWeb Forum
http://www.rici.com/acw/

ARELS
http://www.arels.org.uk

Athelstan Publications
http://www.athel.com

Ballard & Tighe
http://www.ballard-tighe.com/

BEBC
http://bebc.co.uk

Berlitz
http://www.berlitz.com/berlitz_corporate/employment.html

British Council
http://www.britcoun.org

Cambridge University Press
http://www.cup.cam.ac.uk/

Career China
http://www.globalvillager.com/villager/CC.html
Jobs in China, Taiwan, Hong Kong, etc.

Career Opportunities in Singapore
http://www.sg/infomap/employment/
Job links for Singapore.

Cascadilla Press Linguistics Titles
http://www.shore.net/~cascadil/linguistics.html

Central European Teaching Program
http://www.beloit.edu/~cetp

China Employment Centre
http://www.asiadragons.com/country/china/chinajob.htm

China-Net Positions
http://www.asia-net.com/china-net.html

Collins' Cobuild
http://titania.cobuild.collins.co.uk/

Delta Systems
http://www.delta-systems.com

DynEd
http://www.dyned.com

ECC Thailand
http://www.eccthai.com/jobs.htm

Education Jobs
http://www.camrev.com.au/share/edu.html
Job listings in Australia.

Education Job Opportunities
http://www.camrev.com.au/share/edu.html
Educational jobs in Australia.

ELS Job Opportunities
http://www.els.com/intlempl.htm

ELT Job Centre
http://www.edunet.com/jobs/

Employment in Africa
http://www.sas.upenn.edu/African_Studies/Travel/Employment_9976.html

Employment Opportunities for Language Teachers
http://www.csun.edu/~hcedu013/employment.html

Encomium Publications
http://www.iac.net/~encomium/

English Book Centre
http://www.ebcoxford.co.uk

English Teacher Positions in Korea
http://www.ncmc.cc.mi.us:443/esl/jobs.html
Jobs in Korea

ESL Opportunities in Canada
http://www.tesl.ca/jobs.htm
Jobs in Canada

Exceller Software Corporation
http://www.exceller.com/

Exit Studio
http://members.aol.com/ExitStudio/index.htm

Gessler Publishing
http://www.gessler.com/gessler/

Guide to Teaching English in Turkey
http://www.geocities.com/CollegePark/Union/2768/turkey.html

Heinemann ELT
http://www.helt.co.uk/

Heinle & Heinle
http://www.thomson.com/heinle.html

Holt, Rinehart & Winston College Language Publishers
http://www.agoralang.com:2410/hrwcollege.html

Houghton Mifflin Company
http://www.hmco.com/

International House
http://www.international-house-london.ac.uk

International Job Opportunities
http://www.cc.emory.ed/OIA/work_abroad.html
List of teaching jobs.

International Organisations
http://144.96.225.66/internorgs.html
List of volunteer organisations that will assist in finding work abroad.

International Volunteer Opportunities
http://kl2s.phast.umass.edu/~masag/15040.html
Volunteer opportunities.

Jobs-cz
http://www.jobs.cz/english_welcome.html
Work in the Czech Republic.

Job Opportunities in Singapore
http://www.ofs.ac.sg/ofs/jobs.html
Teaching opportunities in Singapore.

JobStreet
http://www.mol.com/recruit/default.htm
Jobs in Malaysia.

KELTIC
http://www.keltic.co.uk

Korean Connection's jobs
http://soback.kornet.nm.kr/~wiegand/2jobs.htm
Korean jobs.

Language Job Market
http://www.vol.it/linguanet/jobs/job.htm
Teaching jobs in Italy.

Lighthouse Publications
http://www.aci.on.ca/lighthouse/esl.html

Linguapress
http://members.aol.com/linguapres/welcome.htm

Macmillan
http://www.mcp.com/

Malaysia Employment Centre
http://www.asiadragons.com/country/malaysia/malaysiajob.htm

Malaysia Online
http://www.mol.com.my/
Job recruitment site for Malaysia.

McGraw-Hill
http://www.mcgraw-hill.com/

Merit Audio Visual Software
http://www.meritav.com/

MIT Press: Linguistics
http://mitpress.mit.edu/books-legacy.tcl

Ohayo Sensei
http://www.ohayosensei.com/
English teaching jobs in Japan.

OK! Software
http://www.mdn.com/oksoftware/

One Small Planet
http://www.onesmallplanet.com
Information about travelling, studying, working and volunteering abroad.

Orchid Land Publications
http://www.ilhawaii.net:80/~orlapubs/

Overseas Job Express
http://www.overseasjobs.com

Oxford University Press English Language Teaching
http://www1.oup.co.uk/E-P/English_Language_Teaching/

Peace Corps
http://www.peacecorps.gov

Peter Collin Publishing
http://www.pcp.co.uk/

Philippines Employment Centre
http://www.asiadragons.com/country/philippines/philippinesjob.htm
Job listings.

Prentice Hall Regents
http://www.phregents.com

Pro Lingua Associates
http://www.bookworld.com/proling.htm

Romus Interactive
http://ourworld.compuserve.com/homepages/Romus/

South Africa Job Web
http://www3.nis.za/jm/jobweb.htm

Space ALC
http://www.alc.co.jp/epro/englstop.html

Stone Bridge Press
http://www.stonebridge.com/~sbp/

Summer Jobs
http://www.summerjobs.com/

Summer Jobs - Hungary
http://www.summerjobs.com/do/where/jobtree/Hungary

Syracuse Language Systems
http://www.syrlang.com

TAI
http://www.taiteach.com/
Information about teaching in Thailand.

Teach English in Mongolia
http://www.asiacouncil.org/Mongolia.html

Teach English in Vietnam
http://www.volasia.org/vietnam.html
Volunteer organisations in Asia.

Teach ESL In Central Europe
http://144.96.225.66/eslceneur.html

Teacher Training in France
http://www.wfi.fr/volterre/teachtrain.html

Teaching Abroad Without a Certificate
http://www.purdue.edu/oip/sa/work/teachl.htm

Teaching English in Asia Pacific
http://asiafacts.kingston.net/

Teaching English in Istanbul
http://www.fptoday.com/cimcoz/teaching.htm

Teaching in Finland
http://www.u-net.com/eflweb/finland0.htm

Teaching in Hungary
http://www.u-net.com/eflweb/hungary.htm

Teaching in Italy
http://www.mclink.it/com/reporter/index.html

Teaching in Poland
http://www.americad.com/

Teaching in Spain
http://www.u-net.com/eflweb/spain0.htm

TESOL
http://www.tesol.net

Thomson Publishing
http://www.thomson.com

Times Higher Education Supplement
http://www.thesis.co.uk

Transitions Abroad
http://www.transabroad.com

Traveller's Guide to the Czech Republic
http://www.czweb.com/czguide/index.htm

UCLES Centres
http://www.go-ed.com/ciltsrsa/centres.cfm

USIS
http://www.usia.gov/education/engteaching/eal-ndx.htm

Voluntary Service Overseas
http://www.oneworld.org/

Volunteers in Asia
http://www.volasia.org/

Volunteer work overseas
http://www.purdue.edu/oip/sa/work/voluntr.htm

World of Reading
http://www.wor.com/

section 10
Index

Where is it?

Activity courses 20
Advanced Diploma in Language Teaching Management *(ADLTM)* 27
Applied linguistics 30
ARELS 62
Argentina 100
Assistant Director of Studies 48
Associations 64
Austria 100

Background books 58
Bahrain 100
BALEAP 62
Bangladesh 101
BASELT 62
BATQI 62
Belgium 101
Berlitz 19
Bookshops 57
Botswana 101
Brazil 102
British Council 63
British Council Offices 126
Brunei 102
Bulgaria 102
Business English 36

Cambodia 103
Careers advice 10
CEELTYLLS 22
CELTA 22
CELTYL 22
CertTEB 36
CfBT 41

Chile 103
China 103
CIEE 13
CILTS 63
City & Guilds 63
Colombia 104
Commissioning Editor 51
Costa Rica 104
Course books 54
Course Director 48
Croatia 104
Cuba 105
Culture shock 45
Cyprus 105
Czech Republic 105

DELTA 26
Denmark 106
Desk Editor 51
Dictionaries 58
Director of Studies 49
DOTE 26
DTEFLA 26

East European Partnership *(EEP)* 14
Ecuador 106
Egypt 106
Embassies 131
English for academic purposes *(EAP)* 34
English for specific purposes *(ESP)* 33
Estonia 107

FCTBE 36
Finance 46

Where is it?

Finland 107
France 107

General courses 20
Georgia 108
Germany 108
Grammar books 59
Greece 108

Hungary 109

IATEFL 64
India 109
Indonesia 109
Internet based resources 57
Internet sites 135
Introductory courses 18
Israel 110
Italy 110

JALT 64
Jamaica 110
Japan 111
JET 12
Jobs in publishing 50
Jordan 111
Junior Course Director 48
Junior courses 20

Kuwait 111

Language development materials 55
LCCI 36
Leisure activities courses 36

Lithuania 112

Magazines/periodicals 59
Malaysia 112
Marketing *(language schools)* 49
Marketing *(publishing)* 51
Masters degrees 29
Mexico 112
Morocco 113
Mozambique 113
Multimedia 57
Myanmar 113

National Insurance 46
Nepal 114
Netherlands 114

Oman 114

Papua New Guinea 115
Peace Corps 14
Pensions 46
Peru 115
PGCE 28
PhDs 31
Poland 115
Portugal 116
Positions within academic institutions 49
Positions within language schools 48
Private language schools 40
Professional development materials 55
Professional purpose courses 36

Recruitment 10
Romania 116

Where is it?

Running exam preparation classes 34
Running homestay courses 34
Russia 116

Saudi Arabia 117
Selection process 42
Senior ELT Editor 51
Senior teacher 48
Setting up a homestay 51
Setting up a language school 51
Short courses 36
Singapore 117
Skill development materials 55
Slovakia 117
Slovenia 118
South Korea 118
Spain 118
Specialising 33
Sri Lanka 119
Sudan 119
Summer schools 20
Summer work overseas 20
Swaziland 119
Sweden 120
Switzerland 120
Syria 120

Taiwan 121
Tax 46
Teacher training 50
Teaching English as a Foreign Language *(TEFL)* 8
Teaching English as a Second Language *(TESL)* 8
Teaching English to Speakers of Other Languages *(TESOL)* 8
Teaching materials 54
Teaching one to one learners 34, 35
Teaching young learners 34, 35
Technology in the classroom 55
TESOL *(Association for Teachers of English to Speakers of Other Languages)* 65
TEYL 35
Thailand 121
Trinity College 23
TESOL Certificate 23
TESOL Diploma 27
Tunisia 121
Turkey 122

UCLES 65
United Arab Emirates 122
United Nations Volunteers *(UNV)* 14
Uruguay 122

Venezuela 123
Volunteering 14
VSO 14

Working abroad 41
Working for yourself 42
Working in the UK 41
Writing 50

Yemen 123

Zimbabwe 123

Section 10
Other Stuff

Advertisers Index

Where's the advert?

Aberdeen College *59*	King's College *33*
Aston University *13*	Leeds University *43*
Authentically English *6, 134*	London Study Centre *62*
Bell Language Schools *23*	Longman ELT *60*
British Council Seminars *37, 124*	Longman Higher Education *98*
Bromley School of English *36*	MS Language Systems *Inside front cover*
Cambridge University Press *52*	
City of Manchester College *42*	Northbrook College *57*
Clarity Language Consultants *47*	Oxford House College *Inside back cover*
CMDT *32*	
Durham University *47*	Oxford University Press *21, 66*
Edinburgh University *43*	Penguin ELT *52*
Exeter University *29*	Pitman *24*
Frances King School of English *35*	Portsmouth University *50*
GLOSCAT *63*	Reading University *48*
Grove House *40*	Regent *11*
Harper Collins, Electronic Reference *55*	St. Giles College *19*
	Students International *34*
Huddersfield Technical College *41*	Surrey University *30*
inlingua *44*	TESOL *38, 49*
Institute of Education *98*	UCLES *4*
International House *16, 38, 52*	UODLE *47*
Keltic *66*	VSO *15*

Section 10

Other Stuff